Her Hooba
and
His Rose

Copyrighted Material

Her Hooba and His Rose

Copyright © 2021 by migebooks/MIGE-LLC All Rights Reserved.

No part of this publication may be reproduced, stored in a retrieval system or transmitted, in any form or by any means—electronic, mechanical, photocopying, recording or otherwise—without prior written permission from the publisher, except for the inclusion of brief quotations in a review.

For information about this title or to order other books and/or electronic media, contact the publisher:

migebooks@gmail.com

ISBN: 978-1-7343378-6-0 (print)
978-1-7343378-7-7 (eBook)

Printed in the United States of America

Cover and Interior design: Book configuration by 1106 Design

By: Dave & Carla

Her Hooba and His Rose

DAVE & CARLA

This is dedicated to love!

Preface

This is a story of love;

the love of two persons and

their families.

It is also about love of a

people for their God, their life

and their purpose.

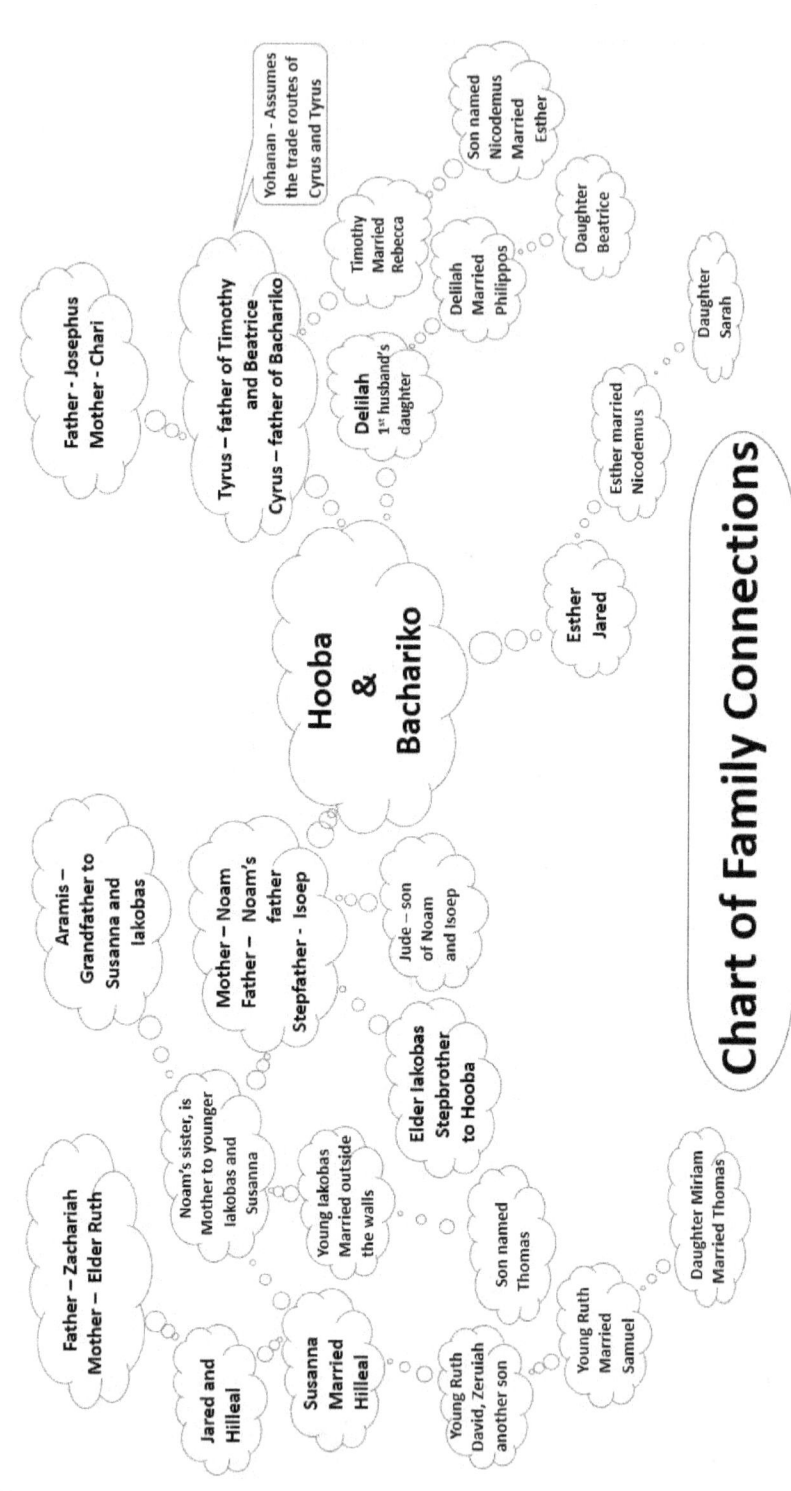

Name Pronunciations

*T*he character names in this story are derived from the languages predominant at the time. Here are examples of some of the pronunciations:

Akeldama -   a h – k e l – d a h – m a

Bachariko - b a - h a - d i c – c o

Bhuti -   b o o – t e e

Hilleal -   h i – l e e - a l

Hooba -   h $\bar{u}$– b a

Iakobas -   y a – k a – bus

Jared -   j e h – r e h d

Noam -   n o – a h m

Philippos - f i l – i- p o s e

Yohanan -   y o – h a h n – u n

Table of Contents

Prologue: 1
Chapter 1: Jared 3
Chapter 2: The Descent 7
Chapter 3: The Deception 13
Chapter 4: The Cloak 17
Chapter 5: Psalms 21
Chapter 6: Recommendations 23
Chapter 7: Isaiah 25
Chapter 8: The Daughter of Cyrus 27
Chapter 9: Pedagogy 29
Chapter 10: Enlightenment 33
Chapter 11: Changes 39
Chapter 12: The Healers 43
Chapter 13: Alone 49
Chapter 14: South to India 53
Chapter 15: Kashmir 57
Chapter 16: A Wise Man 61
Chapter 17: In His Heart 71
Chapter 18: Ascending the Mountain 77
Chapter 19: Jude 85
Chapter 20: Further Up the Mountain 89
Chapter 21: Monastery 93
Chapter 22: Hooba Goes Home 99
Chapter 23: Nine Years Had Passed 107
Chapter 24: Eight Days Home 115

Chapter 25: Home 119
Chapter 26: Hooba Speaks within the Walls 125
Chapter 27: The City with The Temple. .133
Chapter 28: A Man from Queriot. 139
Chapter 29: Kfar Nahum 143
Chapter 30: The Beach 151
Chapter 31: Tracing Footsteps 159
Chapter 32: The Sabbath 177
Chapter 33: Alabaster Skin 183
Chapter 34: Sunday Morning 187
Chapter 35: A Place of Comfort 191
Chapter 36: The Wedding 195
Chapter 37: The Return 201
Chapter 38: The Games 213
Chapter 39: Connivance 219
Chapter 40: Tribulation 223
Chapter 41: Evanescent. 229
Chapter 42: Shrouded 241
Chapter 43: The Lost Sheep 245
Chapter 44: Ameliorate. 251
Chapter 45: Flee 255
Chapter 46: The Vessel. 259
Chapter 47: Trade Routes 269
Chapter 48: They Return 273
Chapter 49: The Times Were Changing. 281
Chapter 50: Revelation 287
Chapter 51: The Ritual Bath. 293
Chapter 52: The Unblossoming of the Rose 297
Appendix 1: List of Characters 299

Prologue

Archeologically, historically, biblically, traditionally oral and by supposition ... what is the history of modern man?

What happened to prehistoric man, six to ten thousand years ago leading to the behavior of modern man?

Communication first began with carvings, then oral stories, then the written word nearly three-thousand years ago.

Great civilizations had risen and then fallen. The story of one small group of people formed and changed the world's beliefs.

Yes, there were Egyptians, Sumerians, Hindus, Persians, Babylonians, Romans and Greeks who held their places in the development of society.

Each of these societies also rose and fell. What emerged was a small faction who became known as those who followed **The Law**.

The Law or otherwise known as The Torah, also referred to as the Hebrew Pentateuch traced the history from the beginning through those called Abraham and then to Moses, who traditionally delivered The Torah to the people. These people escaped bondage from the Egyptians to settle a new promised land, according to The Torah.

The remainder of the Hebrew Old Testament traces their history, their own rise and fall as it relates to the neighboring regions. That history leads them to their last great King David, the following king, his son Solomon and the building of their First Temple.

Each and every time throughout their history, God made a new **Covenant** or promise with those people.

God said, "If you will keep my law, I will be your God and you will be my people."

The Babylonians were responsible for the destruction of the first temple.

The Second Temple period began with the rule of King Cyrus who reestablished the southern kingdom of the people and the rebuilding of the temple. The separate sects of the Pharisees, Sadducees, Essenes and the Zealots developed.

The Persian Empire in 331 BC was waning under the defeat of Alexander the Great as the Greek influence began expanding.

After that time the Roman Empire became the predominant force beginning around 27 BC. The Roman Empire experienced exponential growth beyond its own military ability, therefore, mercenaries were hired from the Island of Cypress. These mercenaries were referred to as the Kittims.

The word Kittim is an accepted term by the people who followed *The Law* which means ***invader*** from another land.

The fall of the Second Temple occurred on August 30, AD 70 as destroyed by the Kittims.

Chapter 1

Jared

I met my brothers at the table. The table was merely made of barren planks of wood with long benches for seating. The cup from which I would drink was nothing more than a carved piece of wood. The plates for eating were woven from the flax plant.

I was the eldest at my table of ten. Thus, I broke the bread and passed it.

I stated, "This is the bread of life, given by God to nourish us."

I then shared the story of Moses. "Moses had delivered our people from bondage and wandered for forty years," I said. For Moses had delivered *The Law* and it is our job to preserve it.

I had spent my entire life preserving *The Law*. Little did I know that at sunset, the start of the Sabbath, I would not have forty more years but rather just forty more hours of life.

During sunset, we retired to our small cubicles to pray and contemplate our God. Before the sun rose again, I descended into my ceremonial bath. I then ate date fruit as there would be no meal prepared before sunset in compliance with our rituals on the Sabbath.

I lay flat on the hard-surfaced floor, face down. The floor was not only hard but cold. It was extremely uncomfortable as I was no longer a young man.

I heard a knock at the entrance to my room.

My thought was: "Who would disturb me on the day of the Lord?"

A young man answered, "Rabbi?"

My thought was that I would not anger. Then, I again thought to myself, there is no duty I can perform, so why bother me?

I answered, "Yes?"

The young man reported to me: "The Kittims are marching from the west."

"Return to your room and pray," I replied.

I stood wearing nothing but a loin cloth as I grabbed my robe and covered my head. I walked slowly because I had never perspired on the Sabbath. In fact, I had rarely seen the sun on the Sabbath for nearly forty years.

I walked the long hall, entered the courtyard and opened the heavy gates without assistance. I could ask no other man to raise his hand to help on the Sabbath, as I walked out into the surrounding community. I had not put on my sandals. To tie the laces on the Sabbath would have been considered to work on the Lord's day.

I again walked slowly through the gates and over the road of rocks to the home of my brother, Hilleal. My brother was feeding their sheep.

I spoke to my brother saying, "Gather Susanna, the children and your neighbors. Bring them within the walls."

I slowly turned and walked back within the walls of our community.

I stood at the gates, guiding the women and children to the Great Hall.

"Make yourselves comfortable and pray. No one must enter the Sanctuary. This building is your sanctuary but that is the sanctuary of the Lord," I said.

Only those in full membership of their community had seen the inside of the Lord's sanctuary and certainly not the women and children.

I told my brother where to find the date fruit, saying, "Please feed your people."

Then, I returned to the wall, standing in prayer until the sun had set.

Then at dusk, I gathered all the others of our community both the priests and novitiates. I advised them to feed all the people who had fasted only on date fruit since sunrise.

I, myself, broke the bread and passed it. I told the story of the Passover once again. It was the story of how God had spared the Israelites at the time of Moses. I attempted to give hope and assurance that God would be with them no matter what happened.

I asked the men to follow me. I walked across the compound to a small wooden storeroom. I opened the door and turned to see Susanna, my brother's wife, standing with the men. There was a fire in her eyes just as on the first day I had met her. I first thought to argue with her. Yet, I had known her for many years and knew her will was stronger than that of ten men.

I called her name, first. I went into the storeroom and returned with the lightest, yet sharpest sword.

And as I handed the sword to her, I said, "Susanna, the innocent never die. May you be strengthened by your God."

I then placed my hand on the shoulder of every man and presented them with a sword. I knew some of these men were not fighters.

I said, "Return to your resting place and to your families. If you hear the bell, take your place on the wall."

I placed one man in the Lord's sanctuary.

I addressed the man saying, "We no longer sacrifice. However, in Abraham's name, if the Kittims reach you and draw blood, throw yourself on the altar thus your blood will purify this holy space."

I also placed two young, strong men outside of the Great Hall where the women and children had gone.

I placed three more men with bells on the north, east and west walls. I positioned myself at the south wall and we waited.

I stood on the south wall ready for war. This was not the war I had prepared for as a young man. My war was to protect *The Law*, the Messiah or the King. We were still waiting for this Messiah or King.

The war we were about to engage in was about change. The old would be destroyed and the new would be in control. If this secret rock was destroyed, how soon would the rock in the city with The Temple fall?

As I stood on the wall, I thought of Hooba; at least Hooba had carried with him *The Law* when he escaped. Even if all perished today, Hooba could still teach *The Law*.

I remembered the young boy ... a peaceful, beautiful boy.

I smiled and thought, "He was like my own son. How pleasing the thought of the student surpassing the teacher."

I spoke aloud: "God, I love that boy."

A tear rolled down my cheek. I rarely cried. Although, I had cried on my own thirtieth birthday knowing it was the day I was in full membership with my community. I had also cried the first day I left a teenage Hooba at the seashore to travel for knowledge. Then, I remembered I cried the day I found an older, wiser Hooba and returned him to our community. Once again, I had cried for their happiness the day my brother Hilleal married Susanna. I thought about how I also cried the first time I held my brother's and Susanna's first daughter Ruth and after the births of their other three children. I shed tears the day I presented *Her Hooba and His Rose* with a rose to symbolize the birth of their rose, the daughter they named Esther.

Chapter 2
The Descent

The wall had been constructed nearly two hundred years prior at the instruction of the leader of the community. Their gates had been crafted of heavy wood at the time. The walls were made of limestone. The purpose of the walls was to protect the holy space of their community and to separate those whose purpose was only to protect *The Law* from the other community members.

The east, west, and north sides of the wall stood ten-foot tall. The south side was just six-foot tall due to the land's topography. It was never intended to withstand battle but rather as a deterrent. Built from limestone, it served their purpose which was not for war.

The gate located on the west wall was closed at sunset and opened at sunrise every day except on the Sabbath. Today, the gates had been closed. Although it was, indeed, heavy to lift by oneself it was constructed only of wood.

During the week the gates were normally open. The brothers of the community had the ability to leave and go to the fields to work and the outside world could come in to deliver what was needed.

The Law had been preserved and was in hiding. It had been sealed and placed in a cool area just two years prior. There had been upheaval with the ruling government and with the Kittims for many years.

My mind wandered to *The Law* and its protection. I knew in my heart that Hooba had the only true oral version and felt assured the written version was secured.

I stood on the wall and feared a battle was about to ensue which could lead to the destruction of the community that I had loved for over fifty years. I remembered my first walk through the large wooden gates.

Just past the age of maturity at twelve years old, I had been delivered by my father to the gates to begin training as keeper of *The Law*. My previous education had been at the hands of the priests under my father's insistence.

That first day, I had been handed a wooden sword. The greeter of the gates handed me the sword and had given me the words from Psalms 23:2 which was part of the wisdom literature of the Old Testament, "He maketh me to lie down in green pastures. He leadeth me beside the still waters."

I was guided to my quarters and was instructed to repeat the passage from Psalms which was 23:3. "He restoreth my soul. He leadeth me in the path of righteousness for his name's sake." Shortly, thereafter, I was summoned for dinner.

Again, I was instructed to recite the two verses from Psalms, aloud. The man who would be head of my table, then recited Psalms 23:4, "Yea, though I walk through the valley of the shadow of death, I will fear no evil for thou art with me. Thy rod and thy staff, they shall comfort me." I was instructed to repeat, aloud, all three of the verses from Psalms.

The entire table of men seated with me then recited Psalms 23:5. "Thou preparest a table before me in the presence of thine enemies; thou anointest my head with oil; my cup runneth over."

Once dinner was finished, my entire table recited Psalms 23:6 which was: "Surely goodness and mercy shall follow me all the days of my life; and I will dwell in the house of the Lord forever."

I was entering the most-strict level of the community's beliefs. I would not marry, and would devote my life to study and preservation of *The Law*. My brother Hilleal, however, received his education outside of the walls. Thus, he would be allowed to marry and have a family to further the growth of the community population.

My training was mental, physical and spiritual. Hilleal and others who resided outside the walls were trained spiritually and physically without the constraints of total mental absorption and commitment. My daily ritual began with ceremonial bathing with full immersion to cleanse my entire body before the first meal of the day. My hands were to be washed for approximately thirty minutes prior to taking food. Our food was also clean. Fluids could not be mixed with animal meat. Those animals had been killed ceremoniously as well ... in a ritualistic manner.

Our minds were purified throughout the morning with the study of *The Law* and with prayer. Near the morning's end, our hands were cleansed once more, ceremoniously before the small fruit meal at midday. There may have been labor in our morning, dependent on the season and after the midday meal, labor continued. Before our evening meal, physical training occurred. That consisted of calisthenics, running, hand-to-hand combat and sword training. Again, our hands were cleansed for thirty minutes prior to preparing the meal which occurred at sunset. Our routine continued every day but the Sabbath. The Sabbath began on sundown Friday evening and ended on Saturday at sunset. This had been my life from the age of twelve until now at nearly seventy.

My life had been completely committed to my community and our God. I thought back to the moments in my life that brought both pride and happiness to my soul. We had experienced festival days when our community joined together for meals and camaraderie. Normally, these revolved around spiritual celebrations. Marriage and the birth of a family member were considered to be a ritual occasion.

As a young man of eighteen years, I hadn't reached the age of which to receive my sword of steel. I had learned above average until this point. However, the rules were strictly adhered to and I could not move forward in my training.

A young boy of six years had entered the community within the walls. Hooba was an exceptional child and above average in learning. The walls had never allowed a boy of this young age to train until now. There were no rules or rituals to pass onto a child of this age.

I was assigned to teach young Hooba the rules and ways of our community. I had no idea what a six-year-old was capable of handling. However, it was not long before I realized that there was nothing the young Hooba was incapable of learning.

The first day, I read Psalms 23:2 through 23:6 to Hooba who repeated it back verbatim without error. It had been my plan to use Psalms as the lesson of the first full week.

Hooba's ability left me no other recourse than to try another plan. I took Hooba out for physical training in the courtyard. He lacked agility with a wooden sword. I kicked a rock toward Hooba hoping for a response. Hooba awkwardly hit the rock with his sword.

I again hit the rock, this time with my own sword. And, the two of us played the afternoon away.

Although I had been trained to use a steel sword from age twenty until the age of full membership which was the age of thirty, it was on my thirtieth birthday that I was permitted to wear on my body a sword outside the walls for that day only.

Hooba was eighteen years old on the day I was dressed complete with sword. I searched to find him in my moment of pride. Hooba was eventually found, holding his six-year-old cousin, Susanna upon his lap. She was laughing uncontrollably at her older cousin. I stood dumbfounded. I was already unfamiliar with supervising a young boy, let alone a little girl.

Suddenly, I found myself laughing along with Hooba and Susanna. I felt a joy in my heart, greater than the joy I had experienced in receiving my sword.

Susanna reached for my hand, a six-foot, two-hundred-pound, shaved-headed warrior/priest, and asked to show me something. I felt completely awkward and at odds with our interaction. But as I knelt down to see what it was she wished to show me, Susanna presented a small stuffed doll. To my surprise, the doll had attached to its waistband a stick representative of a warrior with a sword. Then, she hugged me as I felt myself blush for the first time in my entire life.

I thought to myself: "I have been intimated by a six-year-old girl who has no intimidation for me."

Then, I was jarred back into the reality I now faced, standing on the walls of our community.

Less than eight hours ago, I thought, "I handed this same little girl a sword."

The sun rose in the east. I heard the first bell. Then, the second. Then I heard the third bell. The light from the sun creeped into my view as I saw six hundred soldiers approaching from the south at my wall. I rang the last bell.

They were much closer than I had expected. I could hear noises behind as men inside the community ran to the walls. The next noise I heard was a thud and the wall shook. I looked down the length of the wall to see only six of my men standing on the wall. The Kittims were using a battering ram at the south wall, pounding away at the limestone.

I turned and looked toward the west wall. Another battering ram was approaching the gates. Men were running every direction within the compound.

I heard my own brother, Hilleal, yell, "To the gates!"

A portion of the south wall fell. I turned to my left and saw the gaping hole in the wall whilst three men and one woman, holding swords, stood there at the opening. I ran the length of the wall toward the hole. The years of training and discipline had taught me how to react. I leaped from the wall to outside the community.

I thought, "If I can hold them off, more men will reach the hole in time."

However, the gates fell at that moment allowing two hundred of the Kittim soldiers into the compound.

I took the lives of twelve soldiers before backing myself into the opening in the south wall. A man jumped to my side. He was suddenly pierced by the spear of an enemy soldier, falling to the ground.

I heard Susanna scream, "Jared!"

I spun around with sword in hand, severing the enemy's head from his body. But with every soldier I killed, another one entered the south wall opening. Arrows were passing overhead. I could smell smoke from the burning buildings behind me.

I slashed right and I slashed left. There were body parts laying all around me. The Kittims were climbing over their own dead bodies.

I felt Susanna at my left side.

I yelled, "Go protect the children!"

I then realized Susanna was the only person standing alongside me. I tried to reach out to Susanna with my left hand then realized I had no left arm. I continued to fight.

I felt a sword pierce my abdomen and exit through my back. I stood looking at the sword that pierced me and watched as Susanna forced her own sword into my killer's chest.

I dropped the sword from my right hand. Susanna picked it up and used it to kill yet another Kittim coming toward me. Then, it was as if everything stopped. Twelve Kittim soldiers were staring down at me and the woman standing beside me. No one moved.

I looked at Susanna and remembered her laughter. Then, I heard her screams. I grabbed the sword from within my abdomen and drew it out. I stumbled three steps forward. Again, I felt Susanna at my side. She was holding me up as I swung my sword. And then, she was no longer there.

As I fell to my knees, I saw her laying there.

My last words were: "Susanna, Yea, though I walk through the valley of the shadow of death, I will fear no evil; for thou art with me."

The community fell that day. The Kittim soldiers had taken all eight hundred of the community's lives including, men, women and children. The last life taken by the enemy was a man named Philippos; a man who had walked with and befriended Hooba. He died at the Lord's altar within the Sanctuary.

Chapter 3
The Deception

Like any unmarried young maiden who had reached maturity, she underwent ritualistic purification after her menses. Her cleansing was in accordance with the laws of attendance for prayer services.

Her menses ended always on the Friday before the Sabbath. She would bathe in the garden on that day. The garden was representative of her cleansing and purification for entering her home. The young maiden was then ritually prepared for a meal with her family. Once the meal was finished, the family would cover their heads and leave toward prayer services.

She followed behind her father, her brothers and her mother. She and her sister walked together. Once they reached their destination, the men entered, sitting in the front of the building. The women were to wait outside until all men had been seated. Young, unmarried maidens were not expected to speak unless addressed by their father or given permission by their father to speak. This was the case while at services or at home.

After services, no work was to be performed and they ate a meal of bread and fruit. Sunset brought expectations of the young maiden assisting in the meal preparation with her mother.

The young maiden's first menses had occurred six months prior to this day when her mother had assisted her in the purification bath at its end. It was her fifteenth year. Thereafter, her purifying bath was unassisted.

Another six months passed again. Early that morning while bathing, she noticed a man, standing in the doorway of the garden. He realized when she saw him, that he had been seen. He retreated back into the shadows of the garden. The young maiden was unsure of the man's identity. Yet, she felt shame.

Four more weeks passed again. This time while bathing, she thought she recognized the dark hair of her father. She felt discomfort and was confused.

She called out, "Father?"

No answer came. Once again, the man had disappeared.

Another four weeks passed by. The young maiden tried to hurry along her bathing that morning.

She dried her body and then heard, "Young woman, you will defile the Lord!"

He marched across the garden to where she stood naked. He backhanded her across her face.

Her father looked into her face and said, "You are vile and impure!"

She tried to cover her nakedness.

He again stated, "You should feel shame!"

She would have cried at this moment had she not known that tears would surely bring another strike from her father.

"You are not worthy, nor do you serve me or your God!" he yelled.

He grabbed her towel and threw it to the side away from her.

He removed the tie from his cloak. He ordered her to place her hands on the stone next to the water basin. He lashed three times across her back with the tie from his robe. He grabbed her, spinning her around; his robe was untied at his waist and gaping. He pinned her body against the stone with his forearm. He spread her legs and forced himself inside of her. And as she cried, her father penetrated her even harder. When he had finished with her, he pushed his daughter to the ground.

He spoke again to her saying, "Bathe, for you are vile and filthy! Speak to no one because they will know that you have sinned."

She lay in the cold water, trembling. Then, ceremonially bathed, dried herself off, clothed and covered her head. On this morning, she walked behind her sister to services.

Four weeks again passed. The young maiden did not bleed. That Friday morning before the Sabbath, she again performed her ritual bathing. She was unsure of her body and why she had not bled. She did not know how to tell her mother she had not bled. So, she bathed in her usual manner.

A second month passed without bleeding from the young maiden. After services on that Sabbath day, her father addressed her.

"There is a man who has lost his wife and in need of a mother for his children. You may address him," he said.

The man was much older than the young maiden but with a kind face.

His first words to her were: "You can address me freely."

He was kind and did not raise his hand. She had not known a relationship with an older man like this. Their meeting was brief. However, somehow she felt comforted.

The following week, she heard her father bartering for what she thought was a sheep. She was told again by her father that she could address the mature man. He once more was very kind. He discussed their possible life together. To her, it sounded beautiful.

Yet, she turned to him and said, "You could not want a woman as vile as I. For I have sinned and my father has forced the seed of man within me and I am with child."

And as she cried, the man also cried.

He leaned over, saying to her: "My children need a mother and your child will need a father. This child will be loved by both parents. For the seed of a fallen man cannot tarnish the love of God in your heart. The sins of your father are not your sins or the sins of your child."

He then walked home with the family. Yet, he did not walk among the men.

They approached the young maiden's home as he said to the man's wife: "I find virtue in this young maiden's heart more so than the son of an ass, you call your husband! I pity him on the Day of Atonement. I pray there is a just God. I will not ask that man's permission to marry his daughter. I am not a man without sin. Yet, he is lucky I have not yet thrown the first stone."

The young maiden's mother, upon reaching their home gathered all of her daughter's possessions, packed them and passed them to the mature man who carried them on his back.

The father spoke but one sentence: "We have not finished the discussion on her dowry."

The mature man spun around and said, "You can pay your dowry at your Atonement!"

When the young maiden and the mature man reached her new home, the man said, "I will call you wife."

And she responded with: "I will call you husband."

He opened the door saying, "You shall enter first because I will always put you first."

Their first evening together, the young maiden prepared a meal for her husband. She sat across from him at the table and smiled.

Her husband said to her, "Noam," *meaning pleasant one.*

She responded, "I like that. Isoep," which meant *you add to me.*

Chapter 4

The Cloak

Noam soon bonded with Isoep's two sons. Isoep had always shown Noam respect and affection. However, it became apparent three months after their uniting, Noam was significantly showing signs of being with child.

The women of the community had already begun to gossip. Isoep understood the scrutiny Noam would face from the town's people. He planned for a departure with Noam and his sons right away.

Isoep sold his home. He then purchased supplies for travel and a single donkey. Noam, Isoep and the boys headed on a six-day trip, south where Isoep believed he could find work. He did, indeed, find work in a small shepherd community where he repaired fences and shelters. They found refuge and a new home in one of the repaired shelters.

The time of Noam's confinement approached. Isoep went to the neighboring home and returned back with Noam's new friend Naomi. Naomi assisted Noam with the birth of their new baby boy. That particular evening, the March sky was clear and the stars shone brightly. The neighbors delivered food for the family and gifts of necessity for the new baby.

The young couple planned the trip for circumcision. However, a caravan of travelers to Egypt entered their small community around that same time. Naomi's husband traded with the caravan people who reported to them that the emperor was persecuting their people at The Temple, where they expected to go for the circumcision.

Isoep had no particular ties to this community. He decided it to be a convenience and safer to join with this group in traveling to Egypt. Four days after the birth of Noam's and Isoep's baby boy their journey to a new land began. Isoep and Noam had discussed at length the obligation to circumcise their son on the eighth day.

"God would want our children safe from persecution," Isoep said.

To wait for circumcision would endanger all of them.

They traveled west to the sea and then south along the coast, to Pelusium. Their destination was reached in nearly four months. Isoep found plentiful work in the basin of the Nile. A community of their religious people had already settled in that area. Therefore, they soon found a healer/priest named Josephus to perform their son's circumcision in keeping with *The Law*. Josephus, although from a long line of priests, had traveled to the area to learn healing. A son of Josephus, Tyrus had been in the caravan that traveled to Egypt with Noam's and Isoep's family. He had told them of his father, Josephus. Traveling trade routes was a significant source of income for Josephus's sons, Tyrus and Cyrus.

The circumcision performed by Josephus had been the first in a very long time. He had now devoted his time to the study of healing. Herbs were plentiful in the fertile ground of the Nile basin making them was more readily available to learn about. However, because of the circumcision Josephus had performed, a relationship of fondness developed for this young baby boy, Hooba.

Josephus had lost his wife to death giving him the motivation to learn healing and have time to develop other relationships. Noam, Isoep and their family grew to bond in a family-like relationship with Josephus.

Josephus and Isoep spent many hours telling young Hooba and his brothers the story of their people. Josephus found much joy in teaching the young boys and soon became known to them as *Teacher*. Soon the Teacher began to gather people from the community on the Sabbath. Josephus also began to realize young Hooba's great capacity to learn.

Nearly four years after the meeting of Josephus and Hooba, a caravan came again one day. Josephus could not contain his excitement. His son Cyrus had led this particular caravan along with his wife and daughter. This would be Josephus's first introduction to his granddaughter.

Passover approached as Josephus invited Noam, Isoep and their family to celebrate the ceremonial meal with his family. During the meal, Josephus told the meaning behind the Passover. Young Hooba, just four years old, could hardly contain himself.

During the middle of the story, he yelled out: "They marked the door with blood and the Angel of death passed over them."

There was silence over the abnormality of the child's outburst except for the sound of gasping from those around the table. Josephus quietly went to Hooba and sat beside him.

He asked, "Hooba, what happened next?"

Hooba replied, "The Pharaoh's resolve weakened. Then, the people were released from their bondage and Moses led them away from the Pharaoh."

Then Hooba said, "The Pharaoh angered once again and sent men with chariots to stop the people. Moses raised his staff above the waters and the waters parted. The people crossed the dry bed of the sea. When the Pharaoh's men followed them into the sea, the water crushed down upon them. Then, the people escaped Egypt."

Josephus sat down, poured the wine and broke the bread.

After the meal, he leaned over to Isoep and said, "Your child is truly gifted. We must consider his training."

The next day, all the children played together. Josephus enjoyed the noise of laughter outside his home.

That night, Josephus tucked his granddaughter into bed. He noticed a single rose upon her pillow laying close to her long red hair.

He asked, "Dear, where did you get the rose?"

She responded to her grandfather, "My Hooba gave it to me."

Chapter 5

Psalms

Cyrus and his family had left with the caravan. Since then which was nearly two years later, young Hooba watered Josephus's rose bushes outside his home almost every day. Josephus would simply watch. This was the ritual until a day came when Josephus just had to inquire.

He said to Hooba, "Why do you water the rosebush?"

Young Hooba answered, "I love the rosebush. Red is the color I favor most."

Josephus then asked, "Why did you give my granddaughter the rose?"

Hooba replied, "What good is love if you don't give it away?"

One day soon afterward, Josephus told young Hooba: "I know you will never really forget the lessons that I have taught you but if you do, just remember, Ahav and Ahava to give without expectation, your love."

Noam began feeling homesick for her mother and siblings. Six years had passed since leaving their community. Josephus had convinced Isoep of the need for Hooba to have teaching at a higher level. Isoep was also aware his sons would soon need suitable partners and a larger community would certainly have more eligible young maidens.

The threat of persecution had lessened and a caravan would soon be arriving. If the return to home was a possibility, now would be the most likely of times to leave. Passover was coming and a good reason to celebrate, leave Egypt and return home.

Josephus continued to teach Hooba *The Law* during their six years together. His final lesson was that of Psalms. The lesson was meant for strength and commitment and that God is always with us.

Hooba kept telling Josephus: "Teacher, I will miss you."

Josephus taught him Psalms 23:2 through 23:6.

Psalms 23:2, "He maketh me to lie down in green pastures. He leadeth me beside the still waters."

Psalms 23:3, "He restoreth my soul. He leadeth me in the path of righteousness for his name's sake."

Psalms 23:4, "Yea, though I walk through the valley of the shadow of death, I will fear no evil for thou art with me. Thy rod and they staff, they shall comfort me."

Psalms 23:5, "Thou preparest a table before me in the presence of thine enemies; thou anointest my head with oil; my cup runneth over."

Psalms 23:6, "Surely goodness and mercy shall follow me all the days of my life: and I will dwell in the house of the Lord forever."

Josephus then responded, "Don't miss me, you are never alone. The Lord is always with you."

Chapter 6
Recommendations

Noam and Isoep, under the insistence of Josephus, considered the further training of Hooba. Returning home, they carried a letter of introduction from Josephus written as Hooba's teacher, to be presented to Zachariah, a priest within The Temple who could recommend him for training in protection of *The Law*. Zachariah was also the father of Jared and Hilleal.

Hooba was accepted into the community within the walls at nearly the age of seven. He would be the youngest child ever to be accepted for training. Normally, the age of maturity, which was twelve years old, was the age of acceptance. He met Jared, his new teacher, on that first day. They continued to develop a bond over the next six years of his training.

By the time Hooba reached age twelve, Jared sent a message to Noam and Isoep that their child had reached maturity and was preparing for The Temple. Jared arranged to transport Hooba to The Temple during the time of Passover. Noam and Isoep would travel to meet them both. This meeting also allowed Jared to contact his father, Zachariah the priest, which was a rarity given his oath to the community. Jared also brought a young man with him that day to The Temple from within the walls. His name was John. John, also the cousin of Noam, was in training but had become homesick for his family. He was seven years older than Hooba, yet much less advanced.

Hooba and Jared met Noam and Isoep at The Temple. Hooba was presented by his parents to the priests, as was the custom. Those who attended the Passover festivities occurring after the presentation were Hooba's extended family including Zachariah, father of Jared, and his sons Jared and Hilleal; Noam and Isoep; Isoep's sons and one grandson. Also in attendance were Noam's sister who was with child and Noam's nephew, her sister's son called Iakobos along with Hooba. The family had found hospitality with Zachariah during the Passover time.

During the next few days, Hooba took it upon himself to visit The Temple. Each day, Hooba found Zachariah and the other priests within The Temple. Zachariah was first to start all of their conversations about *The Law*. His intention was to show his fellow priests the vast knowledge and ability of the twelve-year-old boy before them. They were in awe of his realization and comprehension.

One of Isoep's sons agreed to raise Hilleal who was just one year younger than Hooba, until he reached his maturity and ability to go to The Temple. They would live outside the community walls until his acceptance. Hilleal also carried Zachariah's recommendation for further training inside the walls of the community.

After Passover, Noam's sister, who was the mother of Iakabos and soon-to-be mother of Susanna, with her husband traveled along to outside the walls of the community. Iakobos, too, had a recommendation from Zachariah for training at his maturity.

Jared and Hooba caravanned with the family back to the community to continue the training of Hooba.

Noam and Isoep returned to their home village. John returned along with them.

Chapter 7

Isaiah

For days, Jared lectured Hooba on The Book of Isaiah. Each and every day Hooba became more uncomfortable. Some days, Hooba would circle the room as Jared lectured.

On day fourteen, Jared said, "What have you learned, Hooba?"

Hooba replied, "God must be patient." Then, Hooba said, "Last night, the spirit of God spoke to me. The spirit said, *I* am Isaiah."

Jared remained calm, trying not to respond. Then, he calmly spoke, "Was it the prophet Isaiah?"

Hooba's reply was: "No, the spirit was much more direct. Isaiah told me that the sins of the fathers are the sins of the sons. The sins of the enemies are the sins of God's people. If only the innocent can enter The Temple of New Zion, The Temple will be empty."

Jared then asked, "Then, who do you think will worship God on his holy throne?"

"I was taught this was a covenant to our people that those who practice *The Law* will honor God's throne," Hooba answered.

Hooba's teacher responded, "Yet, your Isaiah has guided you to believe that no one is without sin."

Then, Jared followed with: "Is this related to original sin?"

Hooba replied, "How could it be, since the covenant was given to Abraham after the death of Adam?"

Then he stated, "Teacher, then from the Book of Isaiah and the words of my Isaiah, I see no difference between myself and my enemy."

Jared leaned forward quietly and remarked, "There can be only one answer to this. If the spirit from God and the great prophet share this truth then protector of *The Law* does not give you privilege but only responsibility."

Hooba asked, "What then, is the purpose of *The Law* and the covenant with Abraham?"

It took a moment before Jared responded. When he did, he said, "There can only be one purpose. It is my purpose to protect the truth of the existence of God."

Hooba then asked, "Jared, is that my purpose too?"

Once again, his teacher answered, "Hooba, I don't believe so. It is rare but possibly once or twice in a millennium someone so pure will ask that question and seek the answer."

Then Jared continued, "That rare soul will be enlightened enough to teach that there must be more."

"Teacher, what should I do?" Hooba asked.

Jared responded, "Tomorrow, I will raise my sword if I am called upon. Tomorrow, *you* must ask more questions."

Again, Jared leaned forward to Hooba and continued, "At twelve, you baffled the priests, and now at nineteen years of age, you baffled your teachers. There are other teachers and soon, I believe you will baffle them. But you must seek them for knowledge is your purpose. Then, you must seek a knowledge higher than yourself. That knowledge can only be revealed by God."

"Then, what do I do?" Hooba pondered aloud.

Jared then responded, "Rabbi, you teach."

Chapter 8
The Daughter of Cyrus

Josephus's younger son Cyrus, had acquired most of his wealth and contentment through trade. However, most of his happiness came through the love of his wife and daughter. His wife had been born in Greece. He had met her family in Egypt while on his trade route. She immediately caught his eye because of her fair skin and her hair the color of pale cinnamon.

His daughter had inherited her mother's skin and hair unlike the other women Cyrus had seen with olive skin and darkened hair.

His taste for his wife much mirrored the taste he had acquired through his trade of cinnamon and coriander.

Cyrus's fear for his daughter was due to her very obvious ethnic appearance which varied greatly from most of his community's women. He had paid a handsome dowry to her husband. She had been sixteen years of age when he had been approached by a more mature man who showed interest in her as a wife. She had reached maturity by age twelve, yet had the interest of no suitors until then.

Although Cyrus's daughter was treated with love and respect, she never conceived a child with her husband. He had, however, brought a very young daughter into their relationship; he called her Delilah. His wife, Delilah's mother, had died just months before leaving him to raise Delilah alone. Cyrus's daughter assumed the role of mother, affectionately.

Upon the death of her husband just six years later, Cyrus's daughter continued to raise Delilah, her husband's daughter as her own. She was able to support herself and Delilah on her own family inheritance.

Bachariko, as Cyrus called his only daughter, was a little headstrong yet very capable of caring for herself and now a daughter. He would tell her that her nickname Bachariko was because of the *spice* she brought to his life.

She continued to raise her daughter in the religious beliefs of their community.

Chapter 9
Pedagogy

Jared had already begun petitioning his elders to permit Hooba a pilgrimage. He knew that Hooba would never carry a sword. He also knew there was nothing more to offer him in training and was very aware that young Hooba had no worldly experience at the age of nineteen.

Despite the fact that Jared would greatly miss Hooba, should he leave their community, he was very concerned with his being stunted in his knowledge if he remained within the community. It was obvious to Jared and all who knew him that Hooba was a prodigy.

More so than any of the other elders, Jared knew their community was strict which would not allow for Hooba's continued growth. He understood that it was pertinent for Hooba to continue learning as a prodigy and not as a typical student.

Jared had contacted his father, Zachariah, and requested connections to the trade merchants. From there, he dressed in his cloak, wearing his sword beneath the cloak. He walked his brother, Hilleal, to the gate of the walls and hugged him for his brother had chosen to now live outside the walls of the community at his insistence. Jared wished for a different life for his brother not like that of his own.

He packed the belongings of the two named Iakobas for they would also be traveling. Isoep's son, Iakobas, would be staying with Zachariah and taking up the priesthood and the other Iakobas, who was Hooba's first cousin, would be taking up trade. Both would be traveling with Jared and Hooba to The Temple community in the very near future.

Jared spent the following day with Hooba. They packed his second cloak, a single blanket and a leather flask which was inside a leather pouch, branded with Jared's initial of J. It was literally the only personal item that Jared had to give.

The men all went to the hall for their evening meal. It happened to be the Friday night of the Sabbath once again. The next day, they ritually bathed and spent the day in prayer. After sunset, Jared broke bread with the men and enjoyed their last meal together. Jared met the men at the gates after sunrise the next morning with ample food supplies for their journey to The Temple. They set off on foot for the trip which would take about two days.

The men met Zachariah at his home in time for the evening meal and also slept that night in his home. The next day one named Iakobas the elder stayed with Zachariah. Hooba, the other younger Iakobas and Jared set out on foot for the Mediterranean Sea.

Once arriving at the coast of the sea, the men met the two brothers, Cyrus and Tyrus, the trade merchants. Hooba immediately remembered them from his time living in Egypt as a small boy. The men also immediately remembered Hooba. This was Jared's first introduction to the brothers. Hooba anxiously asked Cyrus about his daughter, Bachariko.

Jared couldn't help but notice the smile and exuberance disappearing from Hooba's face when learning of her marriage a year before.

Yet, Hooba turned to Cyrus and said, "Please tell her, I remember her fondly and wish her all the blessings of the world."

Cyrus was taking Iakobas en route to Egypt and Tyrus would be escorting Hooba to Antioch, Turkey.

The time was nearing for the departure. Hooba turned to Jared and said, "Rabbi, friend ... and I would say, *abba* (father). I have valued our time; *ahav* and *ahava* (love, given without expectation). I have nothing to give you. This pouch is my only possession and I must ask you if I may send it to Josephus to thank him for the opportunity he gave me to spend my time with you."

Jared looked into the young man's eyes and simply said, "I would be honored that the man, who sent you to me, received such a gift."

Both men simultaneously reached for the other, grabbing each other's arms and hands which immediately became a strong embrace of arms and bodies.

Hooba turned and began walking up the plank of the boat as Jared walked away.

Jared turned back around calling out, "Hooba, peace be with you."

Tears flowed from the eyes of both men as they parted ways.

Jared continued to walk as the boat set out to sea. Just as the boat disappeared from his view, Jared recited Psalms 23:2 through 23:6 to himself and walked home to within the walls of his community.

Chapter 10
Enlightenment

"If only I could get through the water and to the land, I could get past this boat and the demon that appears to be in my stomach," Hooba thought.

He could also not get past the lack of daily, ritual bathing.

He thought to himself: "I am surrounded by water yet fresh water is scarce."

It had been many days since he last bathed.

The other travelers scoffed at his insistence on hand washing before meals. Hooba's loathing of nonbathing did not compare to the feeling of distain and despair he experienced when expected to assist in unloading supplies from the boat on the Sabbath.

Once the boat had been completely emptied of supplies, the merchants and their wares, Tyrus escorted Hooba to a small temple in Antioch. It was here that Tyrus, Hooba and many of the other men bathed, prayed and observed the Sabbath until sundown.

One of Hooba's first lessons was learned at this time. He now understood why Jared's community had functioned as it had. Because, the community outside of the walls, sometimes observed *The Law* only when convenient.

That night after sunset Hooba learned his next lesson. The complete group of boat passengers, merchants and workers, had their evening meal together. There was prayer. However, some did not participate.

Those who prayed and those who did not continued to respect one another. Those who were ritually clean could eat at the same table as those who were not. Those who had not chosen to eat clean were not condemned. It appeared to be known that all food on the right side of the table was clean and that on the other side was not. It was a matter of each one's choice as to which side their food was chosen. A man seated at the table who was unclean informed Hooba when he nearly chose from the unclean food.

There was no judgment at this table. Hooba had learned a valuable lesson. This brought to mind a lesson from Jared. There is more value in choosing to live the correct path than following blindly.

Hooba thought, "It must be as important to choose God as it is that God chooses us."

That night, Hooba looked for a place to lay his blanket. The unclean man from the table called to him.

He said, "It looks like you would find more comfort close to the fire."

That man then rolled up his own blanket, for he recognized this young man was new to their group.

Hooba placed his blanket in the man's place and thought, "Why is the pagan, called Massa, more kind than the Jew?"

Hooba knelt, lay prostrate over his knees and prayed. He made himself comfortable and fell to sleep.

Before sunset the next day the camp already was bustling. Tyrus found Hooba and guided him to the edge of the camp to a small stream. Other men were also bathing. All of these men again had their morning meal together.

Donkeys and carts were loaded with supplies and merchandise for the caravan going east. Hooba was assigned the care of six goats. That night, after traveling all day, Tyrus asked Hooba if he had ever prepared a clean goat.

Hooba responded, "I have not had that responsibility."

Tyrus then stated, "Here in the wilderness, it is your intention that this goat be prepared clean which is more important than the process. Call on God for purity and do not let the animal suffer."

Hooba said, "I have no skills with the knife or sword."

Tyrus instructed, "You make the cut deep and swift. Hang the animal so the blood will drain. Then, pray thanks to God for the food. Once the blood has ceased to flow, bring the animal to me. I will prepare the fire."

They feasted that evening yet Hooba was not hungry. The next morning he continued to guide five goats toward Damascus.

Once they had reached Damascus they traded, and on their departure Hooba guided four goats and two sheep.

The journey from Damascus to Bagdad took them three weeks on foot. Upon their arrival, Hooba had no animals left to guide. They soon traded and had more goats and sheep.

While in Bagdad, they rested a full twenty-four hours. They then traded both spices and silk. The men were invited to a feast by a local merchant. Hooba had always enjoyed festivals. Shortly before they left for the feast Tyrus presented Hooba with a handful of dried dates.

He stated, "The food at the festival will not be clean. Still, take a small portion so not to insult the host."

There was music and laughter. The pagans among them ate in abundance. For a moment, Hooba felt jealousy.

Then for the second time, he heard Isaiah speaking, "You do not have a jealous God. Why are you a jealous man? Be thankful for the dates."

Isaiah said, "Consider your thoughts or intentions thus they do not become actions."

Then, Hooba again felt Tyus at his side.

Tyrus said, "Do not be alarmed by the Zoroastrians. They will soon be praying to the fire. They are praying to their one God and good is represented by the fire."

Hooba was confused. Was this some type of idol worship?

He heard Isaiah for the third time: "Did not Moses tremble at the burning bush? Is God not everywhere?"

He thought to himself: "If this guardian of God speaks to me in this place then this place must, too, be holy; for they also pray to the God that is all good."

Hooba did not realize he had said aloud, "Praise to my God that is good."

Yet, all looked at him in shock. Then, the pagans, the Zoroastrians and the Jews all clapped. For a moment, Hooba felt shame.

He thought, "How dare I think I own God? This is not my God; this is our God."

In that moment, Hooba felt a presence. It was loving, kind and all accepting.

Hooba again said aloud, "Peace be with you."

The entire group of men responded back, "And peace be with you."

That night, Hooba fell into his slumber with a smile.

To Hooba, every day was the same leaving him hours of contemplation. One day he would recite the Torah to himself and the next contemplate what it all meant.

Early on another day Tyrus woke him. Hooba's first thought went to: "Why should I be awakened so early?"

Then Tyrus reminded him, "Today is the Sabbath and there is a stream to bathe."

Hooba remembered, "It has been a week and I have only washed my hands. Why has God not struck us down? Surely, me forgetting today is the Sabbath must be a great sin."

He again had a thought: "If I would say this aloud, it would be within the right of Tyrus to stone me."

He wondered to himself if when he killed the goat, it had to be swift to be within *The Law*, then the suffering of the goat must matter.

"How could I make a goat walk without water and food on the Sabbath if it still entailed work? To ease suffering on the Sabbath must not be work and to ease suffering must be a responsibility. So, to cause suffering must be the sin," Hooba wondered.

That day while traveling, one goat dropped to the ground. Massa, the unclean man who had become a friend of Hooba, came over and lifted the goat. For the next hour, he carried the goat. There were so many lessons for Hooba yet he had not yet reached the destination of his learning.

Another sunrise and Hooba had risen early. He bathed and he prayed. He finished his work, feeding and giving water to the animals. He then hurried to help his pagan friend finish his work. Together, they loaded another man's cart.

He walked alongside his new friend the entire day. They each noticed and mentioned the beauty of the flowers along the way. The sun shone brightly.

Hooba said to his friend: "I do not wish to appear rude. Who do you believe created the sun and the flowers?"

The friend answered, "The sun god created the sun and the earth god puts forth and creates the flowers."

Hooba did not speak further but rather continued to walk with his friend.

Nearly an hour had passed when Hooba's friend spoke, "Who do you believe created the sun and the flowers?"

Hooba then answered, "I believe God created all of it."

His friend again spoke, "You must believe your God is great."

Hooba responded, "I have felt the love of my God and it is great. It surpasses the love I felt for you when I watched you carry the goat. If I see the strength and love in your heart, and my God is much greater than I, my God, too, sees it."

His friend reacted, "Your God must be great because the sun and the Earth have never reached out to me."

They walked for two more hours alongside one another.

Hooba spoke, "Then my friend, you must be greater than both the sun and the Earth for you have reached out to me and to a mere goat."

His friend said, "Hooba, tell me about your God."

Chapter 11
Changes

Cyrus left his home and village by caravan toward the sea. There was always great anticipation when he was to see his father Josephus. This journey would be entirely by sea unlike his travel for trade in the past.

He felt this would be his last trading excursion as he was beginning to feel his age. A young business associate called Yohanan would accompany him on his final trip. Yohanan's family was also involved in trade.

Approaching the shore of Egypt, Cyrus saw a thin, white-haired man looking out over the sea. He knew immediately it was his father though the years had aged him.

Exiting the boat, Yohanan was introduced to Josephus as the man who would be taking over Cyrus's trade route.

Yohanan addressed Josephus with respect, saying, "Rabbi, Zachariah extends his hands to you."

During their visit Josephus informed Cyrus he had learned much about healing and felt it time to return home. It had been over twelve years of learning. They arrived home a couple of months later.

Upon arriving at the shore of his ancestral home, Josephus first noticed the prominence of the Kittims' presence. Soldiers stood positioned around the port. Their goods were examined and immediately taxed. Cyrus seemed accustomed to this experience. However, Josephus felt discomfort. Things had changed in the years he was away. His home now felt foreign and unfamiliar.

Josephus traveled by cart and ox to the home of his temple. He felt relief once the walls of his city appeared. Then, he noticed more of the Kittim guards stationed along the walls. His heart sank. However, once inside the walls he noticed the city was bustling. They passed through the marketplace where trading and shopping were occurring. Unfortunately, he then noticed a table for tax collection at each market stand.

Josephus traveled through the marketplace to the home of his close friend Zachariah. He was immediately welcomed by his friend who, after their greetings, escorted him to his private bathing facility.

Josephus ritually bathed and then feasted with Zachariah and his wife Ruth. They then slept as the next day was the Sabbath.

Josephus awoke and was up before dawn. He bathed again ceremoniously and ate a meal with Zachariah and Ruth. They, together, left for The Temple.

He thought, "Today, I will be home in the house of the Lord."

While traveling to The Temple, they passed many Kittim guards.

Josephus again thought to himself: "To guard is to work on the Sabbath. This was certainly not necessary."

Standing guard at The Temple, a Kittim guard counted each and every person going into the building. A coin was placed in a till by every man and woman as they entered.

As they waited to enter The Temple and deposit their coins, Josephus recognized the man next in line to drop his coin before entering. It was Yohanan, his son's friend from the boat.

Josephus then witnessed Yohanan's hand throw a coin so hard into the till, it bounced back out onto the ground. The guard bent to reach the coin, only to have Yohanan grind the coin farther into the dirt with his foot. The guard rose up from the ground in anger with his hand raised. It was a second guard who placed his hand on the first guard to stop what would have come to be.

Josephus reflected on what had just transpired. He carefully placed his coin in the till.

After services, when all but the priests had left, Zachariah led Josephus to the Sanctuary. He pulled the privacy veil covering the altar of the Lord to one side. Josephus entered, knelt down and kissed the floor at the altar.

During that same moment in another town, Jared knelt and kissed the altar floor of the Sanctuary in his community within the walls. One thousand miles away, Hooba knelt and looked to the skies, almost as if a veil had been lifted.

"My God, you are everywhere," he thought.

Chapter 12

The Healers

There came a day when Josephus again visited Zachariah and his wife, Ruth. Ruth had a friend also visiting called Joanna. Joanna was the daughter of a man in Jared's community. She and her husband lived outside the walls.

Josephus was introduced to Joanna and during the course of their visit while having a discussion on spices and cooking both Joanna and Ruth showed great interest in Josephus's words on the health benefits of herbs and spices.

Joanna and Ruth learned about healing with herbs and spices for the following six months through Josephus.

During this time, Zachariah became ill with a serious fever causing delirium and his relinquishing of all food. Joanna's husband traveled back to the city within the community walls to bring Hilleal and Jared home to their father, Zachariah.

Josephus treated Zachariah with turmeric and mustard seed. Then, he fed him broth of a chicken, laced with rosemary and tarragon. His fever soon diminished and, once again, he was right in his mind.

When Joanna's husband got to the community within the walls, he told the sons their father was deathly ill and they must go to him at once. But when they arrived home, their father was back to normal health after the treatment by Josephus.

Hilleal and Jared turned to Joanna's husband and Josephus, saying, "You have delivered us and have delivered our father from death. You are saviors."

Joanna and her husband soon returned with Hilleal and Jared where they continued to live outside the community walls.

Joanna continued to practice and heal with herbs and spices. Her friend Hannah also showed great interest in healing and was taught by Joanna. Another young girl from the community named Susanna frequently followed Hannah to her lessons with Joanna. Susanna was the cousin of Hooba, the intimidator of Jared and now approaching the age of twelve.

She had heard that the warrior and priest Jared was ill. She took it upon herself to cook broth of chicken, rosemary and tarragon and walked through the front gates of the walls to deliver the healing broth to him.

A flustered young man named Phillip summoned Jared to the courtyard.

He said to Jared: "There is a young woman in our courtyard asking for you."

Jared entered the courtyard to see a young girl, blossoming into a young maiden. He blushed, nearly as much as on their first meeting, years before, when she had visited Hooba.

Susanna spoke, "I heard you did not feel well, so I came with spiced broth for healing."

Jared fidgeted with nervousness.

Then, he spoke, "No one has cared for me like this, since my own mother when I was a child."

Jared got down onto one knee as to look Susanna in her eyes. "You will be a fine woman and mother, for I see in your eyes the purity of your heart," he said.

Susanna responded with: "Well, are you going to taste it? It is meant to help gain your strength."

Jared stood, reached for the broth and drank it to completion.

He said, "Your kindness has warmed me as much as the broth."

Then, Jared smiled from ear to ear.

"Susanna, you should meet my brother Hilleal. He is close to your age and is free to marry," Jared informed her.

Susanna looked at Jared and responded, "Is he as quiet and shy as you?"

Under his breath, Jared said, "Probably not."

Then, louder, so she could hear him, Jared said, "He is kind, respectful and follows *The Law*."

She then asked, "Is he as tall as you are?"

Jared answered, "In character only."

"Does he come with your recommendation?" she then asked.

Jared responded, "I am sure he is up to the challenge; oh, I mean, yes ... I would recommend you and him."

Then he said, "A man will always watch out for his brother and his brother's wife."

"And, a woman will always care for her husband's brother," Susanna answered back.

"Susanna, with your permission, I will arrange a meeting with my brother," Jared told her. "Peace be to you, my sister," he ended.

"Peace be to you, my brother," Susanna replied.

Susanna and Hilleal soon met at the hand of Jared. Susanna continued the study of herbs and spices for healing with Joanna and Hannah.

One day Ruth, wife of Zachariah, heard from her husband about a young woman who had burned her hand in a fire just the day before. The young woman had been ordered to prepare meals for the Kittims camped outside of the city. The Kittim soldiers had brought and left her at The Temple saying this woman, Rebecca, no longer had value if unable to cook their meals.

Zachariah brought Rebecca home. Ruth meticulously cleaned her burned flesh, applied silver powder and wrapped her wounds.

After many months of treatment, Rebecca regained the use of her hand with moderate scarring. She had been previously captured in Syria by the Kittim soldiers. She had not been raised as a child of *The Law*. However, during her convalescence with Zachariah and Ruth, she learned both healing and *The Law*.

Rebecca attended Sabbath services, seated with Ruth; though, she was shunned by many women due to her Syrian nationality.

Rebecca continued to stay with Ruth and Zachariah, tending to the ill and injured.

Meanwhile, Josephus returned to the city by the sea to visit his granddaughter. He had not seen his Bachariko since her age of six years. He had not been present for her marriage or the death of her husband. Nor had he met the daughter of her husband she now raised as her own, Delilah.

When first he saw the stunning young woman with the cinnamon-colored hair, it brought back the memory of his wife Chari, who had long since passed away and he so missed.

He looked into Bachariko's eyes and saw Chari his wife looking back at him.

"Bachariko, it is a blessing to see your eyes and smile; I so remember them with warmth in you as a child," Josephus said.

"Grandfather, I, too, remember my childhood with warmth. If you look at the northeast corner of my home, I, also, have planted a rosebush," Bachariko informed him.

Her grandfather said, "I have brought you cinnamon to match your hair and spices from the east."

"How long can you stay, Grandfather? For my home can now be your home," she asked.

Josephus answered, "I can stay, as there are no other demands on my time."

Bachariko then mentioned her father would be moving back very close to her home in the near future.

She also said, "Then I will have two men in my life."

"Nonsense, we'll need a third man for you in the near future," her grandfather spoke.

"Grandfather, I have not had that much luck with men," Bachariko admitted.

"Many do not accept me as their nationality, because of my appearance," she went on.

"In fact, many ask what demons inside me make my hair so red," she touted.

"Besides, I have passed my prime and I have been with a man," she said sadly.

They spent hours visiting and catching up on the years spent apart. Josephus met Delilah and formed a bond immediately.

Nearly a year had passed when one day Delilah came home after eating a strange fruit from a tree. Her stomach ached, contracting with pain.

Josephus mixed goat milk, vinegar and wine, giving her the concoction to drink. She expelled the contents of her stomach almost immediately. He retrieved a leather pouch from his room which had been branded with a J. The pouch held herbs and ginger which he ground and added to water to settle her stomach.

Bachariko asked Josephus about the herbs he carried inside the leather pouch. Then, he told her the story behind the leather pouch.

"The pouch was a gift from Hooba. It is filled with all the herbal lessons I learned in the east," he said.

She said, "Grandfather, can you teach me those lessons?"

And, although she had been trying to avoid her next question, she asked it regardless.

"What have you heard from Hooba?" she shyly inquired.

Her grandfather answered, "The boy has learned many lessons and has become a man. Just as I learned lessons in Egypt, he has gone east to learn more lessons."

She again asked her grandfather a question rather reluctantly, "Did Hooba travel alone?"

He answered, "When last I heard, the caravan was filled with only men."

That evening upon retiring for bed, Josephus found a small cup filled with water and a single, floating red rose next to his bedside. He smiled as he remembered so many years ago when first Bachariko had received a single red rose from her Hooba and laid it on her bed pillow.

He left his room, peered into his granddaughter's room only to see another cup, filled with water and a single floating red rose.

And still, the red of the rose reminded him of the cinnamon red color of his granddaughter's hair.

Cyrus, the father of Bachariko, returned to the city by the sea after his last caravan for trade. His cousin also returned to settle in that same city after ending in trade. The cousin's unmarried daughter, Beatrice along with his wife accompanied him on the move.

Being of mixed nationality, Greek and Hebrew, Beatrice related to Bachariko's difficulty in finding marriage and in being accepted. Beatrice had already decided she would never marry and would dedicate her life to religious study and service.

Beatrice and Bachariko became close cousins, nearly like sisters. Beatrice learned healing, herbs and spices along with her cousin from Josephus who was her great uncle and also Bachariko's grandfather.

Chapter 13
Alone

Meanwhile, the day finally arrived when Hooba's caravan reached Kubha. From here, the caravan would turn north along the Silk Road. It had already been a very long journey and many months.

The plan was to stay in Kubha for three days, unload their goods and trade. They also replaced their carts with pack animals for further travel.

Each man received a fur cloak to be worn during the day and to sleep on at night for warmth. The further they traveled into the mountains, the cooler the days and nights became.

The men feasted and some of the men drank the beer of Kubha. Hooba learned to not like the taste of beer.

Once their feast was complete, the men continued to drink, leaving Hooba alone to wander about in exploration of the community. He came upon two men speaking in a form of broken Aramaic. Hooba speaking fluent Aramaic, understood their conversation. He continued to hear the word, *Allah* and knew they were discussing God.

Hooba ingratiated himself into their conversation. The men seemed relieved to now have an interpreter among them as Aramaic was neither of the men's primary language.

The conversation continued to fascinate Hooba. Both men were implying their beliefs were the truth. However, in Aramaic, both nearly matched his own belief. They both mentioned a Godhead who was creator of all that was good. Both spoke of lesser deities who did the work of the Godhead. These lesser deities apparently acted as messengers from the Godhead.

One man quoted the *Avesta* (the sacred book of Zoroastrianism) while the other quoted the *Rigveda* (one of the four sacred canonical texts of the Indus Vedas.) To Hooba, most of their quotes sounded like those found in the Book of Psalms. He began to quote The Book of Psalms aloud.

Each of the men smiled and nodded in agreement.

Hooba thought to himself: "Although these were three different points of view, they all agreed on the beauty and the concepts of their words."

Hooba had not divulged his conversations with Isaiah, the Spirit of God, with anyone until this point. No one had shared conversations with him about having discussions with their lesser deities. Both men aspired to hear more about his interactions with Isaiah.

The Brahman man stood and went into his tent. He returned with a bottle of grape wine to share with the men. Once they had finished the bottle of wine, the Brahmanist offered the flask to Hooba.

Using his broken Aramaic, he said, "Inside the bottle will be the *holy space* for Isaiah." (Brahmanists believe they pray to what's inside the idol rather than the idol.)

Hooba's thought turned to: "How do we place God in the Sanctuary? Is that any different than placing God's holy space in a bottle?"

This remark came after he had been imbibing on grape wine for some time.

Then, he asked the question to both men: "What do you consider to be holy space?"

Simultaneously, they answered, "Allah's creation."

Hooba wondered, "These men have no training on *The Law* yet their understanding is the same as my own."

He asked his next question. "If there was but one ordinance you might name which would you choose?"

Both men mumbled in their broken Aramaic words. Hooba attempted to translate into a sentence what they had spoken. Again, both translations mimicked the other; *honor Allah and do only good to man and no evil.*

He responded back to the men: "If you shall follow that ordinance, what happens?"

The Zoroastrian man responded, "You will become one with the light and fire of the Godhead."

Next, the Brahmanist man answered, "You will become worthy of oneness with the Godhead."

Hooba felt comfort and a kinship with these men.

This led him to his next question. "What becomes of those who do not keep this ordinance?"

The first man again responded, "You will again dwell in evil until you overcome."

The second man answered next. "You will repeat the birth cycle until you undo the evil."

Hooba again responded back to the men: "You reap what you sow."

All three men slapped one another on their backs in agreement.

They asked and answered aloud, "What do we want? Peace on Earth and to return home to God."

Then, "What else do we want?"

All answered with a bit less reverence: "More wine, please."

Hooba found his way back to the camp. There was, indeed, a chill in the air. He laid his fur cloak on the ground as bedding, covering himself with his other cloak. He began to drift asleep but then arose, knelt beside his bedding and prayed.

His words were, "God, you do not belong to the people of *The Law*. You are universal and everywhere. Peace be with these men tonight. May I someday meet them in Paradise."

Then, Hooba thought he heard Isaiah: "Peace be with you, Hooba."

Chapter 14
South to India

The next night, Hooba returned to the home of the Brahmanist man. He confessed to his new friend: "I need to learn more about your Allah."

The man informed Hooba that his son, Aahan, would soon be traveling to the port near Banbhore and then on to Kashmir.

The friend then went on to tell Hooba: "You can find Brahman priests in Kashmir."

Hooba returned to his camp later that evening. He prayed and fell asleep in his cloak of warmth and fur. The following morning, Hooba found Tyrus and informed him he was on a search for God which would be taking him south rather than north along the Silk Road.

Tyrus said, "Hooba, you do not know this territory!"

Hooba replied, "I have met a man called Aahan. He knows the language and the territory. I shall accompany him all the way to Kashmir."

Tyrus spoke with concern: "Hooba, you are entering an area unknown and I fear for you, as even I do not know this territory."

Hooba then dictated two letters to Tyrus to be delivered to his mother and the other one to Jared.

The first letter read, *"Mother, I do not know where I am going or where I will end. My heart is awake with curiosity. I believe I am going where the Lord has sent me. Love, Hooba."*

The next letter to Hooba's dear friend, Jared, read as follows: *"Rabbi and friend, I am learning. I fear not because the Lord is with me. God has opened so many doors and I continue to pass through them. I have learned to ask questions and I have learned to answer them."*

It was signed, *"Admiration and respect, Hooba."*

Tyrus assured Hooba he would deliver the letters to both his mother and his friend.

Hooba sought out his pagan friend, Massa.

He addressed him saying, "Brother, you have made this trip already more educational than I expected. I have learned what is in a man's heart is what makes the man."

Massa turned to Hooba, handing him his staff and spoke, "Sometimes we need a friend to lean on and although I will not be there, lean on me."

Turning to walk away, the pagan man called to Hooba again saying, "May Allah be with you."

He returned to pack his few belongings finding, however, they were already packed along with provisions thrown over the back of a donkey. Tyrus stood next to the animal.

Hooba admitted, "I cannot pay for the animal and the provisions."

Tyrus replied, "You have continually shared the labor of our travels," then handed Hooba three silver pieces.

Then he further said, "One coin is from your father, one coin is from Jared and the third is from me in case you need anything on your travels. Hooba, in some way you have touched us all."

Hooba sat for the noon meal with all the caravan-traveling men. The entire group of forty men then recited Psalms 23:2 through 23:6, for all of them had heard it repeated many times by Hooba. He had, indeed, touched each and every man.

Hooba led his donkey to the home of Aahan. He watched while Aahan hugged his father farewell, then both men headed down the dusty road, south to Kashmir.

A few days had passed on their travels when Hooba again smelled the salty air of the Sea of Oman. They soon arrived at the port near Banbhore. The port was bustling and dirty with a stench filling the air of rotting fish and flesh. The men at the port appeared as rough, loud and unbathed workers. Smoke billowed and loud voices came from the doors and windows of buildings along the way. Painted women with bare midriffs called to Hooba and Aahan as they passed by. One particular woman flashed her breast at Hooba. He cringed, looked up and wondered if lightning was about to strike at any moment.

Aahan leaned over to Hooba and said, "We must find a room here for the evening."

Hooba thought to himself: "It would be better to sleep under the stars."

Aahan then said, "We will have to pay for someone to feed and take the donkeys while we sleep. You will want a room with a door and latch between these people."

Aahan led Hooba into a small building near the end of the road. Painted women, scantily clad were singing, dancing and entertaining. The proprietor guided the two men to a room toward the back. When the proprietor opened the door, there stood four small children. Their mothers were out front, providing the entertainment. The proprietor yelled which sent the four children running out back into the alley with the trash.

Hooba looked at Aahan and said, "Where are their fathers?"

Aahan answered, "Most of them do not have fathers."

Hooba began to anger and then cried, "Are there no responsible men here?"

The proprietor delivered one basin of water to their room. Hooba asked Aahan if he wished to wash first. Aahan washed his hands leaving the water then for Hooba. Hooba picked the basin up and carried it out the back door along with a loaf of bread. He carefully washed each child, broke the bread and gave his portion to the children.

Hooba went back to the front of the building. "Which of you women belong with those children?" he yelled.

The women did not understand his words. They did not know the Aramaic language. Aahan heard him yell. He swiftly came to the front of the building.

Aahan spoke calmly, "Who are the mothers of the children?"

Three separate women danced over to Hooba believing his pity might pay.

Hooba again looked at Aahan and spoke, "How long will a silver piece feed these women and children?"

Aahan answered, "A silver piece will feed them for many months. However, if you give them one piece of silver, they will only pay for their freedom."

Hooba removed two pieces of silver from the small sack at his waist. He gave one to the proprietor and one to the women. He asked Aahan to explain to the women that they were now free.

Hooba had recognized only one word as Aahan spoke to the women. It was *alma*, meaning benevolent mother.

The three women hugged Hooba, throwing themselves at his feet. Quickly, they ran to the back door to see their four children clean and eating. As they turned back to Hooba, he smiled.

Hooba entered his room, knelt on the floor, prayed and cried.

During his prayer, he said to God, "You provided *manna* (edible substance) to Hagar in the desert when she was discarded by Abraham. It is certainly right that I feed these who have been discarded."

Hooba felt a warmth come over him. And then he heard, "They are all my children."

Chapter 15
Kashmir

The next morning, Aahan arose and considered the mere pittance of a cost it was for their room and the boarding of their donkeys. He thought how he had traveled through this port before and had never questioned the activities or the women.

He considered how important it had been that this particular proprietor already knew him. The proprietor could have had taken action against Hooba for his insolence in his establishment but had chosen not to. Then, he thought about Hooba's very fair offer in giving a silver piece for the women's freedom.

The seaside village was rough and under the circumstances, it could have resulted in Hooba's death. There were no rules or law to abide by. Hooba was unaware that each man in the establishment carried a dagger and was willing to use it. Aahan had actually slept with his own dagger in his hand all night, fearful that men of the community might come for any remaining silver. Thus, he himself, paid the small pittance for their room and boarding of the donkeys.

The two men set off on foot, donkeys in tow. They went south and then to the west. They traveled across the southern plateau of Kashmir to the foothills and a small village. Once Hooba saw the small village, he was reminded of his home. It was warm, arid and cleaner than the seaport had been.

Children were playing in the streets and their laughter could be heard. The women were watching their children from the doorways of their homes. He already felt more comfortable.

A round, gray-haired, toothless woman ran out in front of the men, embracing Aahan with all her might. He soon learned this to be Aahan's grandmother.

Aahan pointed to Hooba and the older woman then hurried over and squeezed Hooba again with all her strength and enthusiasm. She began talking a mile a minute. However, Hooba understood not a word. Yet, he continued to smile and nod as if he did.

Hooba realized very shortly he would need to understand this foreign dialect of Kush. The first opportunity, Hooba talked with Aahan about learning the language so he could discuss God with the people of the area. Aahan quickly informed Hooba that the dialect of Kush was just one of thousands of languages included in all of the area.

"The language you will need to know is Sanskrit," he informed Hooba.

"I can teach you Kush and probably twenty parts of Sanskrit but to learn all of Sanskrit you will have to make it the study for the rest of your lifetime," Aahan admitted.

"I suggest I teach you just Kush. If I can teach you Kush, I will then take you to the wisest man of our village and you can communicate and learn Sanskrit with him," Aahan said.

Hooba said, "Please teach me how to say *please* and *thank you*."

"Your first two words to be taught are please and container," Aahan said.

Hooba repeated it back to him in Kush. Then, Aahan pointed to a container and said in Kush, "Please, container."

Then he said in Aramaic: "Follow me."

Each man took a large container and walked to the edge of the community to fill the container with water from a stream.

They carried them back to Aahan's grandmother's home as Aahan said to Hooba in Kush: "Thank you."

Hooba responded back in Kush: "Thank you."

The grandmother prepared a large meal. Hooba was invited by her to sit at the head of their table.

He responded in the language she would understand: "Thank you."

The grandmother proceeded to half-sing and half-speak a prayer before the meal.

Hooba thought with surprise and awe ... "At this place, at this time, this woman is the head of the family and she is allowed to pray. How will I know if this food is clean according to *The Law*?"

Aahan's grandmother had placed an earthen bowl of beans, rice and meat in cream sauce at Hooba's place.

Hooba looked at Aahan. But he was unsure of how to ask such a question.

Aahan said, "It is flavorful and it is lamb which is expensive for my grandmother to make. She considers you an honored guest."

Hooba watched as the grandmother dipped a scoop of the savory dish to her mouth with what appeared to be unleavened bread.

Hooba thought to himself: "How do I dishonor this woman when she has gone to extraordinary lengths to prepare a special meal when I cannot even explain to her the significance?"

He scooped some of the savory dish onto the bread, took a bite and smiled. The grandmother beamed with pleasure.

As the end of the meal approached, Hooba said in Kush: "Thank you; the meal is greater than I deserve."

Aahan realized it would not take his friend very long to learn the language.

That evening, the grandmother offered Hooba her bed. Aahan whispered something into Hooba's ear.

Hooba repeated it aloud in Kush. The grandmother smiled from ear to ear.

Aahan went outside, Hooba followed him out where they set up a small camp next to the home.

Hooba said, "What did I tell your grandmother?"

Aahan responded, "Literally, you told her, *you have treated me as a king but I will not take the queen of this home's bed.*"

Hooba laid down, gave thanks to God and said, "I honor You just as I honor this woman."

The morning came and Hooba awoke to find a bowl of fruit where he had been sleeping. Aahan had been aware of Hooba's customary diet even if not fully aware of the significance of it.

Kashmir

Aahan then asked Hooba if he would like to help repair around his grandmother's home.

The rest of the day he gave Hooba directions in *Kush*. They repaired the roof of her home, the shrubbery was trimmed, the garden was weeded and then Hooba and Aahan prepared a vegetarian meal of rice and vegetables.

Hooba was certain this meal was clean as he had helped to prepare it. He escorted the grandmother to the head of the table and served the bowl to her.

She looked at the two young men and said, "You have made my home a palace."

Hooba sang Psalms 23:2 through 23:6 as a prayer before the meal, in *Kush*. They then ate and conversed in her language. Aahan only corrected Hooba's words three times.

By the week's end, Aahan said to Hooba, "You are ready to meet the most-wise man of my village."

That night as they were falling asleep, Aahan spoke two words and Hooba repeated them back.

Aahan responded in Kush, "That was Sanskrit for *please* and *thank you*."

"One more word that you must learn," Aahan said.

"Upanishads. It means Indus sacred texts," he said.

Night had fallen.

Chapter 16
A Wise Man

Hooba spent four hours a day learning Sanskrit with a wise man who lived down the road, four hours a day with Aahan working to earn his keep and four hours praying to his God. His life cycle was not particularly different than the life within the community walls he had lived for twelve years.

The first day that Hooba had met the wise man, Aahan took him to the man's hut. They looked inside to see a man probably approaching eighty years old, sitting on the floor with his legs crossed.

Hooba's first impression was: "This is a frail, peaceful man whose face has aged and weathered with wisdom."

He was also curious of the man's wry smile. The next moment, however, the man was standing and shaking his hand. Hooba marveled at his agility at such an age. Then, in just another quick instant, he was again seated crossed-legged.

The man gestured for Hooba to sit as he was seated with legs crossed and mimic him with eyes closed in silence.

Hooba began to ask a question but the man in *Aramaic* said, "Silence."

Then in *Kush* he said, "Silence."

Then in *Sanskrit*, he said, "Silence."

Hooba's mind was already racing. He thought, "If this man knows *Aramaic*, why must I have learned *Kush*?"

Next when he spoke, the man again said in *Sanskrit*, "Silence."

Then, again he spoke and said, "Silence" in *Aramaic*.

The man said, "Brahman," in *Sanskrit*.

Then, he said, "Allah," in *Aramaic*.

Hooba once again began to speak only to be silenced with a hand gesture from the wise man. Then, in *Kush*, the man explained that there were only two *Aramaic* words he knew and he had learned them for Hooba.

"In silence, you will learn who you are; your real self/soul or your atman (*Sanskrit*). Then, you will learn about Brahman/Allah," he said.

Again, he spoke, "All else is how these two relate."

Hooba sat quietly with a racing mind. He began reciting Psalms in his head. Then, he began playing games in his mind with Jared.

The wise man inhaled a deep breath and said, "Silence."

He exhaled and said, "Brahman."

He inhaled and again said the word "Silence."

Then once more, he exhaled and spoke, "Brahman."

Soon, Hooba was following the man's breathing and words. No other thoughts filled his mind.

Three hours passed. The man nimbly got off the ground. Hooba got up but rather slowly and with stiffness. The wise man began speaking *Kush* in a rapid manner as if Hooba understood it fluently.

He said, "At age twenty, I knew what Aahan knows about *Sanskrit*. At eighty, I now know, fifty out of one hundred parts."

Hooba, with slight impatience, began to say, "If I only learn one lesson in three hours, it is no wonder it takes sixty years."

The man responded, "If you do not learn the first lesson, how will I teach you the rest?"

The man then sat back down and crossed his legs. Hooba sat, too, and began repeating, "Silence, Brahman," while inhaling and exhaling.

The wise man again rose from the floor. Hooba followed his lead. The man looked sternly at Hooba and gestured with his hand to sit back down. Hooba sat, only to have the wise man leave the hut. Twenty minutes later he returned.

He spoke to Hooba saying, "You are released. I will again see you tomorrow."

The following day, Hooba returned to the man's hut down the road. The man gestured that he be seated on the ground.

In *Aramaic*, he spoke, "Heaven."

Then in *Sanskrit*, he said, "Brahman Moksha." (God's heaven)

He spoke again in *Kush*, then *Sanskrit*, alternating the many words in sentences just to provide Hooba understanding of the basic language. During the lesson, he explained the most valuable lesson is the connection between the atman (soul) and the Brahman (God) which leads you to Moksha (Heaven).

Heaven was the last *Aramaic* word the wise man ever spoke again to Hooba. That same day, they sat and meditated for only one hour then the wise man rose and left the hut once more. Hooba sat for nearly twenty more minutes before the wise man again, returned and released him for the day.

Months passed. During one lesson as it came to an end, the wise man said to Hooba: "You are a quick study. You have almost reached the level that I had at twenty. Only sixty more years to go."

He again had that wry smile.

For nearly two more years, the wise man taught Hooba *Sanskrit* and the principles of the Upanishads (ancient Indus texts).

The first Upanishad taught to Hooba was: "There should be no error in duties to the deity or all others that are lesser deities.

Let your mother be a lesser deity to you.

Let your father be a lesser deity to you.

Let your teacher be a lesser deity to you.

Let your guest be a lesser deity to you.

Perform no works to which you can be blamed and perform them on no others."

The man taught Hooba hundreds of Upanishad verses during those years. The two men no longer spoke in any language other than *Sanskrit*.

The principles of karma, rebirth, responsibility, compassion, personal growth, patience, self-control, even-temperament, respect, nonviolence and love were among the principles taught to Hooba during that time.

Over the next six months, Hooba's teacher said, "Now teach me your knowledge in *Sanskrit*."

He said, "I do not believe to be too old to learn."

The two men had lively conversations. Hooba soon discovered that as he spoke of his God in *Sanskrit*, it appeared to be the *Sanskrit* God as well.

One day, without Hooba regarding much attention said, "Brahman is God and I am one with my atman. (soul)."

The wise man said, "Tomorrow, you will teach the people of our small community in *Kush*."

The next day, the people of their community found Hooba in the center square. He was sitting cross-legged on the ground. For the first fifteen minutes, Hooba sat silently with his eyes closed. Then, he spoke with a wisdom greater than his age. Three hours later, the entire community still stood, listening. The people were in awe of his presence.

He rose at the end, saying, "Peace be with you. Love your neighbors as yourself."

He spoke it all in *Kush*.

The wise man watched the entire time with his wry smile.

The next day, Hooba walked four miles to the next small community; his staff in hand. He sat in the middle of the small community again on the ground. He meditated in silence for nearly fifteen minutes giving all praise to God. Then, he started to speak as the entire community began to gather and listen. All listened as he spoke for three hours.

He finished speaking and again wished, "Peace be with you. Love your neighbor as yourself."

He gathered his staff and walked four miles back to his community. Upon arriving back to his village, he worked the field with Aahan for almost four hours. He then prepared the evening meal. He ritually sang Psalms as their prayer of thanks, this time in *Sanskrit*.

Then, Hooba circling the table, addressed each one of the family members seated there.

To each one he said, "I honor you. I have been blessed to break bread with each of you."

He served the food to every member at the table.

Aahan said, "You are truly a humble man when the teacher becomes the servant."

Hooba responded, "Tomorrow, I will take leave of you. The wise man has told me that I must seek and teach if I wish to continue to grow. I will look forward to the day I meet you again in the house of the Lord."

The next morning, Hooba awoke before sunrise. He bathed in the brook at the foothills. He loaded the donkey with his few possessions as Aahan helped load provisions. The two men embraced.

Hooba said, "Peace be with you, my brother," in *Sanskrit*, with a wry smile.

Aahan replied, "Peace be with you, MY brother," in *Aramaic*.

It had been nearly two years since Hooba had heard an *Aramaic* word.

Hooba traveled for the next year, teaching in every small community he encountered. Some nights, he was invited to meals. Some nights, he went hungry. Yet, each day, he continued to travel to a new community. Every seventh day, he rested and spent his day in prayer to the Lord.

There were days that he was cheered and honored and days when he was jeered and unwelcome. Those were the days Hooba went hungry.

The day came when a wise, older man approached him. The man spoke in *Sanskrit*. Hooba replied to him in *Sanskrit*.

The man said, "Follow me. You have much to learn."

Hooba followed him home. On that first day, the man invited him in. The wise man sat on the ground with crossed legs. He motioned Hooba to sit. For the next three hours, they sat in silence. The man arose while Hooba remained seated.

He said, "You are released and I will see you again tomorrow."

Hooba searched for work but none was found. He returned to the home of the older, wiser man and laid out his bedding on the ground outside the man's home. The man was watching Hooba from his window. He also watched in the morning as Hooba ritually washed in the nearby brook.

Hooba returned to the man's home and waited outside. The man placed a bowl of dates outside his front door. However, Hooba did not take them. He did not take them, because they were not offered to him.

Then, the man returned to his door, saying, "Eat, I am sharing."

He invited Hooba into his home and the two conversed in *Sanskrit*. Hooba began learning some of the subtleties of the language; within the subtleties of the language were the details of the Vedas and Upanishads.

Once their lessons were complete that day, the older, wiser man went to speak with his neighbor. The neighbor then offered Hooba a job and a place to sleep. He would care for the man's sheep.

The nights were much colder in the north. Hooba appreciated the shelter in which he slept.

The man taught Hooba how to shear his sheep. He presented Hooba with wool-lined, sheepskin boots. For the next year, Hooba arose early, bathed, arrived at his teacher's home before sunrise, carried out his lessons, returned to take the sheep out to graze and at sunset he would return back with the sheep.

Soon, the owner of the sheep and his wife invited Hooba to sit at their table.

Each night, Hooba would pray to the Lord. On the seventh day of each week, Hooba would speak to the owner of the sheep and explain that his Dharma (Right behavior or social order) required him to rest on that day.

Every time, the owner would say, "Remind me in a week."

The owner would then take his sheep and walk to the meadow as Hooba spent his day in rest and prayer.

Nearly two more years had passed. One day, Hooba noticed a man with a cart and donkey. The cart was filled with earthenware the man was trading.

Hooba inquired to his teacher: "Who is this man? He appears different."

His teacher answered, "He is a monk from Hemis."

Hooba then asked, "Does he have knowledge to teach me?"

His teacher said, "He is a man of peace. He has knowledge of his soul (atman) yet he does not profess the connection to Brahman."

Hooba responded, "Should we not reach out and teach him of Brahman?"

Hooba's teacher answered, "His *Kush* is weak, his *Sanskrit* is weaker but interestingly, he does speak some *Greek* and some *Aramaic*."

Hooba asked his teacher: "Can I meet this man? It would take time from my learning."

The teacher replied, "If it is within you, seek!"

The following day, Hooba set out to meet the monk. Their conversation was awkward as their conversation was a combination of three languages. However, the monk and Hooba spoke for nearly three hours.

Hooba thought, "This man is more at peace with himself than any other man I have met."

He also thought, "This man speaks of suffering as if it is of no consequence."

The other fascination for Hooba was that in the monk's cart lay four precious alabaster jars. However, the monk spoke as if their only value was in the creation of them and their purpose.

The monk had them filled with his provisions. Hooba wondered how he could speak more with this man.

The next morning, he went to see his teacher. Before he spoke, his teacher said, "Yes, Hooba, you can go."

Hooba ran to catch the monk. The monk advised him he'd be leaving the following day for the monastery in Hemis.

The monk then told Hooba, "You need not have permission to follow me."

Hooba went to the owner of the sheep. He asked the owner, "Would there be hardship if I left?"

The man kindly responded, "No, my son has been ready to take over the sheep for quite some time."

The man's wife brought out a new coat for Hooba.

She spoke, "You will need one below you and one on top of you, where you are headed."

Hooba asked, "Would you need your boots back?"

The man smiled and shook his head to indicate "No."

That evening, Hooba prepared their meal. He substantiated it by saying, "Because I have been honored."

The teacher attended their meal.

Near the end of the meal, the teacher stated, "Teacher, I have learned much from you," as he looked at Hooba.

Hooba replied, "And teacher, I, too, have learned much from you."

Hooba looked at the sheep owner and spoke, "Brother, how can I repay you?"

His response was, "Hooba, bring joy to those around you as you have to us."

Hooba looked to the sheep owner's son asking, "Will you care for my companion, my donkey? The monk says that my donkey is too old to make the trip. I would trust her with you."

The son replied, "I will treat her with the respect that you have treated us."

Hooba said, "Peace be with you all. Someday I will meet you when you enter the house of God."

He then went to the shelter and brushed his donkey.

He said, "Old friend, you have carried me; if only I could carry you up the mountain."

The donkey nuzzled Hooba's hand as he felt a tear roll down his face.

Later, Hooba thought again of his donkey. He had such fond thoughts of her, the one he called Naomi, (*which means pleasantness.*)

Interestingly, his own mother was called Noam, (*which means pleasant one.*) Hooba remembered that these two women had been the most consistent women of his life. The thought of both gave him comfort.

Hooba thought back to his life, traveling from boy to man. There had been times he had shared with Naomi things a boy would normally have shared with his mother. Then, he reflected on those women who had most affected his life.

Two who had been like grandmothers were Zachariah's wife who was also Jared's mother Ruth and Aahan's own grandmother.

"Two had been Mothers," he thought.

His own actual one and his donkey.

Two had been young girls. Both had taught him something about the joy of youth and innocence. They were Susanna his cousin and Josephus's granddaughter Bachariko to whom he gave the rose.

Hooba took just a moment to wonder about these people who had touched his life and what they were now doing. He felt a yearning in his heart and realized how much he missed them all and how much joy they had brought to him.

Then, a thought came to Hooba. That feeling of loss was the same feeling he had when he did not follow *The Law*. The feeling of comfort overcame him when he ritualistically bathed, ate clean, prayed, observed the Sabbath and was teaching others.

There was also a joy he felt in God.

Chapter 17

In His Heart

Noam had been preparing her son for his presentation at The Temple. This was difficult as the boy had no living father. Isoep had passed away before their new son had been born. In fact, he had passed away just shortly after Hooba went to Temple and Isoep had given Jared a silver coin for Hooba, should there ever be need in his life.

Isoep's two older sons had supported Noam and their younger brother after the death of their father. Hooba had not attended the funeral of Isoep because of *The Law* which made it impossible for him to reach their village within the twenty-four hours of his death. Hooba also had never met his younger brother, Jude.

Noam had been thinking back to Hooba's presentation to The Temple. She sadly wondered what had become of her son. Only one letter had been received since his departure nearly six years prior.

She rubbed a silver piece in her pocket and thought how Isoep, knowing she was with child, had given it to her saying, "Here, should our son ever need it."

This was much like when he had given a silver coin to Jared for Hooba.

Noam thought, "How could he have known he would never see Hooba again or meet their son, Jude?"

For the past twelve years, Noam had carried the coin close to her as a reminder of Isoep. She pondered her past life, feeling blessed knowing it had all lead to the good man who had stood up for her and loved her.

Noam had little family remaining in her small community. She considered moving to the city of The Temple where her cousin and one of Isoep's sons now lived. She also considered that her cousin's son or Isoep's older son could become a good male role model for Jude.

There came a time when Noam decided to make the move. She soon became reacquainted through The Temple with her cousin, Zachariah and his wife Ruth.

Ruth along with Rebecca who was still residing with the family, had immediately befriended Noam. Noam felt that this temple and this family could somehow tie her two sons together. She so hoped that a day would come when the two would meet.

Jude did, indeed, however, find his male connection with Iakobas, his much older half-brother who had been learning the priesthood with the Rabbi Zachariah. Soon, Jude, too, was learning *The Law* from Zachariah.

Noam continued to think of Hooba, her first-born son.

"He was boy, then man-boy and now, if only I could know him as a man," she wished.

Each one of Jared's days seemed the same; a spiritual bath, prayer, a new novitiate, studying *The Law* and then working in the fields. Only two things had changed of late. Jared taught a class outside the walls. This allowed daily contact with Hilleal his brother and with Susanna's older brother, the younger Iakobas.

On occasion, Jared would interact with Susanna. Each time they interacted, Susanna could bring the warrior/man to his knees and bring his face to flush.

Jared remembered the day they celebrated Hilleal and Susanna's union.

Susanna had approached him and said, "It is my understanding, if something happened to your brother that within *The Law*, you must take care of me."

She had now stopped mentioning it out loud. However, each time Susanna saw Jared, she gave him the biggest smile, insinuating. And each time, Jared continued to blush.

Jared also remembered the day when Susanna and Hilleal shared the news of their child. Jared had smiled with the announcement, knowing they were both happy.

Each time he saw his brother and wife, Susanna would ask, "If this is a little girl, I wonder if she will make you blush?"

Many days, Jared would train with Hilleal and Iakobas, Susanna's brother. Susanna would watch their sword and physical training.

There came a day when Jared knocked a sword from Hilleal's hand. Susanna, nearly eight months with child at the time, ran to retrieve it from the ground and lifted it into the air. Instinctively, Jared swung to block her sword. He had underestimated her power as she forced his sword from his hand to the ground. The four of them laughed.

Jared thought to himself: "Is this unique to her or motherhood?"

Standing there in retrospection, he then reflected back to the first day he held Susanna and Hilleal's child. So small, she was. His two hands together were larger than her. Then, she cried and Jared blushed just as he had always done for her mother, never knowing how to react.

Susanna had spoken, "She probably needs to be changed."

Jared could only think, "Is there a ritual bath for this?"

Luckily, Susanna had taken the child from his hands. Before leaving that day though, Jared had pulled a small stuffed doll from his pocket that he *himself* had hand-stitched. To the doll's side was a carefully placed wooden sword.

The second thing that had changed for Jared in recent days as he thought about the consistency of his days was that each and every night, he walked the entire wall of the compound. He looked north, south, east and west knowing that in one of those directions was Hooba.

Little did Jared know that soon Hooba would be climbing to one of the highest mountains and climbing to the third story of the tallest building and looking to the west; wondering, "How do I get home?"

Meanwhile, Aahan traveled to the seaport of Banbhore, then to Kabul to visit his father. He had always looked forward to this trip. Although, each time he worried about leaving his grandmother. His grandmother made a feast for Aahan with each trip he made and each time she included lamb just as she had for Hooba. During each feast, the two would reminisce about their days with Hooba. This time, when Aahan reached the edge of the town of Banbhore, he noticed four new, small, clean buildings. Three were homes and each was owned by one of the women whom Hooba had paid the proprietor to free. The fourth building, a school, was filled with children of the community and operated by those same three women.

Aahan thought, "In less than one day, Hooba had changed their lives."

And, as Aahan watched, he noticed sailors and dock workers walking their children to the school. The example of one man had begun to change a community.

The first night that Hooba did not sleep in the stable with his donkey Naomi and the sheep, the owner's son listened to a longful bray throughout the night. The second night, the owner's son gathered blankets and bedding and camped where Hooba had slept, close to Naomi. That next morning, he brushed Naomi as he had seen Hooba do.

He remembered how Hooba had led the donkey and the sheep to the meadow every morning. Naomi had been led by Hooba for six years during all of their endeavors and travels. Thus, he released her from her stall and she immediately walked to the gate where the sheep would be released. He opened the gate for the sheep who began to run and wander about while Naomi stood patiently waiting for her lead. He took Naomi by her rope, leading her into the meadow. The sheep lined up behind Naomi and followed. While in the meadow, Naomi stood watching the sheep almost as if on guard.

He remembered Hooba saying, "Take off her rope and pat her on the bottom because she will wait responsibly until freed."

He then removed her rope and patted her finally on her bottom. She ran after two younger sheep who appeared to be running off. Naomi gently nuzzled them back toward the herd. It was as if she was playing with the two lambs. Then, she went back to the end of the meadow and watched the herd. The same two little lambs again wandered away. She once again ran after them, chasing them back into the herd.

The day came to an end. The owner's son placed the rope back onto Naomi's neck. He guided her back into the shelter. The sheep and lambs lined up and followed behind her.

He later told his father what had happened that day with Naomi and the lambs.

The father said, "Hooba told me the same story after those two lambs lost their mother. Naomi had taken over the role as their mother."

That night, as he fell into slumber, he felt the donkey nuzzle his cheek.

Bachariko, her daughter Delilah, her grandfather Josephus and her cousin Beatrice lived in a comfortable home in the city by the sea. Men had approached the women and the grandfather about marriage. Usually, these were men with needs and many children.

This wealthy community had a matriarchal heritage and the men were much aware of it. Bachariko was comfortable in her own wealth and not in any hurry or need to marry.

Some of the men felt scorned in their inability to coerce marriage from these women. Therefore, some of the men began telling inaccuracies about the women. Included in those rumors was Beatrice's inability to be with child, hinting that Bachariko had mothered Delilah out of wedlock and that their healing practices were based on evil.

Some men went as far as to rumor that Bachariko was not a true woman of their people, having red hair that indicated demons within her.

It had been heard, "She does not cover her head out of respect as our women do. She covers her head out of shame, protecting her skin, knowing God would surely burn her."

Yet, when the people of the community were ill, they turned to the women for healing.

One day, Delilah asked the woman she called Mother: "Why do people hate us?"

Bachariko responded, "Delilah, not all people hate. They fear what they do not know or that which is different. You cannot fear and love at the same time."

Delilah then asked, "Mother, why did God create you different?"

Bachariko answered emphatically, "*She* did not. She created me unique."

Delilah again questioned, "Did God create me to be unique?"

Her mother then replied, "Yes, *He* did."

Delilah inquired, "Why?"

Bachariko then said, "This is a two-part answer. Without our differences, how could God show that he loves us all? The second part is that if someone loves us, how are we sure that they love us in our uniqueness, if we are just as everyone else?"

Delilah said, "I love you, Mother."

Bachariko affectionately responded, "I understand, dear. You know me, accept me and do not judge me."

Delilah asked the same question again: "But, Mother, why do they hate us?"

This time, Bachariko responded with restraint: "They do not know us yet they judge us despite it."

Then she said, "God created us in our uniqueness and is the only one with the right to judge us and loves us anyway."

Delilah said, "Well, Mother, I hate all of them but one little boy who gave me a flower!"

Bachariko responded with a sigh, "Delilah, it is not our job to judge or hate people. It is our responsibility to act as God and love them anyway."

Bachariko was fondly brought back to thoughts of another young boy who had given her a rose many years ago.

Chapter 18
Ascending the Mountain

The sun had risen. Hooba hurried to the edge of town for fear he might miss Bhuti. For Bhuti had told Hooba he would return home today to the monastery.

He found the monk with cart and supplies loaded for his journey. It appeared he was waiting. He sat on the side of the road. The monk spoke as Hooba reached him.

"Why are you running? If it was meant for you to journey up the mountain, I would be waiting," Bhuti said.

The monk then stood. "The beginning of the trip is easier," he admitted.

"Thus, I will meditate over the next hour or two in silence."

Hooba inquired, "How can you meditate and walk?'

Bhuti then asked, "Can't you meditate with your eyes opened? You would miss much beauty on the journey. However, I would suggest if you wish to remain on the right path, your eyes remain open."

Several hours passed in silence. The dirt path seemed to weave and encircle around the mountains. Hooba thought to himself how glad he was of his young age versus the older age of the monk and the terrain.

He admitted to himself, it felt as though his calves would explode with pain. At that exact moment, Bhuti asked a question.

"Are you suffering?" he inquired.

Hooba responded, "Do we rest during this journey?"

"Which journey are you inquiring about?" he said.

Hooba thought to himself: "Is this a riddle?"

The monk answered him with a wry smile, as if he knew his thoughts.

Then he replied, "Yes."

Bhuti spoke, "This is a journey up the mountain, this is a journey of life, this is a journey of suffering."

He then advised Hooba to sit.

He said, "Now that you are seated, is it to your understanding you have the same three journeys? What do you see, hear, smell, feel?"

Hooba responded, "How much detail shall I include?"

Bhuti answered, "As much as your senses can observe."

"I am hot but yet chilly," said Hooba.

"My legs ache but I feel relief," he answered.

"I smell both fresh air and the odor of donkey," he said.

"I see a path up and I see a path down," Hooba finished.

Bhuti asked Hooba, "What is at the base of that blade of grass?"

Hooba ripped the blade of grass from the earth and replied, "There is a root."

The monk breathed a deep sigh then spoke, "You have now taken the life from that blade of grass. Did you have that right?"

Hooba was bewildered for a moment. He was unsure of the question.

Bhuti said, "By all means, feed that grass to the donkey or else there was no meaning in the taking of that life. Now, consider the root. The root is where everything grows. Think back at your answers. You have defined everything as a positive or negative experience. Could that be the root you wish for everything to grow from? If you had not defined the pain in your legs as suffering it would not have been something to overcome but rather just something to experience. Once we understand that suffering is merely an experience, we have reached Nirvana."

He further explained to Hooba: "It's our karma that is the state of our soul as recorded by all of our experiences and actions and our dharma that is the right path and our Buddhist law. Once we understand our karma is equal to our dharma, we are complete. This, too, is defined as Nirvana."

The monk looked at Hooba. "If you have no further questions," he said, "You can now go down the path."

Before Hooba could speak, Bhuti politely ordered, "I believe you should get to your feet for your journey is not over."

The two men continued to climb the mountain. Hooba felt light-headed at times. His breathing had become labored. Yet, neither the donkey nor the monk seemed affected.

Shortly, they came upon a stream. Bhuti advised Hooba to drink the fresh water to his fullest.

"Tonight, we will camp here," he said.

Hooba drank from the stream until he could drink no more.

He thought, "How will I bathe in this icy water?"

The monk prepared a very light meal of vegetables and fruit. Hooba washed his hands in the icy stream. The two ate. Hooba was still hungry as they finished their meal.

Compassionately, Bhuti said, "I am sorry for your hunger. First remember, hunger is a form of suffering. I have shared half of my provisions with you for you were not in my plans for this trip."

The monk sat by the fire in silence. Hooba also sat by the fire and prayed.

Hooba thought to himself, "I am thankful to have two warm cloaks and boots."

Preparing to sleep, Bhuti presented Hooba with oil and spoke, "I suggest you rub your legs. The morning soon ascends upon us."

The sun rose and Hooba attempted to bathe in the stream. However, the cramps in his calves only worsened upon stepping into the icy water. He ritually bathed the best he could.

They ate a small meal together and Bhuti began again up the mountain with Hooba following behind.

Each time Hooba attempted to ask a question, the monk responded, "Save your breath for you will need it."

Unlike Hooba, the monk knew they were traveling up over ten thousand feet to the monastery, his home. After two hours of climbing, Hooba was one hundred yards behind Bhuti. Once they reached fours hours of travel, Hooba was four hundred yards behind the monk.

Finally, Bhuti sat down to rest. He gave Hooba some fruit. Fifteen minutes passed when he again stood to continue.

He spoke, "We have four-and-a-half more hours until we reach the valley. We will stay in that community for the night and have just two to three more days to continue."

Hooba simply nodded.

They continued to climb. Once, Hooba looked back but could see nothing of where they had been. Once, he looked over the edge and could not see the bottom.

In a moment of almost delirium, Hooba thought of the people of Babel trying to build up to reach the Gods.

"I have now experienced so many languages. Babel must be true. For, if God did not spread all those people throughout the world, no one would come here," he thought.

The mountain cast a shadow and it was cold. Then, they rounded the mountain and the sun was closer; it was hot. Suddenly, Hooba realized they were no longer climbing. The monk, now four hundred yards away, had just entered a beautiful valley. Hooba could see people and stone buildings. In the center of the valley, he saw a single tree. Next to the tree was a babbling brook. The people were greeting the monk.

Hooba thought to himself, "Oh, if I can only make it four hundred more yards …"

A man came up the path toward Hooba. Hooba leaned on him as the man nearly carried him the last two hundred yards. He was guided to a stone building where four other monks greeted him. He began to realize that he and Bhuti were laying on the floor with pillows. The monks were serving them warm tea and rice.

The monks conversed among themselves. Bhuti addressed Hooba.

"I'm quite impressed by how you have fared," he spoke.

"You will stay here for a month until I return, to acclimate to the altitude. Walk, meditate and speak to the people during your time here," he told Hooba.

Hooba was given a warm, indoor robe by Bhuti and while he was still in a state of stupor, the other four monks shaved his head.

Bhuti admitted to Hooba: "It is easy to take care of and much easier for you to not identify with your old self."

Hooba flippantly thought, "Great, now I look like Jared."

He rubbed his head and thought, "I think I miss my hair." Then, he heard Isaiah say, "You are all special just none more special."

Hooba fought to pray and then fell into a deep sleep.

The sun rose the next morning. Hooba was allowed to bathe in heated water. He ate a meal with the four monks and Bhuti. They meditated with Hooba and tolerated while he recited aloud Psalms 23:2 through 23:6.

One of the younger monks motioned for Hooba to follow him. He was given a hoe and shown the garden. Hooba looked around and wondered where they kept the animals.

He noticed a small shelter with two donkeys. Bhuti was tying a different donkey to his cart.

He acknowledged to himself, as he limped toward the garden, "They are changing donkeys. However, Bhuti is continuing to walk."

Hooba called to Bhuti, "Peace be with you Bhuti."

Bhuti walked over to Hooba. "We really do not speak this, but from the land south where you have come from … Namaste."

The next day started like the last day.

Hooba asked, "Would there be time that I could teach?"

The four of the remaining monks turned to one another to talk among themselves.

Then, turning toward Hooba, they responded, "Yes."

After the work was done, before the sun had set, Hooba was allowed to teach. He went to the tree in the center of the meadow. He sat next to the brook. People would listen as they came to fill their water containers. Sometimes, he told stories as parables so the children would listen. Each day, a few more stayed to listen. A few brought old, dried flowers and left them at his feet.

He questioned the monks as to the meaning of the old, dried flowers. He told them he had been taught by *The Law* to give your best possible tribute. They nodded in understanding then explained to Hooba that only flowers already dying could be picked. They further explained that life is precious and dying flowers were a sign that life was not permanent. There was still appreciation in the gift of dried flowers.

One evening, the monks were summoned by a woman whose husband was dying. Hooba just listened to the monks. To Hooba, it sounded as if the monks were praying for the growth of the dying man's soul. The man did, indeed, die while they visited. The monks carried his body off to their small temple.

Hooba asked if he might help prepare the body with oils and scents.

The four monks looked at Hooba in dismay. "Why use precious oils and scents on a dead man they asked?"

Hooba asked, "You do not prepare the body?"

The monks answered, "For what, he is dead?"

"Besides," one monk answered, "The scents will confuse the vultures."

Hooba feared asking any other questions at that moment. But the monk continued to give him information about death anyway.

"You would not scent the body, for what is the purpose of the vulture except to eat dead flesh. We honor the vulture, his purpose. For the vulture is more noble than the eagle; it eats only what is already dead. The eagle kills to eat. The eagle celebrates the suffering of another animal. The vulture only celebrates its death."

Hooba looked at his own teaching. He was not to eat birds of prey or any other animal that killed and ate an animal.

He thought, "These animals are declared unclean."

He remembered many of the lessons he had learned in regard to ritualistic killing. If an animal was to be eaten, the kill must be swift and painless. He now understood why these men chose to be vegetarian.

Then, Hooba had thoughts of Jared. He had explained to Hooba how his community no longer sacrificed animals. Hooba also understood the gravity of Jared speaking about the sword. He remembered Jared's explanation of God's lesson to Abraham. God would expect obedience to *The Law* thus Abraham, who was the father of Isaac and the father of the Twelve Tribes of Israel, prepared his own son Isaac to be sacrificed on the altar. However, God, knowing that Abraham would obey, had stopped him.

He said, "I would never ask you for your son, for life is precious."

Then, he thought again of Hagar. Hagar, a slave, who had been impregnated by Abraham and then cast out into the desert with her son Ishmael and were said to not be the chosen ones, God said life was precious and fed them in the desert anyway.

Hooba thought, "No killing can truly be justified."

Now, he also understood why the sword was so heavy for Jared's thoughts.

Nearly a month had passed. Bhuti returned once again with his donkey and cart.

Chapter 19
Jude

Jared's thoughts were, indeed, heavy. He sat and stared at Iakobas in disbelief. The elder Iakobas had traveled from the city of The Temple, back to the community within the walls.

He shared what he had heard and what his mother, Noam, had also told him. Noam had recently moved to the city of The Temple. The city had begun to change with overtaxation, Kittim guards stationed everywhere and citizens being persecuted for petty reasons. But now, the smaller towns and communities were worse. Sometimes the Kittim soldiers ransacked homes and entire communities for unknown reasons.

Political opposition was growing in the smaller communities. Men were meeting in secret from the Kittims. Groups of otherwise non-violent men were now carrying knives. Historically, the men would gather with their families in celebration or at The Temple for prayer.

Now, there were stories of tax collectors being robbed and, even on occasion, Kittim soldiers were being found murdered.

Iakobas said the last story Noam relayed to him was one she had witnessed on her travels to the city.

Noam had said, "I met a man named John. He was a good man, preaching *The Law*. He was meeting with zealot groups of men, teaching them *The Law* and ritual bathing. A band of Kittim soldiers had come upon them as he showed the men how to ritually clean themselves. John told me when the Kittims surprised them, one of their men and one

Kittim soldier had died at the hands of each other. John and his men fled into the wilderness. Then, he said that he feared me traveling with only a young man, as there was so much unrest.

I did not heed his words. We hurried onward to just outside the city walls when we heard men screaming. We saw Kittim soldiers and a small crowd. They had stripped three men of their garments. They were being whipped and hardly able to stand.

Then, Jude and I saw three poles. The men's hands were bound and tied above their heads onto each pole. The bottoms of poles were thrust into a pit, then the poles pushed upright as the men dangled from them.

The soldiers were casting lots for the belongings and clothing of the men. Some of the soldiers were laughing. There were men and women who had thrown themselves on the ground in front of the poles, who were crying and praying. We saw one soldier kick a man on the ground and ask if the man on the pole was his friend. The man had looked petrified. He stood and only denied knowing the man on the pole. Then, the man ran off.

The three men on the poles clawed with their feet trying to hold themselves in the air. Their feet had already become bloody from the wood. One man was crying, one man was begging for forgiveness and one man was yelling out the name of the Lord.

A soldier taunted, "Let your God save you now!"

My son Jude asked one of the women, "What could these men have possibly done?"

The woman with tears in her eyes answered, "One was a zealot, one was a criminal and one was a man of God."

Noam continued … saying she tried to support the women. Then, one of the men collapsed. His shoulder twisted and dislocated as the sound of breaking bones was heard. A woman said aloud, the man was her son. I stayed with her as the soldiers cut the rope, allowing her son to drop to the ground. Jude helped drag the man, her son, away from the wretched place.

Three other women and myself washed the body. A man appeared from the crowd and anointed the body with oil then lifted it into the back of a cart.

I looked around only to find Jude kneeling and crying.

He said, "Mother, why does God not strike them down?"

I had to tell Jude: "This has nothing to do with God. This has only to do with man."

Another man then collapsed and the soldiers let him drop to the ground, as well.

The man with the strongest will, still hanging on the pole, looked directly at Jude and spoke, "Protect my mother as a son should."

Jude looked to the crowd and yelled, "Who is this man's mother?"

An older woman came forward. Jude placed his arm around her and turned her away from her son, still hanging from the pole. And as she cried, her son took his last breath.

Jude walked to the guard and said, "Release this man gently. His mother is watching." Jude caught the man as he fell from the pole and placed him tenderly on the ground.

Noam said, "I went to Jude."

He looked up at me and said, "Mother, this was a man of God. Let me ritually bathe him as he would have expected. This way he will be clean when he reaches the house of the Lord."

Noam then said to Jude, "The man is no longer here."

Jude responded, "But, his mother is."

Men came forward and took the body.

Noam said that Jude then took her hand and guided her to within the walls of the city."

Iakobas looked up after hearing this only to see Jared crying.

Chapter 20
Further Up the Mountain

*H*ooba woke up with the sunrise, ritually bathed and prayed. Then, he went out into the common room. He found a pair of heavier boots and two heavy cloaks laying at his place on the floor.

He asked, "Should I return the cloak I am now wearing?"

The monks answered that he would still be in need of the cloak for inside. The heavier cloaks would help him in snow, wind and hail.

This made Hooba quite curious and, thus, he asked about hail. It was quite difficult for the monks to describe hail. Hooba had never seen frozen water let alone frozen water falling from the sky.

He did, however, understand wind … so he thought. Wind could make the sand sting and the sun feel hotter. All four of the monks smiled wryly.

They told Hooba: "Imagine standing in an icy stream, cold to your bones, pelted with rocks. That is what hail feels like."

Hooba remembered in one community in Kashmir when the people had thrown small stones at him. He could not imagine cold and water that felt like stones at the same time.

Bhuti appeared at the door and yelled, "There is weather to the west. We should prepare and leave immediately."

Hooba walked outside. The sun was shining and it felt comfortable. Bhuti instructed him to get his heavier boots.

"Wrap one of your heavy cloaks around you and put the other on top of the cart," he said.

Hooba's immediate thought was, "This is too warm."

Bhuti didn't even answer Hooba. He just hurried his donkey and the cart to the end of the clearing and meadow. Bhuti was walking even faster than he had on their first trip. The first leg of their trip was on the eastern edge of the mountain. However, within ninety minutes, they rounded a curve and Hooba began to feel rain pelting on his face. He raised the hood of his cloak.

Soon Bhuti came back to Hooba with a pair of woolen mittens and something that resembled a shawl to tie around his face.

Hooba looked closely at Bhuti and thought, "What are the white crystals on his eyebrows?"

Hooba touched his own eyebrows and said, "My eyebrows are both hard and wet."

Within moments, Hooba thought, "Oh, this must be what hail is. Why doesn't Bhuti stop?"

Hooba now understood why the donkey was cloaked and hooded.

He yelled up to Bhuti: "Why don't we stop and let this pass?"

Bhuti yelled back: "Look around; where would we stop? The next safe camp is three hours away."

Hooba then asked, "Why didn't we wait to leave?"

Bhuti answered, "Because I believed we would make it to camp before the weather came upon us."

Hooba looked around and realized the trees had changed from green with leaves to green with needles. He had never seen this type of tree. The trees began to sparkle as if covered with stars.

Bhuti yelled back: "Start pushing the cart."

Hooba realized there was now two inches of fluffy, white covering on the path.

He thought, "This must be snow."

He now understood the meaning of being cold to the bone.

Bhuti was now helping Hooba push the cart. Obviously, the donkey knew the way as he plowed ahead.

They rounded a bend and Hooba saw a large, outcropping of rock. It completely extended over the path. The small outcropping provided them three walls and a roof.

Bhuti yelled to Hooba: "Unload our goods into the rocks!"

Then, he secured the donkey to fit beneath the outcropping.

He looked up into the air and acclaimed, "This may be a bad one."

Hooba helped Bhuti place their cart on its side in the front of the opening, providing shelter. He was driving spikes into the stone and hanging a blanket over the opening, fastening it to the cart.

Hooba thought and apparently said aloud, "There is not much room for a donkey and the two of us."

Bhuti said, "You will be happy later. You will lay on one side of the donkey and I on the other. He will keep us warm."

A pile of sticks and flint were unpacked by Bhuti from his supplies.

Hooba asked, "Are you starting a small fire?"

Bhuti replied, "Not yet, unless I think we will freeze."

Then, he scooped up some snow and placed it in an empty container. He looked at Hooba and said, "I hope it melts in case we need water."

The blanket was already flapping hard in the wind.

Bhuti passed a raw turnip to Hooba and said, "Eat. I cannot cook this turnip. We must save the heat so we do not freeze."

The sun was beginning to set and with it the temperature was quickly dropping. Bhuti took his two warm cloaks and Hooba's two warm cloaks, tying them together into one large blanket.

He told Hooba, "The donkey, you and I will lay beneath this cloak together."

Hooba, not surprisingly, did not sleep well and was extremely cold. However, he could see a hint of light beyond the blanket indicating they had made it through the night.

He called to Bhuti.

Bhuti responded, "Remain beneath the blanket!"

Bhuti peered out from the blanket. Everything was covered in snow. He slipped back beneath the blanket.

He said, "In six or seven hours, the sun will be warm for us to travel."

Hooba said, "I must relieve myself."

Bhuti answered, "Be patient, so must the donkey."

Hooba was curious and also peered out from beneath the cloaks. He now realized that including the inside of the cave, everything else was also blanketed with snow.

Hooba asked Bhuti: "What are you doing?"

Bhuti replied, "I am meditating; aren't you?"

For a moment, Hooba felt shame. He had not thought about prayer or meditation. He thanked God at that moment for the opportunity to pray.

A few hours later, he sensed Bhuti moving. He, too, climbed from under the cloaks. Bhuti and the donkey were out attending to their natural needs. Then, Bhuti returned to start a fire.

He instructed Hooba to hang their cloaks to dry and remove his boots to dry by the fire.

Bhuti said, "Sit close to the fire and have the heat warm you."

He boiled turnips and vegetables, feeding the donkey first. He instructed Hooba to dress and begin loading the cart.

"We have two days to go," he informed Hooba.

Seven hours later, they came upon another community. There was a valley and meadow ahead. The little village was built literally into the side of the mountain.

Hooba asked, "Why would anyone live here?"

"Because one cannot live on the mountain," Bhuti explained.

They ate, they slept and in the morning, they left for the monastery at Hemis. The day was uneventful. Hooba nearly appreciated the burning in his calves versus the cold he experienced two days before.

They rounded a bend on the mountain once again. Hooba could see what appeared to be a tiered, walled community in the side of the mountain. Then, it appeared as if they were walking further away from the community.

Bhuti guessed what Hooba was thinking and said, "This is the only path to our destination."

Two hours later, he again saw the tiered structure in front of them.

Bhuti spoke, "Hooba, it is said, that this is the highest point on Earth. The path that you traveled was no harder than life itself. This represents the highest possible human attainment we call Nirvana."

Chapter 21
Monastery

The first time Hooba saw the monastery from a distance, it appeared to be large and expansive. However, as he entered the front gate, he realized most of it to be just the façade. It appeared multilayered due to it being built into the mountain side. What appeared to be many levels were, in fact, only two.

The main courtyard was no more than one hundred by two hundred feet. Hooba had imagined a great fortress against the mountains, but in all actuality, its walls were merely four-foot tall. The largest structure he would learn was called the Great Hall. Dining, meditation and teaching occurred in the room. There was a room behind the Great Hall which was called the Library. It was certainly much smaller than the library Hooba had used in his community within the walls and contained only one wall of scrolls.

There was a room off to the side of the library, used for cooking. It contained a door leading to the outside.

The Great Hall and the Library had no furniture. Eating, writing or learning was done while sitting or lying on the ground. Various pillows, blankets and animal skins lined the walls.

The remaining parts of the compound included shelter for donkeys, many small workshops and housing. The monastery housed thirty-two monks at its capacity. Four to eight monks traveled at a time trading for supplies or selling wares which were mostly alabaster jars.

Each man had a four-by-six-foot cell with no door. Bhuti had already explained to Hooba that one could have no personal possessions but the clothes on their back and the next day's clothes.

Hooba had already asked Bhuti what he might do with his silver piece for safekeeping. "Silver and gold have no place here," Bhuti answered.

"Why would you need such a piece? All things you need are provided," Bhuti spoke.

"What if a day comes when I must travel?" Hooba responded.

Bhuti replied, "No one has ever left here but to trade or teach."

Hooba then said, "I do not want to give up my silver piece."

"It seems you have formed an attachment to the silver piece," Bhuti accused.

"An attachment is a cause of suffering," Bhuti explained. "It is based on your ego."

Bhuti then said, "I suggest you buy an alabaster jar. Although one would have been provided for free as a chamber pot. I have already explained that an alabaster jar is only good for what it can hold."

Bhuti now wore a wry smile.

"I will take the coin and trade it for supplies on my next trip," Bhuti suggested.

He also said, "The good thought is, no one will use your chamber pot, therefore, should you leave, it will go with you to be traded for a month's worth of food."

Each day at the monastery was exactly the same for Hooba. He had a ritual bath, breakfast and meditation followed by education. Hooba would then tend to the donkeys.

He asked about producing alabaster jars and was told, "It is a skill that takes a long time to master. You have other lessons to master first."

Hooba soon found himself talking to the donkeys more than the monks. He was able to question the monks about the *Four Noble Truths* or *The Eight-Fold Path* which he had learned was their *Law* as opposed to *The Law*. However, when Hooba tried to express his opinion, the monks would look at him as if his thoughts were completely foreign to reality.

Although Hooba understood suffering to be part of life, he considered following *The Law* as not a burden or suffering but rather an honor. Hooba could not understand their focus on suffering. He also understood these monks to be compassionate men at peace with themselves. However, there was a conflict for Hooba between his path which he felt to be joyful versus their path which was to overcome suffering.

He remembered back to playing with Bachariko in Egypt, bouncing Susanna on his knee and playing in the courtyard with Jared within the walls of his community. Those memories brought him joy without any thoughts of suffering.

Hooba believed these men to be incredibly disciplined, yet he understood discipline because Jared had taught him. The wise men of Kashmir had also taught him discipline.

The hardest concept for Hooba was attachment. He understood that which we accumulated had no bearing on what was the quality of the person. Then, Hooba began to understand what he thought was the flaw in their beliefs.

He heard the monks say, "Love your neighbor as yourself."

The monks then broke the statement down to a simple law only related to karma. Their thoughts were about preventing their own karma, their own suffering and their focus seemed completely inward.

Then, Hooba said, "I have attachment. And that attachment is love."

"It's not love other people so you don't suffer due to your karma. It's love other people and there will be no karma," Hooba said aloud.

"It is your only intention," Hooba thought. "Other people matter; it is not about ourselves."

Of course, there was the most glaring difference Hooba deciphered inwardly.

"I have attachment to God, and they have attachment to nothing," Hooba again thought to himself.

One day, they had an exercise. Three hours were spent examining the beauty of a flower. Hooba understood the monks' appreciation of the beautiful flower.

Finally, they asked Hooba, "What are your thoughts on the flower?"

Hooba responded, "I am thankful for the flower."

To which the monks asked, "Why thankful?"

He answered, "Beautiful is what the flower is. However, attachment to beauty does not seem the correct path."

"Thus, I am thankful to the creator of that beauty, for allowing me to experience it," Hooba explained.

He then continued, "I am thankful for the attachment I feel to people and to my God. For in this attachment I experience love and in that I learned the greatest lesson which is to give love without expectation. This brings joy which is much different than avoiding suffering without joy."

The monks began to chatter among themselves.

Hooba thought, "Do they not remember I know their language of Sanskrit?"

Hooba kept hearing the words repeated, attachment, pain, suffering and karma. Then, he noticed the tone in their voices was that of fear. Yet, they appeared to remain peaceful and calm, not allowing themselves any emotion.

"Should you never allow yourself attachment to other human beings or God, you cannot experience love. Thus, it is easy to throw the body on a pile for the vultures and not feel grief or loss," Hooba emphatically stated.

"I understand the body, *is not them*. Avoiding suffering is one way, accepting suffering is another. To avoid suffering is about you and to take on suffering of another is about them," Hooba explained.

Then, he said, "I understand why you approach life as you do. It is the belief of being alone on your paths. You do not believe there is a God and I do; therefore, *I* am never alone. It is not my path to walk in this world alone. My path is to walk the way of love and take everyone along my way with me."

"Why and what is your purpose?" Hooba asked the monks.

"Your focus is too much on the how," Hooba rambled.

"You have your *Noble Truths*, so you exalt yourselves! How proud you must be that you can follow your own rules, he excitedly expressed."

"You submit to your own rules!" Hooba exclaimed.

"So, you truly only love yourself. I submit to God. I love God and I love all others. Because of this I do not suffer and I will not suffer in eternity," Hooba joyfully admitted.

He turned to walk away. Then, he turned back toward the monks.

He said, "I must tell you one more thing. God loves you without expectation. We call that grace. This is my example. This is my action and this is my intention, to love the children of God, the sons and daughters of man, this humanity without expectation; without judgment. I forgive those who trespass against me. So, brothers ... I love you. Peace be with you."

Hooba climbed to the highest point within the monastery. He looked to the west and realized how much he missed his attachments.

Hooba fell to his knees and thanked God for the lessons. The greatest of these lessons was love and always would be.

Many miles away at that same moment, Jared was looking to the east.

Hooba heard Isaiah say in his head: "Go home, Hooba."

Then, he felt an incredible warm embrace and just two words were heard, "Go Home."

Chapter 22
Hooba Goes Home

Hooba arose in the morning, going through his usual routine but knowing the day had new purpose. He began packing his belongings to go home. Bhuti knew Hooba would be leaving soon. Hooba did not stay to meditate after breakfast.

Bhuti arose and followed Hooba out into the courtyard.

He asked Hooba: "Do you know where you will travel?"

Hooba responded, "The only path I know is the one I traveled to get here."

Bhuti then stated, "My understanding is you traveled around the Indus Valley and through Kashmir. If your journey is home, it is more direct through the Indus Valley. There is a better path. Khedenn has just headed down the path that heads to the Indus Valley. We have no donkey for your use. However, since you will be on foot you could swiftly catch him at the next valley. I am afraid your alabaster jar is too heavy for you to carry."

He pulled from within his cloak a small alabaster jar.

He said, "This will be easier for you to carry and you might still trade it for food and lodging."

Hooba reached toward Bhuti for embrace. Bhuti lifted his hand to motion Hooba to stop.

Bhuti spoke, "I already have attachment."

Bhuti then escorted Hooba out the front gate of the monastery and to a different path.

He said, "Hooba, stay on this path, for now it is your path. I understand it is different than mine."

Hooba hurried away, thinking and contemplating all he had learned on his journey for the past nine years away from home.

He soon realized the path down was quite steep. This time it was the front of his legs rather than the calves of his legs that burned with strain.

Eight hours later, he noticed the path was less steep. Soon, he approached a long valley, and in the valley, he saw a small community. He immediately viewed a structure that resembled a monastery. It was slightly larger than the first monastery where he stayed for a month on the path up.

Hooba knew it would soon be meal time. He entered the small monastery, saw Khedenn and took a seat on the ground next to him.

Being respectful to their traditions, Hooba waited to have conversation with Khedenn. Once the meal was finished, Khedenn showed Hooba the sleeping quarters. It was then Hooba found his voice to ask Khedenn if he could travel down the mountain with him to the Indus Valley.

Khedenn said, "I will get you to the lowest valley. From there, you are on your own path. Be prepared to leave at sunrise."

Hooba thanked God and soon fell asleep.

Before sunrise, Hooba was up, bathed, packed and waiting in the courtyard for Khedenn. He helped Khedenn load the cart upon his arrival.

Hooba placed his own pack in the cart and noticed a rattle coming from his alabaster jar. He removed the lid only to find a silver piece inside the jar. He thought of Bhuti, as a wry smile came across his lips.

Hooba thought, "Even if this man is on a different path than I am, he does not judge my path and I will not judge his."

Hooba's and Khedenn's journey began down the path.

Two hours had passed when Khedenn asked Hooba, "Do you want to continue to meditate in silence or do you want to share the story of your journey and your God?"

Hooba had always believed life at the monastery was much too quiet. For the next two days going down the mountain, Hooba shared with Khedenn his life and his God.

Hooba recited large sections of *The Law* and drew comparisons with *The Eight-Fold Path* and the *Ten Commandments* and other teachings the two had in common.

All along their way, Khedenn asked questions. Hooba became more passionate with each of his inquiries.

The Indus Valley approached as Khedenn stated, "I see no suffering in your attachment to God, only joy."

Hooba replied, "I do find joy in my faith and joy in good deeds. Both stand on their own but when the two, that is faith and good deeds, occur together, they truly fulfill *The Law*. What good is it, Khedenn, if someone claims to have faith but has no deeds? Can such a faith save them? And, in the same way, faith by itself if not accompanied by action, is dead. You have faith and I have deeds. Show me your faith without deeds and I will show you my faith by my deeds."

Khedenn looked to Hooba and said, "Rabbi, as you are speaking, you frequently equate faith and love."

"Khedenn, you are a good student," Hooba responded. "Love is both a feeling and an action and faith without deeds is empty."

Hooba and Khedenn then traveled along the monk's small trade route and sold his wares. Every afternoon, Hooba went to the town square and taught *The Law*. Three days passed and all Khedenn's wares had sold.

That evening, Khedenn told Hooba, "I would like to continue with you on your travels to Banbhore. I must leave the cart, the donkey and all provisions here. These belong to the monastery."

Hooba removed his heavy cloaks and placed them in the cart. Khedenn did the same.

Then, Khedenn explained to Hooba: "If I do not return to the monastery, they will send two monks on the trade route next time. They will assume I have left their belongings to be collected even if I have not returned."

They found boarding and storage for the donkey, cart and the provisions. The two men then left on foot with the clothes on their backs, a staff in Hooba's left hand and an alabaster jar in his right.

Over the next month they traveled throughout the Indus Valley. Each day, both men taught the people they came upon. Some days the people fed them. Some days they went hungry. The crowds would sometimes cheer and on some days the crowds only jeered.

Then, one day they finally reached the seaport town of Banbhore.

Hooba and Khedenn entered the village, immediately walking toward the docks.

"I know ... I was uncomfortable, too, when first I came to Banbhore," Hooba said to Khedenn.

Hooba had noticed the uneasiness Khedenn displayed as he looked around to see the conditions of the village people.

Khedenn replied, "It is not only the conditions but the stench. It reminds me of what occurs after the vultures come. Do people actually eat this fish?"

"I assure you, smoked and cooked fish tastes much better than this smell," Hooba laughed.

"Follow me. It has been ten years but I believe I know where we can find lodging," Hooba told Khedenn.

Hooba followed the route down the main road previously traveled years ago with Aahan to find lodging. He entered the same proprietor's shop where years ago, he had paid silver coins to free three women and their children. The same proprietor believed he remembered Hooba.

"When I heard of the man who spoke Aramaic in the Indus Valley, I wondered if it was you," the proprietor said to Hooba.

"You seem to make a mark wherever you travel," he said.

"I did not know you would remember me," Hooba replied.

The proprietor retorted, "I've never had anyone buy three women's freedom in the same day before."

"I hope the women are doing well?" Hooba inquired.

Then said, "I am looking for lodging again for the night."

The proprietor looked at the men and admitted, "I do have a small room for the evening."

Then, he motioned them to the front door.

"Do you see the women and men walking with their children home?" He asked.

"Tomorrow morning, follow the people as they walk their children to school. There, you will discover what happened to the three women you freed," he said.

"You ... have left more than one mark on this community," he told Hooba.

The men ate and retired for the evening. The next morning, both men stared at the one small basin of water that had been provided.

Hooba said, "Yes, that is all we get."

Khedenn had become a ritual bather by this time.

Therefore, he said to Hooba, "Just what, do we bathe with this?"

Hooba replied, "We only wash our hands and splash our face."

Hooba then headed out the door to the street. He heard the laughter of children as they walked past with their parents. Just as the proprietor had said, they seemed to all be walking in the same direction. He smiled, then stepped in line to follow along with the laughing children and their parents.

Khedenn walked out into the center of the street and yelled to Hooba, "Where are you going?"

Hooba responded back, "I'm following the sound of laughing children."

Khedenn simply asked, "Why?"

"Because the last giggling, little girl who sat on my lap was my cousin Susanna and it's been a long time," He yelled back.

Khedenn ran after him but Hooba was nearly three hundred yards away by then.

Hooba saw a larger structure at the end of the road as he approached. The children were all filing in. A young woman stood outside the door.

He addressed the woman and asked, "I am looking for three women. The proprietor said I would find them here."

The young woman looked him directly in the eyes and with a smile and a tear replied, "Sir, you fed me when I was hungry. At the end of the day, I will take you to my mother."

"Is there anything I can do?" Hooba asked her.

"Just wait here," She spoke.

The young woman ran into the building and returned with a loaf of bread. By that time, Khedenn had reached the school and was standing with Hooba.

She said to Hooba, "While you wait, break bread with your friend."

Just a few short hours later, the children came outside to play. Hooba and Khedenn were still waiting.

Khedenn watched Hooba run and play with the children in the yard. He was amazed and filled with joy. Soon, Hooba sat on the ground only to have the children join him, circling all around. He told them stories. Not a single child made a noise while he spoke. The children appeared to be mesmerized and entertained with his words.

Khedenn noticed not long afterward the two women who ran the school were also standing and listening to Hooba. One small girl climbed into Hooba's lap. She patted his face with her hand and Hooba blushed.

The two women spoke to Hooba: "The children must return to their studies."

This brought a sigh of reluctance from all the children.

The little girl seated on Hooba's lap took his hand and said, "Would you like to come in and learn too?"

Hooba looked to the women and asked, "Am I permitted?"

The women smiled and nodded to Hooba, as if granting him permission. Hooba sat on the floor among the children inside the building while one of the women taught. Unbeknown to Hooba, the other woman went to bring back the three women he had freed all those years ago.

Soon, Hooba noticed a commotion at the door. Three older women rushed into the room. One woman ran to Hooba and threw herself at his feet.

Hooba reached down, took her hand and said, "Woman, stand, you should only bow to God."

Another of the women looked at Hooba and said, "Master, what can we do for you?"

Hooba replied, "You have but one master and that is God. The rest of us are here to serve each other."

"Is there any work here that I can do? We are looking for lodging," Hooba inquired.

"We have some small minor repairs but the school cannot afford to pay you," one woman said.

Hooba responded, "We just look for a roof over our heads."

Over the next few days, Hooba and Khedenn repaired the roofs of the school and the homes of the three women. During the afternoons, Hooba and Khedenn taught *The Law* in the fish market.

Chapter 23
Nine Years Had Passed

Aahan, during his trip to visit his father, had passed through Banbhore as he always had. He stopped at the same proprietor that he and Hooba had been to nine years before. During conversation the proprietor, had informed Aahan of rumors about a man who spoke Aramaic, Kush and Sanskrit who was teaching in the Indus Valley.

Aahan could think of no one other than Hooba to fit the proprietor's description.

Aahan thought, "When I return to my father's home, I will send a message back along the trade route with the caravan to Hooba's people. They should be aware of Hooba's teaching and his whereabouts."

Three months passed. The message from Aahan had reached Cyrus who shared the message with his daughter, Bachariko.

She was pleased and comforted to know her childhood friend, Hooba, was healthy and alive. She had such fond memories of the boy who presented her with her first rose.

Cyrus then sent a message to Zachariah at The Temple who shared the message with Noam, Hooba's mother. Iakobas, Hooba's stepbrother, traveled to the community within the walls to deliver the message to Jared. Along with the message were silver coins from Cyrus. The coins were to be used to pay for food and lodging for Jared to find Hooba and return him home to his family. The request for Hooba's return home came directly from Noam.

Iakobas stood in front of Jared delivering the message of Hooba's possible location. Jared stared at him almost in disbelief. It was as if he had returned from the dead. Because, in Jared's mind, he had already been resolved to that possibility.

Iakobas then explained that Yohanan who had taken over the trade routes from Cyrus, knew of a faster route to reach the seaport of Banbhore. It was entirely by sea, once heading south from the city of The Temple.

Jared thought, "Tomorrow is the Sabbath. I will start my journey in less than thirty-six hours."

Jared awoke in the morning, ritually bathed, laid face-down on the ground in his room and prayed, just a little more thankfully.

Sunday morning, Jared and Iakobas traveled to the city of The Temple to meet Yohanan. Yohanan then took Jared to board the boat to Banbhore.

The first part of his journey by sea was relatively calm. However, a storm approached while they were crossing the Arabian Sea. The ship was never at risk but Jared was never sure. This had been his first time at sea and land was nowhere in sight.

Jared considered that if he survived this passage, it might be better to walk home. Two more days had passed when land was announced to the passengers. Eight days in total had passed since Jared began the trip to bring Hooba home.

Jared stood on the deck of the boat much like he had stood on the wall, all the days after Hooba had left, looking east.

He scanned the shoreline thinking, "How will I find him?"

Upon docking the boat, Jared stepped onto dry land. He stumbled to regain his land legs. A man reached out to catch him.

He spoke, "Are you alright, brother?"

Jared stood there surprised, looking into the face of another man with a shaved head. His thoughts were racing. This man looked very different from Jared. Yet, his Aramaic was quite pronounced.

Jared said, "Yes, I am alright."

The monk responded, "Well, peace be with you, brother."

Jared thought, "This man is most different than those from our community."

Then, in an attempt to learn more about this man, he began to recite Psalms 23:2 through 23:6 and to Jared's surprise, the monk recited it back in unison.

Jared asked himself: "Is it possible this man knows Hooba?"

"Do you know Hooba?" Jared asked.

The monk responded, "I know the rabbi."

Jared's mind could not focus. His thoughts were everywhere. "How could the first man I meet know Hooba?"

"It's been nearly ten years," he thought to himself.

"Who is this little man with a beard and how does he know Hooba?" Jared wondered.

"Does he know where to find Hooba?" he questioned himself.

Jared then marveled, "Is this divine intervention?"

Jared's mind then went to his memories of Hooba, the boy, the young man, his brother. But, the monk stood there, waiting patiently. He understood Jared to be deep in thought.

Then Khedenn spoke, "Brother, have you traveled to hear the rabbi's teaching?"

Jared responded, "In a way, yes. I have come to find him."

Khedenn then asked, "Have you traveled far?"

"Yes, I have traveled from Hooba's home to find my brother," Jared answered.

The monk tilted his head to the side and just stared at Jared.

Then, he spoke, "Jared, your brother is not far."

Jared asked himself: "This man knows my name?"

"How do you know my name?" Jared asked the monk.

Khedenn replied, "When you spoke the name Hooba, it was spoken with the same love as when he describes you, the most powerful and peaceful brother he has ever known."

Khedenn looked up as Jared towered above him in stature.

Then, with a smile he spoke, "You are just as he described you, a giant with a warm heart who speaks Aramaic."

"Do you know where I can find him?" Jared asked.

Khedenn's simple response was, "Yes."

Jared's heart was racing and he tried to calm himself.

Then, he asked the monk: "What is your name?"

The monk replied, "Khedenn."

Jared asked, "Khedenn, can you guide me to find Hooba?"

Khedenn turned and began to walk away.

Jared was not sure if he should follow but yelled to Khedenn: "What am I to do?"

The monk turned and replied, "Follow me."

Khedenn had walked just twenty feet when he stopped. Jared ran up to him as the monk just stood still. First, Jared was unsure of what was happening and why Khedenn had stopped. Then he saw, not too far away, a man with flowing dark hair sitting on a boulder under the only tree visible for miles. There were small children sitting on the ground at his feet. There were nearly one hundred people standing and listening to the man. His voice was quiet but confident. There was not a sound to be heard but that of his voice.

Jared wanted to yell in excitement to Hooba but did not wish to interrupt. Hooba raised his right hand up, looking directly into Jared's eyes. He continued to speak for about fifteen more minutes.

Hooba ended his words to the crowd, "Peace be with you."

He stood and the children flocked to embrace him. He reached his hands out to touch everyone in the crowd around him and as he walked through the end of the crowd, Hooba began to run toward Jared. His thoughts were filled with love and thanks to God.

He thought, "My friend, my brother, my rabbi, my mentor. This man is like a father."

Soon, the men embraced.

Jared then realized he had lifted Hooba right off the ground and that he had no wish to put him back on his feet.

He spoke to Hooba: "Rabbi, I see you inspire love in the people just as you have inspired love in me."

Hooba replied, "I love you, too, Rabbi."

Khedenn stood watching and *without any attachments* allowed a tear to roll down his cheek.

Khedenn spoke, "Rabbi?"

Jared began to answer. Then, with understanding and pride, did not speak.

Hooba answered the monk: "Yes, Khedenn?"

"The children will be waiting," Khedenn said.

Hooba motioned for Jared to follow as they walked toward the school. Approaching the schoolyard, Jared noticed many children running out to greet them. Hooba handed Jared a carved, wooden stick. All of the children carried carved, wooden sticks as well. Hooba threw out a stuffed, woven ball onto the ground. The children ran to it, as Jared watched in remembrance. It reminded him of Hooba as a child and their days playing within the walls of the community.

Jared noticed a small child standing on the side of the playground. He had no stick and was watching the others play. Jared ran to the boy and placed him on his back. He took his stick and ran into the yard to play with the children and Hooba. He soon realized that the young boy on his back, along with Hooba and himself, were all laughing in enjoyment.

Hooba shot the woven ball directly between Jared's legs.

Jared thought, "He may not look powerful, but he is nimble. My boy has become a man."

Hooba scooped up another little boy and ran straight past Jared. He sat him down right next to the woven ball. Jared was just about to block the shot when Hooba looked him straight in the eye and the little boy swung with all his might, moving the ball about ten feet.

Jared ran toward the ball but somehow allowed another young boy to hit it before he did. Then, Jared stepped in front of another boy headed for the ball and allowed a young girl to take the remaining shot.

They all sat on the ground, hugging in celebration not only of the game played but of the reunion of Hooba and Jared.

Khedenn had returned back to the home of one of the *freed* women while the game was played between Jared and Hooba. He returned with an invitation from her to the Sabbath meal the next day, as this was Friday afternoon.

The two men, Hooba and Jared, visited until sundown. Then, in the morning, the three men ritually bathed. They ate date fruit and spent the day in prayer. Once the sun had set, they traveled to the home of the *freed* woman.

Before the meal began, Hooba raised his hand, looking straight into Jared's eyes. Jared paused and watched.

Khedenn stood at the head of the table with a twelve-year-old boy. He recited Psalms 23:2 through 23:6 as the young boy repeated it after him. Jared could only smile, holding back his tears of pride.

Hooba stood up from the table, broke the bread and served all that were seated. Then, he served Jared last.

He spoke, "In this case, he who is served last is most honored."

Jared stood. He walked to the head of the table where Hooba was seated. He broke the bread again, and served Hooba.

The table was filled with laughter and conversation. The women shared with Jared the story of Hooba freeing them from the proprietor. Khedenn shared the story of his conversion from the monastery to following Hooba.

Hooba looked at Khedenn and said, "My brother, I will be returning home with Jared. Will you be accompanying us?"

Khedenn answered, "Just as that is your home, this is mine. With your blessings, I would love to continue the work you started here."

Hooba looking at Khedenn, replied, "You are certainly blessed for it is a blessing to carry out the work of the Lord. I look forward to the day when I will meet you again in the kingdom of God."

Looking at Jared, Hooba spoke, "Jared, I need a few days to say goodbye to the children and people. Then, brother … take me home!"

The sun rose and after their ritual of bathing, Hooba asked Jared if he could borrow his sword. Hooba walked to the town's square and went to the single tree by the boulder where he taught. He looked for a sturdy branch and then swung the heavy sword, severing the branch from the tree. He then carved and smoothed the branch with Jared's sword.

He found Khedenn.

Hooba said, "My friend, may this staff and your faith in God carry you as my staff and my faith in God have carried me."

The two men then embraced. Hooba bowed to Khedenn with the respect of one monk to another.

Then he confessed, "Rabbi, I will miss you."

Khedenn bowed, in respect back to Hooba.

He said, "Rabbi, I will miss you but thank you; I now know that God is always with me and I will never be alone."

Hooba answered, "Peace be with you, brother, and where will you go?"

"Peace be with you also, brother. I will go wherever my faith and God will guide me," Khedenn replied.

Khedenn placed his staff on the ground, turned and headed back toward the Indus Valley.

His last words heard were, "This staff is sturdy, just as my foundation and faith are, as you have taught me."

Hooba returned to the town square. Jared met him there and listened as he spoke. The younger rabbi spoke of love and the kingdom of God that awaits all who love. He bid the people of Banbhore farewell and told them of his leaving the following day.

His last words to the crowd of listeners were, "Peace be with you."

Hooba walked with Jared back toward the school. He pulled out his last silver piece from his pocket.

He handed it to Jared and asked, "Will this be enough to get us home?"

Jared answered, "I am hopeful."

Hooba returned to the school and to the homes of the three women he had freed. He bid the women goodbye and then played with the children in the yard once more. He sat with the children and told them stories for his last time, as well. The children clung to his every word.

He looked at Jared and said, "Certainly, those with the innocence of children will also find themselves a home in the kingdom of God."

The next morning, they ritually bathed, ate date fruit, packed and walked to the docks at the seaport. The streets were lined with people and children. The same twelve-year-old boy from their Sabbath meal recited Psalms 23:2 through 23:6 as they waited.

The three freed women kissed Hooba on the cheek and said, "May God be with you on your travels and keep you safe."

Jared took the silver piece and tried to pay for passage on a boat, to one of the sea merchants. The merchant refused payment.

He said to Hooba: "You have done so much for our small community. Thank you for teaching my son Psalms 23:2 through 23:6."

Jared returned with the silver piece and handed it back to Hooba with an explanation. Hooba immediately turned to the three women and handed it over to them.

"Peace be with you and continue God's work," Hooba told them.

One of the women said, "I have been listening to your stories. Every afternoon, after the children play, I will tell one."

A little girl ran out from the crowd. She reminded Hooba of so many little six-year-old girls who had touched his heart.

She looked up at him with large, warm eyes and said, "I love you, Hooba."

Hooba took her hand and guided her back to her parents.

He leaned over and whispered to her, "I love you too."

Jared and Hooba boarded the boat.

Hooba turned to the crowd, raised his right hand and said, "Peace be with you all."

The crowd responded in unison: "Peace be with you."

Chapter 24
Eight Days Home

The first day at sea, the men's stomachs soured again. There was a constant sway to the boat. Jared needed a diversion and was extremely curious to hear Hooba's stories about the past nearly ten years. However, Hooba had questions of his own.

His first question to Jared was, "How is my mother?"

Jared explained that much had changed at home but that his mother was well and now living in the city of The Temple. He also informed Hooba that his mother was now close friends with his own father and mother.

Hooba then asked, "How is your brother Hilleal and my cousin Susanna?"

Jared shared that they were married to each other and had a daughter of their own.

"She is called Ruth," Jared said, "And she is now the age of six."

"Your brother, Iakobas, is studying *The Law* with my father at The Temple," Jared informed Hooba.

Hooba looked into Jared's eyes and sincerely asked, "How did you find me?"

Jared explained, "A man named Aahan sent a letter from his father's home through the caravan on the Silk Road. It landed in the hands of a man named Yohanan who had taken over the route for Cyrus and Tyrus. The letter read of a man who spoke Aramaic, Kush and Sanskrit and was teaching in the Indus Valley and Aahan believed it was you.

Yohanan had delivered the letter to Cyrus. He delivered the letter to my father, then Iakobas delivered the message to me."

Hooba then asked Jared everything he knew about his brother, Cyrus, Tyrus, Yohanan, and Jared's father. Jared filled in the details for Hooba on that which he knew. However, on some, he knew little.

Hooba couldn't resist, "What about Cyrus's and Tyrus's family?"

Again, Jared knew only small details about their family and shared what little he knew. He told Hooba that Josephus had moved home to live with his granddaughter, Bachariko. He believed Hooba would want the information regarding Josephus since he had recommended him all those years before to the community within the walls.

Hooba then asked Jared: "What do you know of Bachariko?"

"I really have no details about Bachariko but that her grandfather lives with her," Jared admitted.

Hooba smiled and remembered the little six-year-old, redheaded girl he had played with in Egypt, nearly twenty-four years before.

Hooba began to tell Jared the stories of his travels over the almost ten years that had passed.

"What have you learned, Hooba?" Jared's curiosity getting the better of him.

Hooba leaned forward and said, "Jared, it may be your purpose to preserve *The Law* but my purpose is more. My purpose is to share *The Law* with everyone."

Hooba looked at Jared and said, "Let me explain it this way. Your purpose is much like *ahava* (Love) of *The Law*. My purpose is *ahav* and *ahava* of *The Law*. (Giving love without expectation.)"

"It is not just something you feel nor is it just something you do; it is both. It must include the *why* you do it. God gave *The Law* through *ahav* and *ahava* and we must follow *The Law* the same way," Hooba explained.

Hooba continued on: "It is not enough to follow *The Law*, you must live *The Law*. It is your intention and choices that matter. Consider Khedenn; within a very short time, he learned of God's love, of *The Law* and all without expectations for himself. He is now living and teaching *The Law*. He has chosen an unconditional love over a life of self-attainment. It is no longer about himself but rather God and others."

Hooba and Jared continued to talk. The captain of the boat approached them. He offered them a fermented grain drink. Hooba explained to Jared that it was stronger than their weakened wine and it required a developed taste.

The captain explained it to be safer than water to drink while on the boat.

Jared was starting to fall asleep after just one mug.

Hooba leaned forward again telling Jared: "You deserve the rest, my brother. Before you fall asleep, thank God for the opportunity."

Jared awoke only to see Hooba at the front of the boat, telling stories and teaching the crew.

He watched him and thought, "This man truly is a beautiful human, even more beautiful than when I first dropped him off at sea. He judges no one and accepts all. He doesn't just share what he knows, he shares what he feels. I am blessed that he thinks of me as his brother, just as he does every man on this boat."

The third day of travel, a storm brewed again. The water was churning and rough as the boat took on some of that water. Hooba, Jared and many of the men carried up buckets of water from inside the hull of the boat, emptying them over the side. Some of the men became frightened however, and Hooba comforted them.

Hooba also bailed the overflowing water and was overheard by a crew member praying to God.

"I am thankful for every moment of this life. I pray that every man on this boat will know the love you have shown," Hooba spoke to God.

Moments passed as the water calmed and the rains subsided. Some men on the boat considered it a miracle.

One of the men asked Hooba: "How did you calm the storm?"

"There never was a storm only a test of our faith. I performed no miracle and was only thankful for what I have. God did the rest," Hooba replied.

The remainder of their travel days were uneventful. Hooba was teaching in the bow of the boat when Jared approached him.

Jared said, "Rabbi, land is visible."

Hooba felt a warmth come over him. He asked himself if this feeling was home … or God that he felt.

Then, he heard Isaiah say, "It's both, Hooba."

Chapter 25

Home

Hooba jumped off the boat. He turned to watch Jared unsteady on his feet.

He handed Jared his staff, laughed and said, "Once you've walked up and down the tallest mountain in the world, this is nothing!"

Soon, they were walking through the gates of the city with The Temple. Hooba first noticed with surprise the Kittim guards standing on every wall.

He looked at Jared and remarked, "I must go to The Temple. Even though God is everywhere it is where I may give God my respect."

The courtyard of The Temple was filled with money changers, tax men and Kittim soldiers. Hooba was appalled. He started to preach in the middle of the courtyard. His voice got louder the longer he spoke.

Nearly speaking at the top of his voice, he said, "You disgrace the covenant and the home of God."

Two Kittim soldiers began to approach Hooba. Jared placed his hand on his sword. Iakobas appeared from nowhere and hurriedly led Hooba and Jared through The Temple doors.

Hooba hugged his older brother, Iakobas.

Iakobas leaned over to Hooba and said, "Outside those doors is Rome. Inside these doors is home."

Zachariah stood at the front of The Temple veil near the Sanctuary. He greeted his son and Hooba.

Hooba bowed his head and said, "Rabbi, I have come to kneel at the altar of God and thank him for my life's experiences."

Zachariah replied, "Young man, this is holy space, the holiest of holy. It is only available on Passover."

Hooba replied, "Rabbi, with all respect, it has been ten Passovers since last I stood in this holy place and what I have learned is that we must tear down the veil in front of the Sanctuary and allow the people and God to live as one together."

"We are not the owners of God," Hooba then said. "We must share God with everyone."

Zachariah took a deep breath then smiled.

Then he spoke, "Rabbi, I hear the truth of God within you."

Zachariah turned to the veil and tore it off the wall to the Sanctuary. Hooba then entered the Sanctuary, laid on the floor in front of the altar and prayed.

Zachariah walked toward his son Jared and said, "Son, you have done well with this one."

Jared replied, "Father, I believe this was always within him."

Hooba stood up from the ground and said, "This Temple is a place for the people. I will take God to the people and create a new temple or kingdom outside of these walls; for the kingdom of God is for all people and not just for those who enter the door."

Hooba then turned to Zachariah saying, "Rabbi, can you take me to my mother?"

Zachariah answered, "Yes, Rabbi, follow me."

Iakobas ran ahead as Zachariah, Jared and Hooba as they walked toward the home of Zachariah.

Iakobas entered the home and began looking for his mother.

Once reaching her, he grabbed her hand and said, "Mother, follow me. Your lost son has returned home."

Noam said, "Hooba?"

"Yes, he is at the door, Mother," Iakobas answered.

Noam rushed to the entryway. She flung open the door to see Hooba standing, facing her. Zachariah and Jared stood close by.

Hooba said, "Mother, I now understand what it is like to be away from home. I want to thank you for the sacrifice you made when I was a child, allowing me to train and grow in the love of God. For you allowed your son to go and I now know what it is like to miss those that you love. I want you to know that even as the boy becomes a man, he still loves his mother."

Ruth heard the commotion. She came to the door surprised to find not only her son but Noam's son.

She said, "We must celebrate and prepare a feast for our sons have returned home."

Hooba responded, "I look forward to the celebration of my family. However, at this meal, I will honor my brother Iakobas for I respect the care he has given to my mother."

The women went off to prepare the meal. The men visited, ritualistically washed their hands and prayed.

The men went to the table. Everyone of the men sat down but Hooba. He remained standing. The three men looked at Hooba, wondering why he had not seated himself.

Jared leaned over and whispered to Hooba, "Why are you just standing there?"

"I stand to honor the women who prepared our food," Hooba replied.

Jared leaned over to Iakobas and informed him: "Hooba is standing to honor the women who prepared our food."

Iakobas then stood along with Hooba and Jared.

Iakobas leaned over to Zachariah and relayed, "Hooba is standing to honor the women who prepared our food."

Zachariah looked around and then stood.

The women entered and placed the food on the table. Hooba personally seated Noam, Ruth, and Rebecca as the three other men stood.

Hooba then seated each man individually.

"I first seated the women and then the men out of respect for every woman and every man who treated me with love and respect on my journey. I do this to honor all of you and the divine female and male I see in our creator."

Hooba picked up the loaf of bread and handed it to Zachariah.

"As is the custom, this is your house," Hooba spoke.

Zachariah pushed back his chair and walked to the end of the table. He handed the loaf to his wife.

He said, "I believe this house is also yours."

Ruth broke the bread and passed it to all of them and Hooba thanked God for allowing him to have a meal with his family.

They all conversed throughout the meal. Hooba informed his mother that he would be traveling the next day to the community within the walls with Jared.

"I will return shortly," he told his mother, "But, I have an obligation to the community."

He continued, "My purpose is not within the walls but rather to share the message."

Jared and Hooba set off on foot the next morning. Upon arrival to the community, Jared and Hooba first went to the community, outside the walls. They visited the home of Jared's brother Hilleal and his wife Susanna.

Susanna immediately embraced both of the men and, as expected, both men blushed.

Jared told Hilleal: "I want you to gather all of the men. I want them to come within the walls tomorrow when Hooba will speak."

Jared turned to Susanna with a smile on his face and said, "I am sure you will want to come also."

They all noticed then that Hooba had stepped outside of their home. He was found in the yard bouncing their daughter Ruth on his knee.

Hooba thought to himself: "Ah … she reminds me of young Susanna and Bachariko at that same age."

Susanna's friend Johanna appeared and began carrying on conversation with her.

Susanna turned to Hooba and said, "Johanna would like to come with us to the community within the walls tomorrow."

Hooba said, "Please do. All are welcome."

Later, Hooba overheard the women talking about spices and herbs.

He leaned over and asked, "Where did you learn of these spices and herbs?"

The women all responded, "Through Ruth. Ruth learned through Josephus."

Hooba then asked, "What do you know of Josephus?"

The women in unison answered again: "He lives with his widowed granddaughter, and they share their healing with many people."

Susanna whispered to Hooba, "It is said the granddaughter has cinnamon-colored hair."

Hooba responded, "I know because I met her at the same age as when I met you and your Ruth."

"All three of you had the same delightful laugh," Hooba admitted.

Hooba and Jared left the home of Hilleal and Susanna to enter the community within the walls. That evening, Hooba sat at Jared's table. A young man seated next to Hooba stood and recited Psalms 23:2 to 23:6 and Hooba smiled.

Chapter 26
Hooba Speaks within the Walls

*T*he next morning, Hooba awoke at sunrise, ritually bathed and prayed. He ate with the brothers. He greeted Jared with an embrace.

He was smiling ear to ear. Jared thought to himself, how peaceful Hooba looked.

Hooba looked at Jared and said, "Today, I would be presented with a sword. However, if presented, I would turn it down. My passion is my sword. My passion is my purpose. I will share my message."

Hooba said, "Jared, I have learned much within these walls. But, nearly as much outside. I have experienced love at the hands of children, strangers, friends and if I tell you also God, I hope you do not doubt me. I have returned home and experienced the love that I missed with my family and you, my friend. Now, I must share what I have learned. That is my passion. That is my purpose."

"My friend, I support you on whatever your chosen path. I see that your maturity and experience has changed you," Jared spoke.

Hooba responded, "I will miss you my friend but I must go. To not share the love that I have experienced is to not love at all."

Jared looked at Hooba in just a little bit of sorrow.

He said, "Rabbi, it would be selfish of me to hinder your purpose or your passion. I will be just thankful for the last few days. I see peace and joy in your heart and that is all a friend can really ask."

Jared and a dozen of the other men within the walls opened the large wooden gates. The community people outside the walls and all of the men within the walls gathered in the courtyard. Hooba walked person to person, embracing each one. He walked over to the steps of the Great Hall. He flung both doors wide open and disappeared within the building.

Fifteen minutes later, Jared entered the building, looking for Hooba. He found Hooba praying in the Sanctuary.

Jared said, "Hooba, the people are waiting."

Hooba slowing stood up from the ground. He removed the veil in front of the Sanctuary then slowly and carefully folded it and placed it in the center of the altar.

Hooba spoke, "The only thing that should be sacrificed is that which keeps man from God."

He walked out onto the steps of the Great Hall. The men all stood to the front of the courtyard. The women all stood to the back. Hooba walked straight through the center of the men, parting them much as Moses had the Red Sea. He then led the women directly up the middle to the front of the courtyard, near the steps.

Hooba looked up and out, to see Jared and Hilleal standing on the wall. Then, he looked down to see Susanna holding the hand of Ruth her daughter, standing right in front of him. Ruth ran up the stairs and took his hand. Hooba smiled and thought of the innocence of children. He picked her up and carried her back to her mother. Susanna smiled.

Hooba thought to himself: "This is not the time to blush."

He picked up his staff and said aloud, "This will be my sword. I will lean on it and my God in my journey."

Then Hooba addressed the crowd.

"My brothers and sisters, I came to you as a child, no experience in *The Law*. I played and ran as a child. I was loved by my mother, my father, my teacher. I loved because *I* was loved.

"I have experienced the joy of love from a child who did not know *The Law* but only love. I have bounced a child upon my knee and I have been loved by this child simply for being. I have heard laughter and joy. There is beauty in the joy of their innocence. I have seen love from the innocent, the pagan and the stranger. This love is universal.

"I have learned the lesson of Abraham that the innocent shall not be sacrificed to God. Do not sacrifice love or life because life and love are precious. Love must be experienced.

"I have known the story of Solomon and the Judges; the abomination of the sacrifice of the innocent children, those not of royal birth burned in the Valley of Gehenna. There is no value in the sacrifice of innocents.

"There are but three things, *The Law*, the God of love and the love of God. We were given *The Law*. We were given God's love. We were given free will, freedom to choose love and there is no earthly power, ruler or circumstance nor experience not even death that can separate us from the love of God. So, how can you not follow *The Law*?

"My brothers, I understand why you must preserve *The Law*. However, without God, *The Law* is meaningless. Faith in God requires *deeds*. Faith without *deeds* is empty. *Deeds* without faith are empty. I know your faith by your *deeds*. I know your love by your actions. Your light will shine through you. Your good *deeds* will glorify your God and you will be the example of God's love.

"I do not teach to abolish *The Law*. I teach that you must fulfill *The Law*. However, your love and righteousness must surpass the pharaohs, the rabbis and all other teachers of *The Law*. Then you can enter the kingdom of Heaven. However, if you set aside *The Law* or teach others to set aside *The Law* you will be called last to Heaven.

"Blessed are the poor, the meek, the hungry, the humble, merciful and pure of heart, even if they do not know *The Law*. For each of these has invited me to the table and to each I will invite to my table.

"So, what of *The Law*? Do not retaliate. Do not judge lest ye be judged. Invite all to your table. Love your enemy or stranger as yourself. You shall not murder. Do not give false offerings or sacrifices. If you are selfish, jealous or conceited, your offering is meaningless. Settle with your adversary because your stubbornness will be held against you. Do not swear an oath or make a contract because if you have love, none is needed.

"It has been said, *"An eye for an eye,"* but that is God's judgment and not for man. Love your neighbor and your enemies as you love yourself.

Then, we will return to God as the sons and daughters of God. We will return like the children, in innocence.

"Give to the needy but do not announce it in The Temple for that is hypocrisy. Do not proclaim your righteousness, live it. Do not store your treasures for yourself; share of yourself. Do not pray in The Temple if you do not pray in the streets and behind closed doors, for nothing you do in unseen. Your eyes are a lamp unto you. If all you see is darkness then all you know is darkness. If all you see is suffering, then all you are is suffering. If all you see is love, then God is within you.

"Do not worry. Be thankful for today is the day to live love. Seek love in all things. Give love in all things. Be love in all things.

"The gates to Heaven are narrow but never closed. For from God you have come and to God you will return. It is only you that chooses any other path. Good fruit comes from good trees. Flowers bloom when watered. A wise man builds his home on solid ground.

"Love is patient and kind. It is not boastful or rude. It rejoices in the truth. Love never ends. God is love.

"I honor those who preserve *The Law* but I must teach it. We must return to the love and innocence of a child. I will pull back the veil on the Sanctuary. God is not only in the Sanctuary. Love cannot be this neatly packaged. It must be freed, given and experienced.

"Tomorrow, I will walk through these gates. Yes, brothers, protect *The Law* but, brothers, God is love. *The Law* is God. *The Law* and God must be shared.

"Love … agape, ahav, ahava. These words may sound different but are all the same. My brothers … God, Allah, creator, the Alpha and the Omega. These words may sound different but are all the same.

"Peace be with you my brothers and sisters. My journey has just begun.

Hooba walked down into the crowd.

Still up on the wall, Jared whispered to Hilleal, "You must go with him."

Hilleal looked down to Susanna. Their eyes met. Susanna nodded back up to Hilleal. She knew at that moment what he was saying.

Johanna had already asked Hooba if she could walk with him. Susanna scoured the crowd. Ruth was already walking with Hooba, holding his hand. Susanna's brother Iakobas, who was also Hooba's cousin, was asking Hooba to walk along. This younger Iakobas looked up at Jared and signaled that he, too, would be following Hooba.

Families began walking through the gates to the community outside the walls.

The men within the walls were overheard asking one another: "Is this the great teacher?"

Jared climbed down from the wall. He went to the small warehouse on the perimeter of the courtyard. He took Hilleal's sword from its honored position. He returned with the sword and presented it to Hilleal.

Then, he turned to Iakobas who had not yet reached the age of receiving his sword. Jared unstrapped his own sword from his side and gave it to the younger Iakobas.

He said, "You are traveling with a man of peace. However, the roads are no longer safe."

Jared approached Hooba.

"Be safe, Rabbi, my friend," he said.

Then Jared thought, "I have a man from inside the wall, a man from outside the wall, two women healers, a small child and a man whom I would proudly call my son, my family … leaving on a journey with uncertainty."

Jared looked back at the gates as the crowd was leaving. He wondered why he hadn't noticed this before. The other Iakobas, Hooba's older brother, was standing in the gate. Jared rushed to the gates to meet him.

He asked, "Did you hear your brother speak?"

Iakobas answered solemnly, "Yes, Jared, I did. I must speak to Hooba."

Hooba was watching his brother Iakobas from a distance. He noticed the look on his face. He rushed to embrace his brother.

Iakobas whispered in his ear: "Hooba, will you tell him Zachariah has died?"

Tears welled in Hooba eyes. He then asked, "Ruth?"

Iakobas responded, "She is alright."

Then Hooba asked, "Our mother?"

Iakobas answered, "She and Rebecca are tending to Jared's mother Ruth."

Iakobas then said, "Zokef the Pharisee now claims primacy at The Temple. I know this is a bad time to share this. I am now not favored at The Temple. I left Ruth, your mother and Rebecca with Yohanan."

Hooba said, "Go talk to Jared. I will be right there."

Then, he walked over to Susanna.

He said, "Susanna, prepare a meal for the family. Jared needs family right now. I will bring him with me."

Hooba walked over to Jared. He told the younger Iakobas to follow Susanna and that she was preparing an evening meal.

Hooba said, "Jared, death is just one type of departure. It is not the end. Your father has departed this world. This does not end your relationship. You will see him again."

Jared began to sob. Then, he felt a tug on his cloak.

Susanna's daughter Ruth smiled up at Jared and said, "It is alright to cry when you are sad. Don't worry, we will keep Hooba company."

Jared got down on his knees next to Ruth, still towering above her.

He looked up at Hooba and said, "There really is something beautiful in their innocence."

Jared then turned back to young Ruth and added, "Thank you, Ruth; that does make me feel much better."

Ruth took Jared's hand in hers, then Hooba's hand in her other one and said, "My mother is preparing a meal; it is a celebration."

The three, with hands still entangled, young Ruth, Jared and Hooba passed through the gates of the community within the walls together and while they did so, Jared and Hooba recited Psalms 23:2 through 23:6 in unison.

On entering the home of Hilleal and Susanna, Susanna threw her arms around Jared and kissed him on the cheek. It was the first time she had not seen or expected him to blush.

They were all seated to eat as Hooba passed the bread to Jared.

Jared broke the bread and then said, "I have been so blessed to be invited to this table. This table has brought me great joy."

Jared set his eyes upon each one around the table and remembered them one by one as children. He smiled within.

He asked himself: "How has a man with no wife become so blessed by the children in his life?"

Jared turned to Hooba and said, "Hooba, you are so correct. What is *The Law* without the love?"

Hooba and Jared walked back toward the community inside the walls. Hooba shared more details with Jared about the situation at The Temple. He informed Jared that both of the Iakobases would be traveling along on his journey due to the unrest in the area.

Hooba then said to Jared: "My mother and your mother, along with Rebecca, will be joining this journey. We cannot leave them alone in the city. I will care for your mother as if she was my own."

Before sunrise the next morning, Jared had been up and ritually bathed. He was in the courtyard when the sun began to peek over the wall. He had already been to their small warehouse and gathered supplies and the smallest but sharpest sword.

He believed that Hooba may be willing to carry the small sword on his body. He then went in search of Hooba with sword in hand. Hooba took one look at the sword Jared carried and shook his head to indicate no.

They walked back into the courtyard where the sun now shone above the walls. The men were just opening the gates for the day.

Jared looked at Hooba and said, "Please, be careful out there."

Hooba smiled back at Jared and said, "I have been teaching now for almost ten years. It's not that dangerous," he said with a laugh.

Hooba's eyes then focused on a rock on the ground in the courtyard. He looked at Jared then turned his staff over and smacked the rock straight at Jared.

Jared took the tip of his sword and flipped it right back to Hooba.

Hooba walked over to Jared. They embraced, yet neither man said a word. Hooba turned and walked to the gates. Then, he turned back around one last time, raised his right hand and spoke.

"Peace Be with You, Rabbi," he said to Jared with the most heartfelt respect.

Jared could only reply with emotion, "Rabbi."

Hooba walked out the gates of the community within the walls. He took with him the clothes on his back, his staff and a small alabaster jar in his pocket. Jared climbed the walls and watched until he could no longer see Hooba.

Iakobas (Hooba's cousin), Johanna and her husband, Susanna and Hilleal with Ruth on his back and Hooba began their journey back to the city of The Temple.

Chapter 27

The City with The Temple

*I*t was alarming to Hooba as they approached the city to see Kittim soldiers standing on and around the walls.

The guards at the gates questioned their reasons for entering the city.

Hooba yelled out, "My father has recently passed and we have come for my mother."

The guards waved them through without response. They walked directly toward the house of Yohanan where Noam, Ruth and Rebecca awaited.

They were met at the door by Yohanan. Hilleal, Susanna, Ruth and Hooba went to find the elder Ruth who still dressed in black to offer their condolences. Hilleal conveyed to his mother immediately the love he brought from her oldest son, Jared.

They soon broke bread with the evening meal. Hooba explained to his mother what he proposed to do on his new journey. He invited the three women, Ruth, Rebecca and his mother to join them.

He looked to them and spoke, "At times like this, you should be with family."

Hooba told the women of his plan to head south to the country, then head north to the communities by the sea. Yohanan was moved by the passion Hooba possessed.

He said, "I have the means, the carts, the donkeys and the tents if you will allow myself and Miriam my daughter to walk with you."

Hooba thought inwardly: "This idea is good. The older women should not walk for long and Yohanan has been on many caravans and is capable of setting up camp, cooking for a group and instructing others if necessary."

"Yohahan, it will be an honor to have someone traveling with us with your experience," Hooba said. "And again, I thank you for assisting my mother, Ruth and Rebecca."

Yohanan replied, "I will bring four other men to trade on the southern route which should strengthen our numbers."

Hooba again voiced his appreciation to Yohanan.

The next morning, Hooba took off for The Temple on his own, once completing his morning rituals. Upon entering The Temple square, he again noticed Kittim soldiers stationed in various places. There were also tax collectors, people selling their wares and then his focus went to a foreign woman who was attempting to purchase bread.

The soldiers and the merchants were ridiculing this woman. Hooba instantly found himself in conversation with the merchant.

"Would you allow me to buy bread?" he asked. "Do I look more hungry than this woman?"

"Are those Kittim coins of more value if they come from my hand?" He went on.

"It is not her kind who have hung people outside the city on trees," he taunted.

Hooba stated, "If this woman goes hungry, she is more likely to enter the kingdom of God than you!"

Hooba began educating the crowd of listeners.

"I have traveled many miles, where I was the stranger. I was fed, when I had no food. I was clothed, when I had no clothes. I was offered a fair wage when I had no money."

One of the merchants spoke out to Hooba: "This woman is not clean. Why should we waste clean food on her?"

Hooba took a deep, long sigh and thought, "I must learn to control my temper."

Then, he said aloud: "Hagar was a foreigner who Abraham took as a slave. Thus, her son by Abraham was, too, a foreigner. Undoubtedly, you would consider them to be unclean. However, God fed them with manna from Heaven when Abraham cast them out into the desert, and never once asked if they were clean.

"Hagar did not worship idols. Ishmael honored his mother. Neither coveted the riches of Abraham. What is purer than the love of a mother for her son? It appears that Hagar followed *The Law*, although considered to be foreign," Hooba stated.

A man from the tax-collectors table approached the merchant. He paid the merchant for a loaf of bread then turned to the foreign woman and handed her the bread.

Hooba knew how a tax collector was viewed by the people. They ranked as low as murderers and prostitutes in their eyes.

"Who is most humble, the woman who seeks to feed herself or the tax collector that feeds her?" Hooba asked the crowd.

He addressed the crowd for nearly forty minutes. The entire courtyard of people had circled around to listen.

Hooba, nearing the end of his teaching, said, "I do not judge for judgment is God's. However, at judgment I suspect it will be easier for God to judge this tax collector, this hungry woman and a foreign slave and her son, than many of those listening in this square. Thankfully, we have a loving and forgiving God and the day of atonement is not today."

The merchant walked back over to the woman and handed her a loaf of bread.

Then, he yelled, "Is there anyone else here in the crowd who is hungry?"

"My mother is hungry but too ashamed to ask," a little boy admitted.

The merchant asked, "Where did that voice come from?"

One of the Kittim soldiers answered, "The small boy is over here!"

Another man came forward and said, "I can pay for their loaf of bread."

The merchant replied, "If you pay for one loaf, they will get two."

The tax collector quickly closed up his stand, walked over to Hooba and asked, "Rabbi, where will you be speaking tomorrow?"

Hooba answered, "I do not know, but I will invite you to dinner tonight because just as you have shared bread with a hungry woman, I will share bread with you."

Hooba turned to the hungry woman and invited her also to join them for dinner. She fell to her knees to thank him.

"Woman, stand up!" Hooba requested.

"Do not bow to me; bow only to God."

The tax collector reconciled his books, turned in his collections and followed Hooba home to the house of Yohanan.

The Pharisee Zokef, the one now claiming primacy, had been watching and listening the entire afternoon in the courtyard.

That evening, Yohanan welcomed the two new visitors; a hungry foreign woman and a tax collector to his table.

The senior Iakobas, Hooba's brother, immediately asked, "Hooba, do you consider that this makes our table unclean?"

Hooba responded, "Many a stranger has invited me to their table. They both have an understanding of love and they both seek something. If both love and *The Law* are required to enter the kingdom of God, does it matter which comes first? Your cleanliness is your responsibility."

Yohanan added, "I have had many good men that worked for me who had no understanding of *The Law*. I have already heard rumors from today Hooba, of how you have stirred up the courtyard."

The foreign woman then spoke, "Hooba rescued me today and showed me compassion. If his God moves him that way, I want to know more of his God."

"I also heard of your adventures, Hooba. Some of the nationalists overheard you and they have said you put the tax collectors and soldiers in their place," Iakobas relayed.

It was then that the tax collector spoke up, "I did not witness Hooba putting tax collectors and soldiers in their place but rather witnessed them being inspired by his message. I imagine if he believed one of the soldiers to be hungry, he, too, would have been invited to this table."

Hooba then explained, "My intention is to inspire, to include and not divide."

The elder Ruth interjected, "The women today were also talking. One commented on your respect for women, Hooba. One woman went to the Pharisee Zokef and asked when you would be speaking again and one woman said she witnessed a Kittim soldier attempting to help a young child in finding their mother."

The younger Iakobas then spoke up, "It appears you stirred things up very quickly, my cousin."

Hooba answered, "I hope all throughout the city of The Temple, this same discussion is taking place at many other tables; the old, the young, the women, the men, the hungry, the pagan, the unclean and the clean. The first step will be when we all talk to one another."

Again, the foreign woman spoke, "What must I do first?"

Hooba answered, "It is simple. Love one another."

Hooba began to teach. He said, "I want you to consider this. Faith in God is much like love of God; both are an action and a feeling."

Noam asked the foreign woman, "Do you have a place to sleep this night?"

She answered Noam: "I do not, but I fear I have used too much of your hospitality by now."

Susanna added, "Well, that is just nonsense. Young Ruth will sleep with us and you may have her bed."

Yohanan turned to the foreign woman and offered, "We are about to travel extensively. My house will be empty. Would you be willing to watch over my home while we are away?"

The tax collector smiled and added, "Is there room for one more traveler?"

Hooba returned his smile and answered, "Yes, we will continue to make room at our table."

Yohanan also replied, "As our group enlarges, we could use a person responsible with money and numbers."

Hooba asked Yohanan, "How soon will we be prepared to leave?"

Yohanan answered Hooba, "Two days will have us prepared and ready."

Iakobas the brother, asked, "Where is our first destination?"

Hooba asked, "Iakobas, what is your suggestion?"

Iakobas said, "There is a man in the southern area I wish you to meet."

Hooba then responded, "Then, south it will be."

Hooba thought to himself: "I have one more day to teach in the courtyard."

Chapter 28
A Man from Queriot

The caravan left two days later. Each night, they set up in a different, small community. Each day, Hooba taught as his reputation began to proceed him.

Often, an entire small group from one community would follow the caravan to their next nearby town. When the crowds were very large, Hooba would sometimes teach for close to ten hours without stopping. But, when the crowds were smaller, Hooba enjoyed making time to play with the children.

What had begun as a small caravan, increased in size to thirty-two travelers by the time they reached Queriot.

Their first day in Queriot, Iakobas the brother, arranged an evening encounter with Hooba, to meet twenty men of the community who were in favor of nationalism. They were adamant about ridding their country of the Kittims.

Hilleal attended the meeting with Hooba. He would not allow Hooba to attend without accompaniment of a sword. Hilleal's sword meant there were, in total, twenty-one swords in attendance. Everyone but Hooba carried a sword.

Throughout their meeting, Hooba remained diplomatic. He spoke also of *his* own mission, which was love. The men repeatedly attempted to change the conversation to love of *country*.

Hooba went through all the many foolish battles of their people throughout history, from the Philistines to the Babylonians and to the Assyrians.

He said, "There are no winners in battles like these. The battle I seek is the one within your hearts. It is the battle for your soul."

A man named Akeldama, the apparent leader of these men, was quietly talking with several others toward the back of the group.

He was telling them: "The people will follow this man. I will travel with him because, along with this caravan, we will meet many more who feel as we do about the Kittims."

Akeldama spoke aloud so Hooba would hear his words.

"I hear great wisdom in your words. We must bring the people to God," he said to Hooba.

However, to himself, Akeldama thought, "A united people, even under God, will be stronger. I will pledge my sword to God to defend *The Law*."

Hooba replied, "We will welcome your input. However, neither God nor *The Law* will need to be defended. In teaching *The Law*, I preserve it."

Hooba and Hilleal walked back to their camp.

Hilleal said to Hooba: "I do not believe Jared would look on this man with favor. Jared would never raise his sword as the first action; only the last possible action."

Hooba agreed, "Yes, Hilleal, but this, however, is the type of man I must change."

The next day, as Hooba spoke again to the crowd in Queriot, Akeldama and four of his men stood among the crowd. Akeldama did soften in his heart as he listened to Hooba's words.

He thought to himself: "This is a good man and there is much to learn from him."

The next morning, their small caravan had increased in volume to forty travelers. One of the new travelers was, indeed, Akeldama.

The next day they traveled from Queriot north to the plateau. They moved from one small community to another small community and each time, the crowds grew and gathered while listening to Hooba teach. Leaving the plateau area, the group traveled more north to the midcountry. From there, they headed even farther north to the land by the sea. It was nearly four weeks until they reached the sea.

One day, Hooba was approached after speaking to a crowd by the shore. A woman approached him.

"Rabbi, my name is Beatrice. I have traveled here to care for a sick friend. I find great wisdom in your words. Will you pray for my friend?" she asked.

Hooba responded, "Can you take me to their home? I have healers with me."

Beatrice looked at Hooba and replied, "I, too, am a healer."

Hooba thought for a moment to himself: "I'll get my healers. They are well trained and are capable of helping her friend."

Then, Hooba called out, "Ruth, Susanna, will you follow me to help heal this woman's friend, who has taken ill?"

Beatrice led the group to the home of her friend for healing. Upon arrival, Hooba went immediately to pray with Beatrice's friend. Susanna accompanied Hooba to examine the woman.

Ruth asked Beatrice, "What have you done to heal your friend?"

Beatrice replied, "I have been steaming roots for aromatic healing. I have also used herbal remedies."

Beatrice then detailed the herbs she had used to Ruth. Ruth listened and thought about the similarities in their herbal remedies.

Ruth asked, "Have you tried turmeric, rosemary and chicken broth to reduce the fever?"

Beatrice quickly responded, "That was the first remedy I gave my friend."

Ruth looked directly at Beatrice and began, "I believe the next course would be..."

And both women simultaneously responded, "Mustard packs."

The two women, stared at each other in awe.

Each woman thought inwardly: "How does she know what I know?"

Ruth intently looked again into the eyes of Beatrice and asked, "Have you been to Egypt?"

"No, but I have trained with a man from Egypt," Beatrice replied.

"Have you been to Egypt?" Beatrice asked.

Ruth replied, "I was trained by a friend of my husband and Hooba, whose name is Josephus."

In Beatrice's excitement, she quickly responded, "My cousin and myself trained with her grandfather, Josephus of Egypt."

The two women ran into the room where Hooba and Susanna were with the ailing woman. Susanna was already applying a mustard paste. Hooba had laid both hands on the woman's shoulders and stood praying.

Ruth and Beatrice, upon entering the room, noticed the labored breathing of the ill woman. However, as they watched, her breathing became more calm and less noticeable.

The woman looked up and said, "I am thirsty."

Beatrice said, "These are her only words of the past two days."

Beatrice implied that her friend's words were due to Hooba's praying.

Hooba spoke up, "It is not I, but rather God and you women who have cured her."

Ruth walked nearer to Hooba, smiled and then spoke, "This woman knows Josephus," as she motioned toward Beatrice.

"Beatrice, do you know where Josephus is?" Hooba asked.

Beatrice responded, "Why yes. Josephus and myself live with his granddaughter, Bachariko."

Hooba smiled as he thought of a sweet, six-year-old girl with cinnamon-colored hair.

Hooba's plans the next day had been to travel farther north to Kfar Nahum. However, his thoughts remained on the six-year-old little girl and her grandfather Josephus who lived not far to the south of where they presently were. Hooba understood the next day being Friday, they needed to reach Kfar Nahum before sundown and the Sabbath beginning. Yohanan had connections and friends in Kfar Nahum and connections at The Temple. He knew he must settle the caravan before he could think about traveling south.

Chapter 29
Kfar Nahum

Early the following morning, Hooba was up to ritually bathe in the sea. Yohanan found Hooba standing on the seashore, preoccupied, watching the sunrise. Yohanan placed his hand on Hooba's shoulder and spoke.

"Hooba, today will be a busy day. We must travel, unpack, and settle before the sun sets," he said.

Hooba simply nodded. Yohanan informed him that arrangements had been made for him to speak at The Temple the next day. Again, Hooba just nodded.

Yohanan stated, "Hooba, my friend you are very quiet today."

Hooba replied, "Yohanan, we are all tired. Everyone will need a rest in Kfar Nahum."

"Is this all that concerns you?" Yohanan asked.

"No," Hooba answered.

"Sometimes I look at the crimson color as the sun rises and it reminds me of how many days I have traveled and how far I have come since I was a child. There have been so many sunrises. Do you remember laughing as a child?"

Yohanan responded, "I do, my friend and rabbi."

"Yohanan, there lies my problem. Even to my family and friends, I am friend and rabbi, brother and rabbi, cousin and rabbi. I am son and rabbi but never just Hooba," he sadly admitted.

"The last time I was just *Hooba*, I was six years old."

Yohanan sensed a longing in Hooba … the man. He embraced Hooba and attempted to give him comfort.

"My friend, we will be leaving soon," he reminded him.

Then Yohanan went to find Noam.

Noam was packed and waiting to leave with the caravan. Yohanan approached her.

"I spoke with Hooba and there appears to be a loneliness in his voice," he told Hooba's mother. "He speaks of childhood laughter and I fear he feels the heaviness of his responsibility."

Noam and Ruth had been watching over Yohanan's daughter Miriam.

Noam looked at Miriam and mumbled, "I understand Hooba's thoughts as he talked about childhood laughter."

Ruth said, "I noticed a smile appear on Hooba's face when he mentioned Josephus and Bachariko the other day."

Noam and Ruth began a conversation about Josephus and Bachariko living close by, just south of where they now were. Yohanan merely stood and listened.

Noam looked to Ruth and spoke, "You know, it is biblical that no man should be alone."

Yohana yelled to Iakobas across the camp: "Can you lead the caravan to Kfar Nahum? Ask for a man called Massa on your arrival. He is a friend of Hooba and will help you locate an appropriate camp."

Yohanan turned to Noam and said, "I am probably the only one to have sailing experience among us. We are at the shore. The community to the south is at the shore and so is Kfar Nahum. If I travel by ship, I will be there by Sunday if they will come with me."

Yohanan commissioned a fishing boat and headed south. The caravan started off and headed north.

The caravan traveled north while Iakobas found Hooba with the travelers. He informed Hooba that they had a surprise; his old friend Massa, was meeting them in Kfar Nahum.

Hooba smiled and replied, "It will be good to see an old friend."

He looked at the staff in his right hand and thought, "My friend, you have no idea how many times I have leaned on this gift."

Hooba struck out walking ahead of the entire group. A few hours later, in the distance, Hooba glimpsed one single man walking toward them. Soon, both men picked up their pace.

Massa yelled, "Hooba!"

Hooba answered back, "Massa!"

Massa then yelled, "I knew it was you by your scrawny, little body. You still don't eat, do you?"

Then, he laughed, so he would show no emotion.

"Apparently, you do not walk as many miles, because I can see that your appetite is still very good," Hooba goaded.

And, then as they reached one another, the two men embraced. They walked the next five miles beside each other, catching up on all the missed years.

Massa explained to Hooba where their camp would be located just south of Kfar Nahum and positioned on the edge of the sea.

"I hear tomorrow you are teaching at *my* temple," Massa informed Hooba.

Hooba looked up at Massa and smiled as a single tear ran down his check.

Massa spoke again, "You know, you never completely explained entirely *The Law* thing. I had to accommodate my walk for almost a week afterward," he wryly smirked.

Hooba laughingly said, "We've learned a lot since Moses. We now perform circumcision on infants."

They set up camp quickly upon their arrival and began to prepare the meal before the sun could set and bring on the Sabbath. Hooba smiled as he saw Massa kneel at the water's edge to ritually wash his hands before they ate.

Yohanan could see the shore quickly approaching. The docks were clean and the boats neatly tied. He looked up on the small bluff ahead and could see what had previously been Cyrus's home. The surrounding homes were much larger and had more land than what was common in most communities.

He quickly ran down the beach toward the bluff upon exiting the boat. He knew his time was limited until the sun would set, bringing on the Sabbath.

There was a small stone path cut into the bluff that led him to the street level of Cyrus's home. He pounded on the door only then realizing he was unsure of what he would say.

The door flew open. Standing in front of Yohanan was a relatively fair-skinned woman with cinnamon-colored hair. Yohanan stood in shock. He wasn't sure who this woman was and if she was, indeed, a keeper of the home.

Yohanan hesitated then spoke, "I am looking for Josephus."

The woman responded back, "My grandfather is resting."

Yohanan then knew she was Bachariko and not the keeper of the house.

He said, "I have come for your grandfather and you."

"And, why would I go with you; is someone ill?" Bachariko asked.

"No one is ill," Yohanan quickly confirmed.

Bachariko responded, "My grandfather is resting. If there is no important business perhaps you could come back later as it will soon become the Sabbath."

Alarmed, Yohanan then responded, "No, no, if I could have just a minute of your time, I will explain. I have come with information about Hooba."

Bachariko replied, "I think we can make the time."

"Grandfather, we have a visitor," she yelled.

A thin, older man appeared in the doorway.

He said, "Set the table; this man is a friend. We need to feed him before the Sabbath."

He looked to Yohanan and said, "Let me show you where to bathe your hands before the meal."

Josephus set a small fire in the fireplace.

He said, "We need to eat. I think the conversation will take longer than when the sun sets."

Josephus recited Psalms 23:2 through 23:6, broke the bread and served Yohanan, Bachariko, Delilah and Beatrice.

The first words from Beatrice who had just returned that day were: "I met healers and a man named Hooba on my trip."

Yohanan quickly interjected, "I just came from that same man, Hooba."

Josephus asked, "How is the family? Tell us about Hooba and his mother."

Yohanan gave a brief summary of what he knew of Hooba's life in the past many years. Then, Beatrice talked about her interaction with Hooba and healing her friend.

Josephus began speaking about Hooba as a child. During the entire conversation, Bachariko sat quietly, listening but not speaking. She slowly got up, went into the next room and returned with two small, wooden boards wrapped in parchment and tied together with a bow. She sat down and slowly untied the bow.

She unwrapped the package, separated the boards and said, "I remember his laughter and when he gave me this rose."

Delilah said, "Mother, you never told me the story about a boy who gave you a rose. However, you made me tend to the rosebush out at the corner of the house my entire life."

Bachariko said to her: "Delilah, sometimes the gift you are given when it is pure and innocent is a gift you never forget. Just as I received this rose, I received you. So, I have taken care of this rose, a gift and you, both being pure and innocent."

Yohanan said, "I, too, have a young daughter and I also care and nurture her."

Bachariko spoke again to Delilah: "I had you nurture the rose so that you could learn to love and someday nurture your own child."

Yohanan jumped back in: "That reminds me of a conversation I had at sunrise with Hooba. He remembers the laughter of a six-year-old girl with cinnamon-colored hair when he was that age. That brings me to why I am here. Hooba is a great teacher and is touching the people with his words. Yet, when he heard the names Josephus and Bachariko, it changed him. There is nothing missing in his teaching but I believe if he sees you, there will no longer be anything missing in his heart."

He continued, "I may have been rash in my decision. However, this man is my friend and I believe it will bring him great joy to see you both. So, with little forethought, I commissioned a boat and came to get you. On Sunday morning, the boat will leave for Kfar Nahum where Hooba is with his caravan."

Josephus smiled and said, "I'm up for a boat ride. It has been a long time since I looked at the beautiful coast of the sea from that vantage point. I do remember what a delightful and bright boy he was."

Bachariko said, "Grandfather, I have a daughter!"

Beatrice interrupted, "I can stay with your daughter or your daughter and I can come with you."

Delilah was not silent. "Mother, I have never been anywhere. Beatrice and myself will care for Grandfather."

"I am a mother. I previously had a husband. Hooba and my grandfather were close. I suppose it would be fun to see an old friend," Bachariko admitted.

Josephus interjected, "I think it is settled. We should go."

Yohanan informed everyone then that the boat would leave soon after sunrise on Sunday. He advised them all to pack lightly as there would not be much room on the fishing boat.

Josephus said, "We will have to pack lightly. Tomorrow is the Sabbath and, therefore, we cannot pack until after sunset."

Everyone left to go sleep but Bachariko. She sat at the table and stared at the withered, dried rose.

She thought, "I am not a young woman. In fact, I am older than this withered, dried rose."

Then, she carefully placed the rose back between the two wooden boards, wrapped them in parchment and tied a bow around them.

She went to her room. Laying on her pillow was a single red rose cut from the rosebush in her yard. She smiled.

Then, she yelled, "Grandfather, you did not cut this rose on the Sabbath, did you?"

Josephus replied, "Just like you who did not wrap the rose back up on the Sabbath."

Once Josephus was certain Bachariko had fallen asleep, he went to her door. The rose was still laying on her pillow.

He whispered, "You look as beautiful as when you were six. Besides, when Hooba was a boy, I told him if he needed to water the rosebush on the Sabbath, it was okay. It is always okay to do God's work on the Sabbath."

Meanwhile, Hooba prepared to speak at The Temple of Kfar Nahum. As he entered the courtyard of The Temple, the first thing he noticed was no Kittim guards to be found. There was, however, one Kittim tax collector stationed at the front door.

He thought to himself: "This is an improvement although a small one."

He entered The Temple. His family, friends and members of The Temple entered as well. He looked through The Temple to see all men seated in the front and women and children all seated in the back.

He thought to himself: "This is not a battle I will take on today."

He began to speak, "Sometimes a young man will wander in the wilderness, not unlike the people of Moses. In this place, on the edge of the Promised Land, my friend Massa also entered the Promised Land. Massa, however, never learned about God in a temple. Moses did not deliver The Ten Commandments in a temple. God was not just in a temple. God was the burning bush on a mountain and for my friend he was introduced to God by a sheepherder along the road. So, this temple is literally Massa's Gil Gal … the place he entered the Promised Land. But God is not just in this temple. God is not behind the veil at the Sanctuary. God had already entered Massa's heart along the road."

Hooba then said, "Open the back doors to The Temple. There are people outside the doors that need to hear."

He turned and carefully removed the veil from the Sanctuary.

"You all follow *The Law*. Love of God is that fire burning in your soul just as it was in the **burning bush**," he went on.

"Just as the stranger helped me on the road, I found God to be in all of us. It is our responsibility to keep *The Law* and to try to bring Heaven to Earth here in this Promised Land. But, the kingdom of God is truly not of this world. You reap what you sow and when you sow the love of God, you will reap the kingdom of God ever more. Tomorrow I will teach, tomorrow I will preach … on the shore," Hooba finished.

Sunday morning they walked to the dock. Each had one simple bag but Josephus carried a second bag; it was a leather pouch branded with the letter J.

While they boarded the small boat, Bachariko felt a cool mist off the sea. She looked to the east and saw a magnificent sunrise.

She thought, "This really will be a beautiful day."

She raised the hood of her cloak and thought, "The sun will certainly burn my fair skin."

The boat left for Kfar Nahum.

Chapter 30

The Beach

Hooba had a meal with his family and friends and after their meal, he walked alone to the beach. He took off his sandals to feel the water cool his feet. He allowed the warmth of the sun to bathe his face.

He thought, "I am grateful for such a beautiful day."

He could hear people behind him as they began to gather. He heard bits of conversations and realized they did not know it was he that was about to speak.

One man was overheard to say, "I hear he is an impressive orator."

Another man said, "He has a commanding voice."

"I heard he towers over all other people," another man said.

A mother spoke, "He is very good with the children."

"I heard that he and his witches can heal the sick," a woman interjected.

Then, a man said, "I heard the Kittim soldiers are trembling."

"I heard he is a man of God," was said by yet a different man.

Hooba again thought to himself: "I just spoke yesterday in their temple, and this was their impressions?"

He heard the voice of a small boy say, "He held my hand, looked into my eyes and said God loves me. He was very kind."

Hooba thought to himself once more: "If only everyone was as innocent as the children."

He began to walk among the crowd which had grown to nearly fifteen hundred. He injected himself into a few conversations.

"Do you think he'll talk about the wrath of God?" Hooba added to one group.

Hooba couldn't help but insert into one discussion: "I heard he can move mountains with just his words."

As he approached the front of the crowd, he found it nearly impossible to get through. The people were pushing and tightly packed into the spaces.

He began telling people: "I think he's down on the beach."

This caused some of the people to move and turn, allowing him to reach the front of the crowd.

A tall man jumped up on an outcropping of stone. Hooba walked up to him.

"Can you see him out there?" Hooba asked.

The man replied, "No, I am looking for my wife."

Hooba reached up with one hand and asked the man, "Can you help me up there?"

The tall man reached down and pulled Hooba up onto the stone.

He looked up to the man and asked, "How do you think I should get their attention?"

He responded to Hooba: "Are you the rabbi?"

Hooba replied, "No, I am the servant."

The man then caught Hooba's peaceful smile.

Hooba began to quietly speak to the twenty or thirty people standing just in front of him, who could easily hear him. Soon, it was fifty who stood silent; then two hundred. His voice was peaceful, calming. Then, the entire crowd was watching and trying to hear him.

At the very moment the entire crowd became silent, Hooba spoke in a voice that everyone could hear.

"The days in this life are measured but not the days in the kingdom of God. For this is the day the Lord has made. The sun is shining, it is beautiful and warm with a cool breeze from the sea. Today, we should be thankful and glad."

Hooba then asked, "Where is this man's wife?" as he gestured to the tall man standing next to him.

People began to whisper to one another as Hooba simply watched and waited. The woman slowly worked her way from the back of the crowd through to where they were.

Hooba asked the question, "Why do two people who love each other have to be separated?"

"Just as this man and woman should not be separated, God should not be separated from man," he said.

"As I have brought these two closer together, my words are meant to bring you closer to God. Just as this crowd has separated this man and this woman, it is us who separate ourselves from God. It is our actions and our intentions that bring us closer to God. So, what can we do?

"We can follow *The Law*. We can love God with our whole hearts, minds and souls."

Hooba continued to speak to the crowd for the next thirty to forty minutes. He did not notice the small group who had worked their way down the beach from the dock who now stood and listened.

"I have heard people talk about God's wrath. I would say, what about God's steadfastness? Is it that God has ever failed us? Or is it us who have failed God? Did God create Sodom and Gomorrah? Did God create Babel? I think not. I believe those are creations of man. No, God created The Garden of Eden and man turned away from it and *The Law*. God will create a new Eden and invite us back. I see no wrath in that, only forgiveness. I see a loving God.

"A man has two sons," Hooba spoke. "One son stays home and works his father's farm day and night and provides for his father an incredible harvest. The other son takes his father's money and travels the world and wastes it. When the second son returns, the father rejoices and has a great feast in his honor. This man loves both of his sons. Yet, this man has even greater joy when the lost son is returned. Some will say the first son was disrespected. I will say it is the father's right to judge his son just as it is God's right to judge his children.

"Today, I walked through the crowd," he began.

"I heard innocent children. I tell you; you must be like the innocent children of God. Present yourself back to God as the humble servant. One way to act the humble servant is to follow *The Law*. Yet, there must be a second part to being a humble servant. You cannot separate the action from the feeling. They do not exist alone. The steadfastness and forgiveness of God is representative of God's love. So, I share with you that you must love God with your whole heart, mind and soul and you must love your neighbor as yourself. For, God is love and love is patient and kind. Love revels in the truth."

A man in the back yelled, "I am a fisherman. What do I do to gain eternal life?"

Hooba looked to the back of the crowd. Then, he paused. **He caught a glimpse of a woman with cinnamon-colored hair and his heart smiled.** He stood silent.

Then, he looked at the fisherman and answered, "Fish, follow the law, love your family, love God, love your fellow man."

Hooba raised his staff as if to metaphorically divide the crowd. He climbed down from the rock and walked his way through the middle of the crowd as they separated.

He motioned the entire crowd to be seated, continuing to speak. Then, he finally reached the group of his friends, family and new visitors who had remained standing.

Hooba nodded to Josephus, then smiled at Yohanan. He turned to Bachariko who was holding the hands of the two young girls, Miriam and Delilah. Suddenly, a gust of wind blew, causing the hood of Bachariko's cloak to fall back from her head. Her cinnamon-colored hair flew up and landed way below her shoulders.

A man in the crowd yelled, "She has no husband. Look at her hair. She must be bewitched."

Hooba turned, pointed his finger at the man and firmly asked, "Sir, are you without sin? This humble woman has just come here to listen. Yet, I have told you of God's love. Is it this woman or you who have just sinned? If you are without sin cast the first stone. Is it an eye for an eye? What has she done to you? If you cast the stone will the crowd cast a stone on you?"

He yelled, "Susanna, walk to the front so that your husband will follow you!

"For that man up there has his wife with him and you should have your husband with you!" Hooba shouted.

"Doesn't it say in the Torah a man will leave his parents and a woman will leave her parents and the two will cling together as one flesh?" Hooba asked the crowd.

"It also says in The Ten Commandments, to honor thy mother and they father," he went on.

"In fact, I honor all women. For without a mother there are no fathers," he stated.

Hooba then escorted all the women in his family and friend's group to the front with himself. He turned around and walked back into the crowd. He took young Ruth's hand and Miriam's hand, whose hand was holding Bachariko's and thus Delilah's in her other hand and led them to the front of the crowd.

He walked, saying, "You cannot enter the kingdom of God if you are not humble and innocent like these children."

Hooba climbed back up onto the rock from where he had been speaking. He addressed the crowd.

"You revered King Solomon for his temple. What respect did Solomon have for the women and children? He took seven hundred wives and three hundred concubines. Yet, he dared talk of love," Hooba expressed.

"Give your love of justice to the king, Oh God. Help him judge your people in the right way. Let the poor always be treated fairly. May the mountains yield prosperity for all and may the hills be fruitful. Help him to defend the poor, to rescue the children of the needy. May the king's rule be refreshing like spring rain on fresh-cut grass, like the showers that water the Earth. May all the godly flourish during his reign. May there be abundant prosperity until the moon is no more. May God reign from sea to sea. Desert nomads will bow before him. His enemies will fall before him in the dust and all nations will serve him."

"These are the words of Solomon," Hooba touted. "But what are his deeds?"

"Solomon built his temple on solid ground. Then, he built temples to other gods for his wives. Should not have Solomon built his own temple on his integrity?" He asked the crowd.

Hooba stated, "Yet, we say Solomon built God's house.

"I say to the man who accuses this woman. Tear out the corner of Solomon's temple and cast it at this woman if you can. I believe God would rather see that temple built with hypocrisy fall, than see one strand of this woman's crimson-colored hair fall to the ground," Hooba affirmed.

Hooba took a long, deep breath.

"My brothers and sisters, forgive me my anger and I will forgive your transgressions against the innocent. It is not for me to judge, but for God. If you are transgressed, turn the other cheek. Do not raise your voice or hand in anger. Enjoy the fruits of your labor but remember the reward is in the kingdom of Heaven. Again, love is kind, it does not put on airs, it does not anger, it rejoices in the truth," he declared.

Hooba recited, "The Lord is my shepherd; I shall not want.

He maketh me to lie down in green pastures: he leadeth me beside the still waters.

He restoreth my soul: he leadeth me in the paths of righteousness for his name's sake.

Yea, no matter which valley I walk, I will fear no evil: for thou art with me; thy rod and thy staff they comfort me.

Thou preparest a table before me in the presence of mine enemies: thou anointest my head with oil; my cup runneth over.

Surely goodness and mercy shall follow me all the days of my life: and I will dwell in the house of the Lord forever."

"Peace be with you," he ended.

He climbed down from the rock. He went straight to Bachariko and took her hand.

He looked straight into her eyes and said, "To stand in your presence brings me great joy. Forgive me my passion. You are my fondest memory," he apologized.

Bachariko staring back into Hooba's eyes recalled, "My memories are also fond. I still carry your rose."

The crowds were gathering around and clamoring.

Then Bachariko, still holding his hand, smiled at Hooba and advised, "Go. There will be time later. The people need you."

His hand lingered in hers. He turned and walked through the crowd, greeting the people. The next time she saw Hooba he was up and standing on the rock once more. This time, he was holding a small child who had wandered away from their parents.

Bachariko found the mother of the lost child and brought her over to Hooba.

Looking up, she informed him, "Rabbi, I have found the mother."

Hooba passed the little child down to his mother. He reached down and took Bachariko's hand pulling her up onto the rock with him.

He told Bachariko: "Do not look up to me or call me Rabbi. As children we were equal; I would expect nothing else as man and woman."

She replied, "But, I honor the man you have become."

"But I honor the woman you have become," he replied back.

Bachariko teased, "Do you know you are still holding my hand?"

Hooba responded with a question, "Yes, do you consider it inappropriate or too forward?"

Bachariko laughed back, "No, I do not consider it too forward but are there others who will think it to be customarily inappropriate?"

He yelled down from his rock to Josephus: "I only wish to honor your granddaughter. May I hold her hand?"

Much to his surprise, he heard Josephus answer back: "Hooba, I'm surprised you haven't embraced her yet!"

Hooba, in one fell swoop, picked up Bachariko, swirled her all the way around and carefully placed her feet back on the ground. It was then that he noticed the faces of Yohanan, Noam, Ruth, Susanna, Hilleal and Iakobas standing with smiles.

Bachariko then whispered, "Hooba, you must meet my daughter, Delilah."

He whispered back, "Was that appropriate in front of your daughter?"

Hooba again jumped from the rock.

He said to Delilah: "My name is Hooba and your mother is my very good friend. Can I be your friend too?"

Delilah asked, "Do you swing all your very good friends like that?"

"Well, I do tend to get a little excited when I haven't seen you for years," he joked.

"Well, you've never seen me," she admitted, as she held both hands outstretched.

And with that, Hooba picked Delilah up off her feet, spinning her completely around a couple of times.

Delilah catching her breath said, "My mother said you were fun as a child. I was a little concerned because you seem quite serious when you are speaking."

Hooba divulged, "I share from my heart so sometimes my passion shows, thus, when I am joyous, you will see joy and if I am frustrated, you may see frustration."

"My mother said you were cute, and I still think you are," Delilah confessed.

"Do you think your mother still thinks I'm cute?" Hooba half whispered to Delilah.

Bachariko was standing directly behind Hooba. She silenced her daughter with one finger to her lips.

She thought to herself: "How do I answer this question? I hardly know him, yet he moves me. Is it his presence or is it the man?"

Then, Bachariko, with a glint in her eyes, leaned forward and whispered into his ear: "Yes ... she does, Hooba."

Not realizing she was standing behind him Hooba began to blush.

Their family and friends had heard the banter. Everyone was talking and laughing. They were talking among themselves trying to relay their story of the past twenty years, filling each other in on the particulars.

Noam reminded Hooba: "The sun will be setting soon and no one has eaten."

He answered his mother's concern: "Why don't you all go and begin to prepare the meal; I will follow shortly. I would like to see the beauty of the sunset."

Bachariko informed her grandfather: "I could stay with Hooba if he would escort me and show me the way, if you think it is appropriate."

Josephus answered, "I think this is a fine young man; a man of God."

The others hurried off in preparation of their meal. The crowd had dissipated, leaving Hooba and Bachariko standing alone on the beach.

Hooba stumbled to find his words. "I, I, I, don't know what I am supposed to do. The sunset is beautiful. You are beautiful. I, um, I ..."

Bachariko took his hand. "I think you are doing fine. It starts just like this. I heard you talk and I think that now we should just be thankful for the moment."

They both stood thankful; they both prayed to themselves, thanking God, holding hands and smiling.

Chapter 31

Tracing Footsteps

The men and women were tired. Hooba knew their caravan of travelers was in much need of rest. Yet, he was on a mission. He was aware that his destination of Gil Gal was in reach.

He thought, "If this area is the land of milk and honey and Gil Gal is the entrance to this land, then I must travel to where my people entered. I was trained to preserve *The Law* and this is the land of *The Law*. Then, Gil Gal could be called the gate to the covenant of God.

"If Abraham and Moses are the deliverers of *The Law* and this is where *The Law* first entered, and if I am to teach this law, then I must travel to Gil Gal and experience the Jordan River where the chosen people first crossed."

Hooba, remembering that he would again be speaking the next Sunday on the beach of Kfar Nahum, spoke to Yohanan.

"Yohanan, how far is it to Gil Gal?" Hooba asked.

"The people are tired, Hooba," he replied. "A large group of travelers could not be back in time for next Sunday."

Yohanan continued to answer Hooba saying, "However, the road between here and there is smooth and well-developed. A small group going by cart or wagon could travel to and back within four days time."

Hooba then asked, "Would there be time for me to speak along the way?"

Yohanan replied, "Likely, one or two hours each day."

Yohanan sighed. He could hear the determination in Hooba's voice. Then, he spoke, "I can be prepared to leave within the hour."

But Yohanan was also thinking, "I will need men with swords."

"I need Susanna to go, to appropriately bring Bachariko along," Hooba thought to himself.

Then, immediately considered: "I hope both women will accept my invitation."

Yohanan, already considering the manner of Hooba's thoughts, replied, "If your mother can watch young Ruth, then she will have a purpose and, thus, I will invite Hilleal and Susanna to come along. I will also invite the younger Iakobas to join us. He requires less rest."

Hooba immediately went to find Bachariko. He found her at breakfast with Beatrice and Delilah. Hooba explained the shortness of his next trip and that Susanna and Hilleal would be traveling along.

Delilah immediately asked if she could stay with Ruth.

Beatrice responded, "I believe I would be the appropriate chaperone to accompany Bachariko and my brother lives in Gil Gal. I have not seen him for many years."

Bachariko appeared to be excited with the invitation.

While she looked straight into Hooba's eyes she spoke up: "I really haven't unpacked, so, I would be glad to go. We have just been reunited after many years. I would not look forward to being separated for four more days."

The cart, pulled by two donkeys, took off for Gil Gal. Yohanan and Iakobas rode in the front. Hilleal, Hooba, Susanna, Beatrice and Bachariko rode in the back.

Hooba and Hilleal had assisted the women into the cart. Hilleal had appropriately seated himself next to Susanna. However, Beatrice had placed herself next to Bachariko. Susanna and Hilleal, after noticing, slid themselves over, leaving a space for Hooba to sit next to Bachariko.

Yohanan yelled back, "It will be nearly six hours until we reach a community where you can teach, Hooba. We will camp there tonight."

Susanna and Bachariko carried on a lengthy discussion about child rearing. Susanna conveniently mentioned her own childhood experiences with her cousin, Hooba. Then, Bachariko also told her experiences with Hooba in Egypt when they were children.

Susanna frequently mentioned Hooba and Hilleal's brother Jared, and how easy it was to tease them both and cause their faces to blush.

Bachariko agreed. "I, too, remember how easy it was to make Hooba blush."

Then Susanna said, "Just watch this … and she kissed Hooba on the cheek."

They all laughed and Hooba blushed. Hilleal and Beatrice, all the while, conversed in a serious manner about *The Law*.

Every now and again, Hooba interjected his words into Hilleal and Beatrice's conversation. But for the most part, he laughed and enjoyed Susanna and Bachariko's banter.

Meanwhile, in the front of the cart, Iakobas leaned over to Yohanan and said, "I know this is my cousin, but these other women … they do talk endlessly."

Yohanan replied and had a lesson for Iakobas: "I love the sound of their laughter. I miss my wife. Iakobas, do you notice the laughter in Hooba's voice? I once laughed like that when I was young."

Iakobas then asked Yohanan's opinion: "What do you think of Bachariko?"

Yohanan replied, "In one way, she is more independent, confident and wiser than Hooba. Yet on the other hand, Hooba is more confident and wiser than any man I have known. I would put Hooba up against any man. However, he does have an innocence in all worldly things. I think what I appreciate in her, within just a few short days, is that I have discovered this is a woman of character who would not exploit Hooba's innocence. In fact, what could be any better, but I think she would celebrate his innocence."

"I don't quite think on your level, Yohanan, but I have seen Susanna with Hilleal and I see a little bit of the same thing," Iakobas admitted.

He said, "I have seen Susanna with Jared. She would do anything to protect him. He would do anything she asked; but she would not ask."

Yohanan looked at Iakobas and laughed, "I may have underestimated you. There is some hope for you. There just might be the right woman who could mold you into something too!"

From the back of the wagon, Susanna yelled, "Yohanan, don't give my brother too much credit!"

Bachariko jumped in, "It does appear that the men inside the walls have a fair bit of innocence to deal with."

Iakobas blushed.

Hooba, pointing to himself, asked, "Me?"

Bachariko answered while snickering, "Yes, you! You far better understand *The Law* and the house of God than do I. But it is yet to be seen how you will do with the House of Bachariko. According to the tribe of Benjamin, the house is mine."

Hooba chuckled, "Well, in that tribe of Benjamin, who do the children belong to?"

Bachariko replied quickly without giving a thought, "They would be ours."

Then she blushed and Hooba grinned from ear to ear. Everyone else held back from grinning. All those seated in the back of the cart had eyes straightforward not muttering a word.

However, Yohanan and Iakobas widely smiled at each other.

Hilleal stood up in the back of the cart and leaned forward to talk to Yohanan and Iakobas.

"There's a cloud of dust behind us," he informed them.

"As large as the cloud appears, I fear it is many men on horseback."

Yohanan advised loudly so that all could hear, "If we are stopped, no one show your sword! Beatrice, we are on the way to see your brother."

He pulled the cart to the side of the road. Sixty Kittim soldiers passed by on horseback.

Once the soldiers were far away, Hilleal mentioned, "We have not seen many Kittim soldiers for months now."

Soon, they came upon the small community of Tynhar. Although they were prepared to camp and for Hooba to speak to the people, twenty Kittim soldiers were camped on the edge of the town. Yohanan led them to the opposite side of the community to camp for the night. Hooba walked alone into the center of town to speak. Once they were unpacked, Yohanan sent Iakobas to look for Hooba. He was found in the middle of the community speaking with twenty members of the community while being observed by eight Kittim soldiers who stood listening.

Several of the Kittim soldiers were eating chicken and arrogantly throwing the bones into the street.

Hooba spoke to the crowd: "Let me help you clean up these bones so they do not draw anymore rats to your community."

He turned and addressed the guards directly. "I believe you represent the emperor who is the government of this province. Would he not consider it disrespectful to treat his province this way?"

A guard spoke up, "Little man, we are in charge here."

"I do not judge man by the size of his stature but by his heart," Hooba responded. "I respect your occupation. You are to guard these Kittim citizens."

Then, Hooba continued to address the crowd.

The soldiers started to walk in and among the crowd. The people began dispersing.

A man walked over to Hooba and said, "Rabbi, thank you for speaking here. It has been so long a time since a man of God was present."

A guard addressed Hooba, "Rabbi, why are you so far from a temple?"

"The kingdom of God is so much greater than just a temple," Hooba informed him.

"If the kingdom is so great, where are its guards?" the soldier taunted.

Hooba smiled, turned and said, "Iakobas, let's return to camp."

On their return to camp, Iakobas informed the group of the happenings with the crowd.

Yohanan with concern, advised Hooba, "I believe you should not go off on your own."

Hooba replied, "What would you do, fight to your death, three against twenty while I speak to a crowd of twenty?"

"Hooba, just beware. Kittim soldiers with no leaders have no conscience," Yohanan reminded him.

Bachariko walked over, took Hooba's hand in hers and asked, "Will you please be careful for me?"

Hooba replied to her, "I will. My war is not with them."

Hilleal whispered to all of them, "There are four Kittim guards outside our camp, watching us."

"Let no one wander off tonight and we will leave first thing in the morning," Hooba instructed them.

They all sat around the fire talking and soon Hooba fell asleep with his head resting in Bachariko's lap.

Beatrice mentioned to Bachariko, "He looks quite comfortable with you, my friend."

To which Bachariko responded, "And I am comfortable with him."

Beatrice shook Bachariko awake as the sun rose the next morning.

She told her, "You have fallen asleep next to the man. I must remind you of your honor."

Hooba responded back to Beatrice: "I would not dishonor her. However, I have been awake for over an hour and did not want to disturb our closeness."

"There are laws related to this, Hooba," Bachariko reminded him.

"If Josephus was here, I would deliver a betrothal gift today," Hooba announced.

Bachariko voiced her thoughts, "You must remember that I have a child for which I am responsible."

"Are you ready to receive a betrothal gift for my daughter's hand also? She is at the age of maturity and will need a father's approval to be betrothed," Bachariko asked with conviction.

Hooba thought for a moment. Then, he looked at Yohanan and Hilleal.

He asked them, "What is it that you look for in a man for your daughters?"

Yohanan was keen to answer, "He must be kind and respectful. He must make her smile. He must be thoughtful and believe that same way, if he had a daughter. I would want him to be just like you, Hooba."

Susanna interjected, "Before I went too much further into the conversation, Hooba, I would ask the woman if SHE wanted to be betrothed."

Hooba turned to Bachariko. She lifted her finger to her lips in a motion to silence his words.

"We should discuss this on our return to Kfar Nahum," she suggested.

Bachariko spoke again to Hooba saying, "I was married to a good man and he treated me with respect. This daughter is his with his first wife who died. He trusted that I would do what was in her best interest.

So, I will have two criteria for my betrothed. He must accept this daughter as his own and secondly, this marriage must be more than a good man and respect. And Hooba, there is more criteria that I require. I must get to know your mother and she must approve of me."

Iakobas jumped in at that point stating, "I now understand why it may be better to stay within the walls of our community rather than abide by all the rules of betrothal."

The group laughed for a moment, lightening the subject.

Bachariko leaned over and kissed Hooba on the cheek. He blushed yet another time.

Soon, they were in the cart and on their way to Gil Gal. For the next six hours they talked and laughed while Hilleal observed two Kittim soldiers following them the entire way.

Yohanan announced, "We are approaching Gil Gal."

"Please let us camp at the River Jordan," Hooba replied.

And with that suggestion, Yohanan steered the cart toward the River Jordan.

Hilleal then reported, "Our friends are still following us and have been for over six hours."

There was a camp with many tents as they approached the river. They were occupied by Kittim soldiers.

Yohanan responded, "I believe we just found the other forty soldiers who passed us yesterday."

Hooba asked, "Do you suppose the two soldiers behind us are just going to meet the others?"

"No, now that we have arrived upon the other Kittim soldiers, our two friends have left us," Hilleal shared.

"If they have been watching us, then they know we are here. Let's set up camp close to the river also," Hooba suggested.

They erected two tents by the river. Hooba stood right on the bank.

With excitement, he said to everyone, "Moses stood right over there, as he pointed. In that land, God spoke to Moses. For forty years, our people wandered to this very spot to cross this river. Everyone who crossed this river became ritually clean and entered the Promised Land. The next part of my journey is to cross this river."

He took one step into the water. He turned and looked directly at Bachariko.

Then he spoke to her. "For the last twenty-four years, I have been on a journey that is my own. But now, I would like to take you on the same journey. Bachariko, come join me in the water and we will cross the river together."

Bachariko eased her way down into the water. They slowly walked across the narrowest portion of the river to the other side. Hooba climbed up the bank once they reached the other side, then reached down to help Bachariko up onto the bank.

Hooba did notice as he helped Bachariko from the water that her cloak now clung to her wet body and he smiled. He removed his head scarf and handed it to her to dry her body which she immediately placed around her shoulders to cover her breasts.

He led her up a small hill and then both turned back, to look across the river as Moses would have done. Bachariko looked at Hooba.

He said, "That land was to be Heaven on Earth, a free land where we could live and praise God."

Bachariko added, "And now, right down where we camped, the demons occupy the land."

"But casting out demons is not my purpose. My purpose is to sing the praise of the Lord," he told her.

Suddenly a feeling of warmth passed through them. Bachariko looked to Hooba.

"Did you feel that?" she asked.

With a tear in his eye, he looked back at Bachariko and said, "No, Bachariko, I heard it."

"What was that she asked?"

"That was God," he answered.

Bachariko just nodded.

Then, he took her hand and said, "Let's cross the river one more time and we will again enter the land promised to us together."

Once they reached the other side, Hooba climbed up the bank ahead of Bachariko. He asked her for his head covering. She removed it from her shoulders and tossed it up to Hooba. He dipped it down into the water, then reached down and took her hand. As she stood on the bank, he knelt down and used his head covering to wash the sand from her feet. Then, he washed his own feet. After finishing, he threw his head covering back into the river.

He said, "We are now ritually clean and have brought none of that land to this land."

The others of their group had been watching Hooba and Bachariko.

Hooba addressed his group. "At this place, a thousand men were circumcised. They had traveled for forty years. When they stepped into this holy place, they renewed the covenant of God with Abraham, which was that our people would be the chosen ones. Our people are to preserve *The Law*. I have washed our feet and I have discarded my head covering in respect for their actions. Now, if I can only teach the people to live *The Law*. Then, through God's love, they will gain everlasting life in God's kingdom."

Hooba reached out and took Bachariko's hand.

He said, "There is still time to teach."

Their group of seven walked into Gil Gal. Beatrice went off to find her brother. They found the town center and half a dozen Kittim soldiers standing by.

Hooba began to speak. "I am here to speak of the kingdom of God."

Bachariko reached up and touched him on the chest as if to tell him to pause and think about his next words.

She spoke, "We are the peacekeepers. The kingdom of God is in our hearts. Do not raise a sword against any man. Forgive even those who transgress you. Let them know you are of God by your actions. Love your enemies as yourself. Love is kind, love is patient."

Hooba then spoke. "The first law is to honor the Lord thy God with thy whole heart, mind and soul. The second law is to love thy neighbor as thyself. These two laws entirely sum up *The Law*."

A man in the crowd said, "What about the Kittims?"

Bachariko shot another *look* at Hooba.

"What would a man gain if you owned this entire land and lost your soul?" Hooba replied.

"The kingdom of God is greater than this land. This land is nothing more than a possession and the commandment says to not covet another man's possession. The only thing you truly own is your soul which you should give to God in love."

Hooba continued to relay to the crowd many stories and parables for two more hours.

They walked back to camp after Hooba was finished. Susanna approached Bachariko.

She said, "Women do not usually teach."

Bachariko, eager to respond to Susanna, said, "I know, women usually must teach by example. I could have tried to remain quiet and peaceful, however, men are foolish. If my actions were inappropriate, it was an example at least of the appropriate things to say."

Then Bachariko continued, "What was the worst that could happen? Some man in the crowd would have rebuked me and then Hooba would have defended me instead of attacking the Kittim soldiers."

"What if it had angered Hooba?" Susanna inquired.

Bachariko smartly answered, "Then, he is not the man who asked me to walk across the River Jordan together."

She quietly then leaned over and whispered to Susanna: "And, when we return, I will say *yes*, because this is the man I thought he was."

The next morning, they were all up early and packed for their trip back to Kfar Nahum. Hooba was determined to be back before the start of the Sabbath. On the Sabbath, Hooba was to speak at The Temple. He then planned to teach on the beach on Sunday.

Beatrice had invited her brother to return with them to Kfar Nahum. He had been impressed after hearing Hooba speak and wanted to hear more of his message.

Hooba thought excitedly to himself: "I have other reasons to return before the Sabbath. I must meet with Josephus and Delilah."

Soon, they were back in the cart being pulled by the donkeys toward their destination. Fifteen minutes after they had left the camp, Yohanan yelled back, "Well?"

Hilleal replied, "Four Kittim soldiers are, indeed, following behind us."

The younger Iakobas asked, "Rabbi, do you have any commentary on the Kittim problem?"

Hooba then replied, "The Kittims are not part of my message. However, I will comment.

"Each and every time the people have fallen, an outside force has taken over and controlled our people. Each and every time, the people's faith and the Lord have returned the land to them."

Iakobas then asked, "Did not David lead his people against the enemy?"

"David was a king. I am a teacher. If God called on King David, I do not know. However, God has called on me and I am fulfilling my purpose," Hooba then explained.

Iakobas said, "I am being trained with a sword."

Hooba sighed a long, deep breath, loud enough for all to hear.

"Iakobas," Hooba reminded him. "You were trained with a sword to preserve *The Law*. You have also been trained with the pen to copy and preserve *The Law*. If you would like to write the Kittims a letter, do so."

Iakobas asked, "Then, why am I now carrying a sword?"

"And why am I not?" Hooba replied.

It was Yohanan who spoke next. "Rabbi, we all carry the sword. For we believe you to be the most complete copy of *The Law*."

Hooba responded, "Then we must correspond with our brothers within the walls. They must make more and better copies. These copies must be secured and preserved."

He went on. "I respect the oral tradition but without a written copy, the oral tradition is too easy to corrupt. I am just a man and all men die and with them, their knowledge dies. And, that is why I teach as many people as I can reach."

Bachariko added her opinion. "Hooba, this talk is morbid. I have just reconnected with you and now you have yourself dying."

Hooba explained, "It is not my intention to die and if you will have me, I plan many, many more years with you. However, I noticed you have been paying attention and if for some reason I could not speak, you would be more than capable of sharing the message."

Susanna then spoke up. "But Hooba, what if we have to fight to protect the innocent?"

Hooba said, "Consider King Saul. He was fighting for who he believed were the innocent. Then the Lord said he should destroy all of the bounty of war, yet King Saul had hungry people. He saved some of the spoils of war to feed his people, displeasing the Lord. Now, I cannot judge King Saul. Only God can judge, yet, God is loving and forgiving. God may have justified King Saul's actions. However, King Saul threw himself on his dagger when he displeased the Lord. I do not know if God justified Saul in taking his own life. This is why we pray for the souls in Sheol, going through Atonement. The gates of Heaven may be narrow but they are never closed. Is one mistake enough to slam the gates of Heaven? Our people have made mistake after mistake, built false idols, some of them based on their own ego. Yet, God has given our people chance after chance. With our history, with our God, I can only believe that King Saul would be given the same chance as our people."

Hooba faced Bachariko and said, "This is why it is not good for man to be alone. If King Saul had been close to his wife, she would have told him what a foolish man he was."

"A man should listen to his wife," Hooba added.

Bachariko replied, "And a woman should listen to her husband."

"And a man should love his wife," Hooba said.

Bachariko responded, "And a woman should love her husband."

Beatrice's brother had been quiet up until this point.

He looked at his sister and said, "Are these two always like this?"

Beatrice answered, "Yes, it is how it seems; somewhere in all of this, there is always a lesson. And, somehow the lesson always comes back to these two."

Beatrice's brother turned to her asking, "And, just what is your role in all of this?"

"Believe it or not, I am the chaperone," she answered. "And, I take my role very seriously. Just as I take the role of older sister seriously. Brother, I see that you, too, are unmarried and I know a wonderful young woman named Rebecca that you should meet."

She went further, "Brother, I think you, too, need a woman to let you know when you are foolish."

Everyone at that point was laughing, forgetting the Kittim soldiers behind them. The rest of the trip was uneventful until they could see in the distance, Kfar Nahum.

Suddenly, the Kittim soldiers sped up and rode on each side of the cart. One soldier yelled to Hooba.

"Rabbi, I am glad to see you only have one recruit from this trip," he said, as they raced past the cart, heading for Kfar Nahum.

They all remained silent for the remainder of the trip until reaching camp.

Upon arriving at their camp, Iakobas, Hooba's older brother, Akeldama and Josephus all greeted them. Josephus had concern for his granddaughter's safety. Iakobas was concerned for everyone's safety. And, Akeldama's concern was with the one hundred Kittim soldiers camped on the other side Kfar Nahum.

Akeldama said, "The hundred soldiers arrived shortly after you left, four days ago. A group of them left and headed in the same direction just after your departure."

Hooba spoke, "We encountered them and we were, indeed, watched."

The elder Iakobas stated, "The crowd that listened to you last Sunday has swelled to twice its size hoping to hear you this Sunday. The Kittims will be there, watching and listening."

Noam ran to Hooba, "My son," she said, "I am glad to have you home."

"Mother, I soon need to speak with you," Hooba urged.

The elder Iakobas said, "Rabbi, we will soon have trouble feeding the large crowds who come to hear you."

Hooba yelled to his mother that their conversation would have to wait. Then, he asked Yohanan to follow him to the beach. The fishermen were unloading their boats when the two arrived. Hooba began right at that moment to teach.

Some of the fishermen had heard him speak the Sunday before. One fisherman asked a question.

"Rabbi, you are speaking next Sunday. Why are you here, especially for the fishermen today?"

Hooba answered, "I have a mission to teach. You have a mission to fish. I am trying to feed the soul. I need help to feed the man. I beg you, cast your boats back into the water. Redeploy your nets. We must feed these people who wait to hear me speak in two days. It is the humble who feed the hungry that will enter the kingdom of God."

Three of the fishermen spoke, "Rabbi, we will put our nets out, two, three, four times a day if that is what we must do to feed the people."

Some of the other fishermen grumbled, "Who will reimburse us for our time?"

Hooba replied, "Your reward is not of this world."

The grumbling fisherman then exclaimed, "It is not our fault these people come to listen to you!"

A woman's soft hand took Hooba's hand. He turned to see Bachariko standing next to him. She spoke.

"I will pay you double your daily wages," she offered the fishermen.

A young boy approached them.

He said, "I work on one of their boats as he pointed to the grumbling fishermen. I will work for free."

Hooba smiled at the young boy. "What is your name?" he asked.

"My name is Philippos," he replied.

Again, Hooba smiled. "When I was a young boy, a wise, strong man named Jared, took a special interest in me. Philippos, would you like to learn more about *The Law* and the love of God?"

Philippos replied, "Rabbi, please feed my soul."

Hooba looked at Bachariko.

She said, "Yes, there is room for one more at the table."

"Philippos, follow me, it is time for your first lesson," Hooba directed.

The young man followed them back to the camp. During their walk, Hooba taught Philippos Psalms 23:2 through 23:6. By the time they arrived, Philippos had memorized the verses completely.

Bachariko leaned over to Hooba and observed, "He is a bright young man. He very much reminds me of you."

Hooba replied to her, "Bachariko, do you think your grandfather would recommend him to the community within the walls? He will need a recommendation."

She answered with a question. "Have you considered they might take your recommendation?"

Hooba wore a confused look. "They need a man or priest of high standing for a recommendation."

Bachariko smiled, and thought to herself: "Simple, beautiful, humble man ... you have no idea how you move them."

―――

That night, as they sat around the dinner table, Hooba asked young Philippos to share what he had learned. Philippos began reciting the Psalms verses he had memorized. And as he reached 23:6, Hooba,

Iakobas the elder, Iakobas the younger, Hilleal, Yohanan, Susanna, Ruth, Rebecca, Noam, Josephus and Bachariko all joined in.

Akeldama was also seated at the table. He leaned over to the younger Iakobas and whispered, "What is this?"

Iakobas answered, "It is a prayer; a rite of passage."

Akeldama said, "How is it that I do not know these words?"

The younger Iakobas replied, "You have been invited to this table and Hooba has repeated those words hundreds of times."

Then, in his mind, he asked, "Have you not been listening?"

Before Iakobas could speak any words, Hooba broke the bread and first served every woman at the table. Then, every man was served. The last man to be served was Akeldama.

Hooba leaned over Akeldama while serving him and whispered, "This young man was ready today; when you are ready to lay down your sword come to me and I will personally teach you the verses."

During dinner, Hooba told his mother he required a private conversation with her after the meal. Nearly in that same moment, Bachariko asked her grandfather for a private conversation with he and Delilah. Meanwhile, Susanna, Hilleal, the younger Iakobas, Yohanan and Beatrice listening to the requests for private conversations, exchanged glances and smiled at one another.

Immediately after the meal, Hooba walked off with Noam. Noam immediately began rattling off all of the events that took place while he was away. Hooba's palms were becoming sweaty yet he tried patiently to listen to his mother. Noam looked at Hooba, grinning from ear to ear. She was well aware of what Hooba's intentions were. She purposely went on and on to tease him.

She looked at him and asked, "Well, do you have something you need to discuss?"

Hooba stammered, "Mother, do you believe it is good for a man to be alone?"

"You have been traveling with a group of forty people for months. When do you spend any time alone?" Noam quizzed her son.

"No, Mother ... like a partner," Hooba clarified.

Noam then asked, "You mean like Yohanan?" She continued to tease.

"Mother, do you ever get lonely since father died?" Hooba asked.

His mother looked at him and smiled. "No, Yohanan is too young for me," she giggled.

It finally occurred to Hooba that his mother had been purposely goading him which meant she knew what he was attempting to discuss.

Noam then said, "Yes, Hooba, I miss your father. I was lucky to find a good man who would love me. You know, I was with child when your father married me and he had children already. You know your father loved you as his own? He made, what was a very difficult situation, beautiful and loving."

She continued, "You know Hooba, there are things between a man and a woman. You must make yourself vulnerable and my situation was already vulnerable. Hooba, Bachariko may feel very vulnerable, so you must ask yourself if her situation in any way affects how you feel. I am thankful that it never affected your father nor did his previous wife affect me."

Noam took both of Hooba's hands in hers and looking straight into his eyes, she said, "Tell me your thoughts as you think of Bachariko."

"I cannot bear to be apart from her," he admitted.

"When her hand touches mine, I want to sing," he continued.

Then he innocently asked, "Mother, have you seen her eyes dance?"

"My son, I have seen both of your eyes dance," his mother replied.

Hooba said, "She is not like other women."

Noam then shared, "Your father told me that once and you need to tell her that. Because, if you tell her that and she believes it, she will know that you are not just like any other man. You know she is older, smarter and stronger than I was when I married your father?

"These should be qualities you admire. She knows things that I did not know when I married. And, in some ways, you have been sheltered and she knows things that you do not know. On the other hand, you have had many great adventures and have spent time developing yourself. Do not expect her to change you or you to change her. She does have a strong will, Hooba."

"Do you see a problem that I do not, Mother?" Hooba asked.

Noam answered, "No, I do not. I think Bachariko may be exactly what you need. Do you see a problem, Hooba?"

He replied, "No, I do not."

"Then Hooba, I believe your father and I would both approve," his mother confessed.

Meanwhile, Bachariko had captured Josephus and Delilah for a personal discussion.

She began, "Grandfather, I know you knew Hooba as a child and you have been introduced to him as a man. Is it fair to ask you to judge him after such a short time of knowing him as an adult? I do not find him impulsive but decisive and we have become close. I am assuming, based on his decisiveness, he will soon ask you for my betrothal."

"My dear, my first question is to ask where your heart lies?" Josephus asked.

She responded, "If you ask where my heart lies, I will answer that it lies in the clouds; my heart is flying … as it is so high. Sometimes, I feel as if I am floating when I am with Hooba.

"This is why I ask you, Grandfather. I have never felt this way. Am I moving too fast because I have a daughter to consider?" Bachariko admitted.

Josephus replied, "With your grandmother, I knew in a moment, yet we knew each other a long time before our betrothal. We had much to consider, both being of different faiths and different cultures. She was stronger than most of the women I had known. Her skin was fair like yours and I was trained by Zadokite priests so the pressure was there to not marry her because of our differences. In some way, I have shame for thinking I might not marry her. So, when I see you with Hooba, he does not appear to see any differences in the two of you and he does not see that you were married before or that having a child is an obstacle. He is a man of God and he sees you for the beautiful, strong woman that you are."

Bachariko responded, "Yes, he respects me for who I am and I respect him for who he is."

"Then, it appears to me that your heart and mind are in the same place," he answered.

Bachariko then turned to her daughter and spoke, "Delilah, it has always been just you and me for so long."

Delilah replied, "Mother, you have always spoken of my father with reverence and respect and I have known him only through you. Yet even in your voice, there is something different when you speak of Hooba. You know, Hooba treats me as if I am highly valued; because you are of value, I am valued. It is as if he believes you are a gift and I somehow make the gift even more precious. I can only hope that someday, I and my children will feel that way about their father."

Josephus interrupted, "I only wish I had married your grandmother sooner."

Bachariko stated, "Thank you. If he asks you, please say yes, Grandfather."

Chapter 32
The Sabbath

As the sun was setting, Hooba thanked God for the people in his life ... Jared, Hilleal, Susanna, Yohanan, both the Iakobases, his mother, his father, Josephus, Delilah and Bachariko. Then, he thought again of Bachariko; her laughter, her cinnamon-colored hair, her beautiful eyes and her alabaster skin.

"Alabaster ..." he thought. "I have an appropriate betrothal gift for Josephus," Hooba remembered. "I still have the alabaster jar given to me by Bhuti."

Then he thanked God again. "Thank you for Massa, Aahan and his grandmother, Khedenn, Tyrus, Cyrus and all of my other wise teachers. I have been truly blessed."

Hooba's prayers continued. "God, my entire life has led me to now."

Hooba looked over at the alabaster jar and noticed its soft, smooth exterior. Then, he was reminded of Bachariko. She, too, was soft and smooth.

Then, he thought of the wisdom of Bhuti. "The value lies in what the vessel carries," he remembered.

Hooba fell into slumber with a smile on his face.

The morning came and Hooba arose. He performed his usual rituals while thinking about his teaching in The Temple that morning. He believed he had been speaking too much about Moses. His intention today was to speak about Genesis and Leviticus.

"Genesis is about man and woman leaving their parents and clinging to each other," he thought.

"Leviticus is all about ritual cleansing," he also remembered.

The time approached for Hooba to head off to The Temple.

The families began to arrive and Hooba met and greeted each of them.

He said to each family upon arrival, "Today, all families will sit together … a man with his wife."

He began, "What is the covenant with God? We will be his people and God will be our God. In the beginning, God provided the animals and the garden. But God provided more. God knew life would be difficult, so God created man and woman in his own image that man and woman would leave their family and cling to each other. Thus, we would have suitable partners when life became difficult. Man and woman could share love just as mankind should love God. They would be partners, each subservient to the other, giving love freely.

"Now, we need to talk about two words," Hooba continued.

"Avera and Khata. Both are words of various translations in the book of Leviticus. Avera means sin or transgression. Khata is to fail or fall short of a goal. These two words are used interchangeably in Leviticus. Think of these two words. Sin or transgression sounds like an evil act. Yet, to fall short of a goal does not sound evil. Think about Leviticus as being about Atonement. We talk so much about an eye for an eye, yet, think about these two separate words. A sin or transgression almost needs to be punished. However, in Khata or falling short of a goal, one needs encouragement. Yet, in Leviticus, both words are interchangeable.

"Now, let us go back to the man and woman in Genesis," he continued.

"God's love for us is perfect. We cannot be perfect, because we are not God. Thus, is it possible that we will fall short? Are we punished or encouraged? Why do a man and a woman cling together? To encourage each other when they fall. We no longer sacrifice at the altar. Why?

"It was an action. Atonement is about having an action that brings us closer to God. It is about encouragement to do better. A dove or a goat is not responsible for our actions. Sacrificing them will not take away our responsibility for our actions.

"So, why do we choose to eat clean?

"Why do I ritually bathe? Because, I must take care of myself physically if I am to give love back to God.

"Why must I keep the Sabbath? Because I rest and pray. Because I must take care of myself spiritually if I am to give love back to God. So apparently, I am responsible to care and love myself, if I am going to give love to God. So, if God loves us and encourages us, then the example is that if a man loves his wife, he will take care of himself, love himself and encourage his wife.

"Maybe in the book of Genesis God is saying, *to be human is difficult, but I have given you a partner to love and encourage.*

"So, did God punish Adam and Eve? Some would say yes. They were placed outside the garden. Or, did God give them another chance outside the garden with each other to love and encourage? Some would say this is punishment. However, I would say it is forgiveness and compassion.

"Then, what is the real message of the book of Leviticus? First, to acknowledge that we fall short of the goal. The second consideration is to acknowledge that we are responsible for our actions. The last acknowledgment is that God loves us and encourages us to be better.

"What is the covenant with God? We will be his people and God will be our God."

The end of the Sabbath grew near, as the sun was beginning to set. The smell of smoke permeated the air as well as the smell of food. The fishermen had been very successful in their catch. Their camp had tripled the size of the population of Kfar Nahum with people waiting to hear Hooba speak the next day on the beach. The fishermen would be feeding all the waiting people.

Hooba's thoughts became, "If we can feed this many people, hopefully, I can feed their souls."

Then, his thoughts drifted back to the alabaster jar he carried within his cloak, "Now is the time; I must find Josephus."

Hooba entered the tent of Josephus and spoke, "Rabbi, I come with the deepest respect. I have both a request and a need. There is so much more I need to learn."

Josephus smiled as he had been waiting for this moment.

"Son," he said, "I have been preparing. Ask what you will."

"I own nothing but my staff and this alabaster jar," Hooba offered.

He continued, "I have learned many things. One is that this alabaster jar is nothing but a beautiful vessel. The value is what can be carried inside. When I look at this, it reminds me of Bachariko's beauty outside and the beauty that is inside. I offer this as a gift, not a dowry as is the custom of our people. I ask for her betrothal and I ask you for your wisdom. You had many years with the same woman. Are there secrets that I do not know?"

Josephus replied, "Hooba, I accept your beautiful gift for I know that it represents a humble purity from your heart. I know you seek respect for the custom and appreciate the respect you are giving me. You know that Bachariko, Delilah, your mother and I have already spoken. We all seek nothing but happiness for you two.

"Now, you asked me a second question and there are so many answers to that question. My first piece of wisdom, and I mean this with all respect ... be flexible. Women are difficult to predict. What seems so easy for you to understand can have many interpretations for a woman. How can something so beautiful and loving respond in such confusing ways? In fact, the response can change based on the time of year, the time of month, the day of the week or the moment of the day," Josephus explained.

Hooba looked at Josephus with confusion. Josephus simply smiled back. Then he went further.

"Hooba, I will try to explain in words you will understand. I have heard you speak that no man can take an oath to anything but God and in this God has shared a specific wisdom. God is the Alpha and the Omega ... all powerful, never changing, consistent and loving. I know this may sound different but because of God's consistency, it is easier to make this oath. Now, I will try to explain women. With all due respect, they are the Omega, they are always changing and never consistent, yet they are loving. So Hooba, there is not just one oath you can take. For Hooba, every year, every month, every day and every moment, you will need to make a choice. So, in every moment, invite her, love her, respect her, show her and if you completely understand, explain it to some other man," Josephus laughed.

Hooba was overwhelmed by the explanations of Josephus. He was lacking confidence in the clarifications.

Josephus bantered, "Fear not, Hooba. Love can overcome many things. I, too, was naïve when I married my wife."

Hooba then asked Josephus, "Rabbi, may I ask you a question that could cause you discomfort? In my formative years, I was raised by a celibate man. Jared frequently blushed around the women he was close to. And, he never discussed, except in a modest manner, interactions with women. Bachariko has been with a man and I have never been with a woman."

Josephus thought long and hard before he answered. "First remember, I told you, no year, no month, no day, no moment is the same with a woman. So, if your concern is that she has been with a man, your moment will be different."

Hooba asked, "What do I do?"

Josephus encouragingly answered, "When you hold her hand, can you feel the softness of her skin? Can you feel it affect you?"

Hooba replied, "Yes."

Josephus continued, "Women are soft like that over their entire body. Touch them, and they will respond and so will you. Learn from each other. Do not be afraid to ask her what she likes and do not be afraid to show her what you like. Be tender and respectful but remember, God created you to respond to each other. Let your passion guide you."

Josephus went on, "Hooba, the woman you are being betrothed to had a mother who had explained all of your questions to her. She understands some of what you may not. Let her guide you."

Hooba and Josephus headed to the meal table. Josephus grinned when he saw Bachariko looking in his direction to which she returned the smile.

Bachariko couldn't help but look directly into Hooba's eyes. She thought his eyes to be wide-opened and with panic.

Hooba asked, "Josephus, would you like to break the bread?"

Josephus broke the bread, serving Hooba and Bachariko last.

He then announced, "Hooba presented me with a betrothal gift today."

Hooba spoke up, "After a very lengthy conversation, I believe Josephus has accepted me as a suitable partner for Bachariko, if she will have me."

Bachariko took his hand and said, "Stand with me."

Then, she addressed Noam, "It will be an honor."

Bachariko then addressed her grandfather, "I respect your judgment."

She looked at Hooba and said, "I have prepared our tent."

Chapter 33

Alabaster Skin

Hooba took Bachariko's hand after dinner and led her toward the beach. She reminded him that her tent was in another direction.

Hooba said, "But, the moon is over the water right now."

What Bachariko did not know was that Susanna was on the way to her tent with purpose. Hooba had given her a single rose with instructions to place it on Bachariko's pillow.

Hooba and Bachariko stood at the water's edge. He looked to the north and the south and could see no stirring of any people.

He turned to her and said, "If I may, I would kiss you now?"

Their lips met for the first time although Hooba allowed his lips to linger on hers much longer. Bachariko reciprocated by kissing his neck.

Hooba unconsciously sighed a little and thought to himself: "I did not actually realize one could kiss a neck. Her lips are, indeed, very soft."

Bachariko gazed up at him and asked, "Have you seen enough of the moon?"

Hooba answered, "Yes, I just needed to see that you are as beautiful at sunrise, sunset and in the moonlight."

Bachariko took Hooba's hand and led him back to her tent. As they reached it, she asked Hooba to sit upon the ground outside the tent. She stepped into and out of the tent, returning with a pitcher of water. She knelt at his feet and poured the water over his feet to cleanse them. She sat next to him, handing the pitcher over to him.

She instructed, "Now, wash my feet. My mother taught me this. Just as you have your ritual bath, we will enter this tent cleansed together."

He slowly removed her sandals, seeming to enjoy the ritual of washing her feet.

Bachariko then said, "We will jump over the threshold together."

Once inside, she removed the scarf from her head, allowing her cinnamon-colored hair to cascade below her shoulders.

"Your hair is beautiful, Bachariko," Hooba whispered.

She lit a single candle and then noticed the rose laying upon the pillow. She turned her eyes toward Hooba as a single tear ran down her cheek.

"You remembered the rose, Hooba," she said with emotion.

Hooba replied, "The rose is the most beautiful flower and that is how I think of you. You are like my rose."

He brushed the hair and then the tear from her cheek and kissed her lips one more time. Then, he kissed her neck.

"What is that smell?" he inquired.

Bachariko admitted that it was scented oil and, "I prepared myself for you."

"I have never been with …," he began to say, but Bachariko stopped him from speaking.

"I have never been with you," she whispered back.

She loosened her cloak, allowing it to fall to the ground. Hooba had never seen the undergarment of a woman. He noticed how the candlelight flickered against the white of her skin and the white of her undergarment. Then, she methodically removed Hooba's cloak.

Hooba fidgeted slightly.

"Do not be shy in my presence. You are beautiful," Bachariko spoke.

He reached for her, allowing less space between them. She was so close that he could feel the shape of her body as it pressed against his. And she could feel his breath on her neck then realizing they were breathing in sequence. She felt her undergarment loosen. It fell to the ground as she realized it was not of her doing. His lips were now kissing her shoulder as he pulled her yet closer.

"You are softer than I could even imagine," he said quietly.

His hand traced down her back as she tried to comprehend whether it was his hand or her body that now trembled. She took his hand and reclined her body onto the bed. He followed with his own body.

They continued caressing one another. Bachariko wrapped her body completely around Hooba's. She felt a pressure and gasped, pulling his body as close as she possibly could.

Chapter 34

Sunday Morning

*H*ooba awakened with Bachariko still at his side. He heard voices and activity outside of their tent.

He thought, "Why is there so much activity this early?"

Then, he realized that there was already too much sun for the time of day he thought it to be. He also noticed the alabaster jar was now sitting next to their bedding. A single red rose stuck out of the top of the jar. Next to the jar was a familiar leather pouch, embossed with the letter J.

Hooba whispered to his wife, "Bachariko, the rose …"

She nuzzled up closer to Hooba with no intention of rising.

"Bachariko … the rose!" He said even louder.

She thought to herself: "He's calling me his beautiful flower."

"I like that," she said aloud.

"I like it too … wait, what did you like?" he asked.

"You called me your rose," she replied with a sweet affection.

Then, Hooba heard a voice from outside their tent.

"You know, you two missed breakfast," Delilah yelled in.

Bachariko and Hooba shot each other a glance. They were slightly embarrassed yet not embarrassed at all because of the love they felt for one another. However, Hooba scrambled to dress immediately. He pointed to Bachariko to notice the rose in the alabaster jar.

"I guess we have not been completely alone this morning," she chuckled.

Then she yelled, "Delilah, come into the tent."

Delilah peeked her head under the flap, grinning from ear to ear.

Then she said, "Great-grandfather had me bring these two gifts. I placed the rose in some water in the jar and I placed the pouch next to it. He said both had served their purpose. He asked me to relay to you that those gifts represent two of the most precious people he has ever known."

Delilah then added, "Great-grandfather also told me the story of the rose, once again. So, when I saw the rose laying next to you, it made me smile. That's why I placed it in the jar."

"You know, sometimes he calls me *His Rose*," Bachariko said.

Hooba thought to himself: "I think this name will stick."

Delilah stood with both hands on her hips, "As the most responsible member of this family, I think I must remind you that in a little less than sixty minutes you are to teach on the beach!"

She was looking at Hooba directly. The three of them quickly headed to the beach.

"Watch this," Hooba smirkingly said to Delilah.

"Have you seen the rabbi yet?" he asked a couple in the crowd already waiting.

"I heard that he is over six foot tall," he interjected into another group's conversation.

Bachariko joked with Delilah: "He has other good qualities!"

Hooba soon found himself standing up on his familiar rock. He shared parables with the group as he looked across the crowd of nearly five thousand people. And within that crowd, he saw fishermen, tax collectors, businessmen, families and children. One parable he told was about watering a rose to nourish the love.

Delilah looked up at Bachariko and said, "He really is sweet, you know. He's talking about you."

Bachariko whispered back, "I knew that was for me."

Hooba noticed a wall of one-hundred Kittim soldiers at the north end of the beach and one-hundred Kittim soldiers at the south end of the beach. It was almost as if the crowd was being contained, surrounded by the soldiers.

Hooba noticed Akeldama and a group of men heading toward the Kittim soldiers to the south. Immediately, his thoughts were that of concern.

Hooba yelled over the crowd, "Akeldama!"

He began reciting Psalms 23:2 through 23:6 loudly in the hopes of gaining the attention of Akeldama.

Hooba thought to himself: "Now is the time to lay down your sword and learn the verses."

Akeldama after hearing him just thought, "Now I appear more important. He has singled me out."

Young Philippos walked over to Akeldama and quietly recited the verses, so that Akeldama could hear and repeat after him … which he did.

Hooba spoke for two more hours.

Then, he addressed the fishermen. "Please, let out your nets once again as we have an even larger group to feed."

Once Hooba finished speaking, Bachariko and Delilah joined him and headed back to their tent. As they approached it, Delilah spoke.

"Hooba, Ruth said I can stay with her again tonight."

Hooba blushed.

Chapter 35

A Place of Comfort

K far Nahum was a beautiful community situated on the water. It reminded Bachariko of her home. *Her Hooba* and *His Rose* frequently walked the beach in the evening. Each night, he would admit how the sunset reminded him of her beautiful hair.

Every night after returning from the beach, once they reached their tent, Hooba would wash the sand from Bachariko's feet before entering it.

A particular evening, one of the fishermen, Zelo, appeared at their tent. He reported that his mother was sick with arthritis and was unable to get up. Hooba and Bachariko hurried along with the fisherman to his home. Hooba prayed with Zelo while Bachariko administered herbs orally and oils topically to his mother. Two hours later, the fisherman's mother rose from her bed. She had been given turmeric for the inflammation and oil as liniment.

During those two hours, Bachariko had inquired with the woman the probability of available homes in the area. She was a local woman and knew which homes were available. It just so happened that the small home next to them overlooking the water was now ready for occupancy.

Once Bachariko and the woman emerged from the bedroom, Bachariko mentioned to Hooba that the crowds and the food were noticeably abundant in this community. She also touched on the fact that the surrounding communities had been receptive to Hooba's teaching.

Bachariko then reminded Hooba of their contentment and the beauty of the sunset during their evening walks.

"Hooba, I fear that any area closer to the city of The Temple will have more Kittim soldiers to contend with," Bachariko explained.

Then she added, "My daughter needs a home, not a tent."

Zelo spoke up not knowing of the conversation his mother and Bachariko had had in private. "The home next to ours is vacant."

Hooba looked to Zelo and asked, "Is there work to be found on your boat?"

Bachariko said, "Hooba, I have the means."

"The price will be small, because of what you have done for my mother," Zelo answered.

Zelo then added, "I own the vacant home next door."

Then he began, "Your wife has been …"

Bachariko shushed him immediately. She did not want Hooba to be aware she had paid the fishermen for the fish to feed all of the people.

"Rabbi, you should teach, not feed," Zelo stated.

Hooba turned to Bachariko and said, "My Rose, I needed nothing and I did not remember that you might."

"Husband, I merely need a place to plant the rosebush," Bachariko responded.

"Hooba, I share so much of you. Please do not think badly of me for wanting to spend time just as us," Bachariko admitted.

"It is my place and my desire that you find refuge in me," she added.

Hooba then asked Zelo, "Is it possible to see the home?"

They all walked outside and next door to the vacant home. The entry room was large with a table to accommodate twenty people. One end of the home was the kitchen and to the back were three additional rooms. Two of the rooms were much smaller and Bachariko immediately assigned them as one for her father and one for Hooba and herself. The larger room, Bachariko assigned to Delilah, Noam, Ruth and Beatrice.

Behind the small home was a stone path that led directly to the beach. Ironically, at the end of the path, lay the rock Hooba had stood on to preach to the people on the beach.

"This will be the rock upon which I build my church," Hooba announced.

Hooba took Bachariko's hand in his own as they walked back toward their tent city.

"Bachariko, are you pleased with this home?" Hooba asked as they walked.

She replied, "As pleased as I am with my husband."

"A woman should be able to spend time with her husband alone without sharing a tent," Bachariko teased.

"When you wash the sand off my feet living in this new home, at least I won't step back onto a sandy floor," she laughed.

Many a week had passed; many meals with family and friends; many small trips to the neighboring communities. Each and every Sunday, Hooba taught nearly five-thousand people on the beach, standing on the rock. Every morning without fail, Hooba walked down the stone path to the shore. He looked to the north and saw the Kittim soldiers training. He would look to the south and see Akeldama training with his men.

Each morning, Hooba thanked God for the life he had and that neither of these groups had yet raised their swords.

Over the next year, Hooba's reputation grew. Rumors of skirmishes occurring outside the city of Kfar Nahum became more abundant. Each week, Hooba preached more about having peace. The number of Kittim soldiers doubled, then tripled.

Two Passover meals or two years had gone by when Noam mentioned wanting to attend the wedding of a friend. Bachariko told Hooba that they should go along with his mother to the wedding.

"The trip will be long and it could be at least four weeks before we could teach again on the beach," Hooba answered.

"Tensions here are high. Some of the crowds will disperse, leaving the Kittims more at ease," she offered.

Hooba thought, "I can teach along the way. It will calm the situation here and help the fishermen who have been working to their limit to feed the crowds."

So, Hooba set off to find Yohanan.

"Yohanan. Gather those closest and invite them to dinner at my home tonight," Hooba advised.

A Place of Comfort

The women began preparing the evening meal. Bachariko approached Hooba.

"There are two hundred people standing on the beach wanting to follow you south to the wedding," she said.

Hooba looked over the group. Almost one hundred of them consisted of Akeldama's men. He stomped right over to Akeldama.

"I will not march an army of one hundred men south," Hooba insisted to Akeldama.

"It will appear to the Kittims that we are ready to fight," he went on.

"I am not building an army. I am building a church," Hooba roared.

Akeldama replied, "Rabbi, I just want to bring men to protect the caravan."

Hooba responded, "Then, you can bring four!"

Hooba turned to Yohanan. "How many can we feed on this trip?"

Yohanan replied, "We can feed forty yet we will have at least eighty."

"Yohanan, will you please ask young Philippos and a few of the other young fishermen to travel with us so we can feed the large group of eighty," Hooba asked.

Hooba then asked Yohanan, "Can you please order your finest wine for the wedding?"

One more Sunday arrived for Hooba to teach his people. Then, the band of eighty followers left to head south for the wedding. They traveled town to town and, in each, the crowds grew larger.

Hooba could not possibly have known what was happening in Kfar Nahum while they were gone. Akeldama's men had fought with the Kittims after they left. Twelve Kittim soldiers had been killed. Thirty of Akeldama's men had lost their lives. The remainder of Akeldama's men had disbanded and dispersed across the countryside. Hooba's and Bachariko's own home had been ransacked. Some of the community people had also been killed by the Kittims.

Men had been pulled out into the street by the Kittims and asked, "Where does your allegiance lie, with your ruler or your Rabbi Hooba?"

Zelo had been one of those men.

Regrettably, he had responded, "My allegiance lies with my ruler."

Then, Zelo abandoned his mother, stole a Kittim horse and rode south to find Hooba's caravan.

Chapter 36

The Wedding

The caravan arrived in southern Levant where the wedding would take place two weeks later. The celebration had already begun as family and friends gathered. Hooba's group arrived shortly before the Sabbath. They observed the day and on the next day, Sunday, Hooba taught the wedding crowd.

On the third day of the week which was Tuesday, the wedding took place. Hooba had instructed Yohanan on that day to fill jars with water because the wine had not yet been delivered. He did not want his large group of eighty people to drink up all the wine provided by the hosts.

The betrothal or the couple's commitment to marry had occurred nearly six months before. Although it was not legally binding by secular rules it was binding under *The Law*. They had completed the first part of their marriage. Today, their marriage ceremony would be the legal part of their contract.

The ceremony had been completed and the celebration in full swing when the wine ordered by Yohanan finally arrived. The guests all commented on how wise the hosts had been in saving the finest wine for last. There was great laughter and joy.

Hooba gazed into the eyes of Bachariko. "Do you miss this celebration?" he asked.

She replied, "The celebration is only in our love. My commitment is solely with you and God."

Hooba smiled, nodded and kissed Bachariko on her cheek.

Precisely at that moment, a horse carrying Zelo ran straight into the celebration.

Hooba immediately jumped up and grabbed the horse by the reins in utter disgust.

"Zelo! You are interrupting this couple's joy," he declared.

Hooba led the horse and Zelo out of the celebration. Zelo then spoke emphatically.

"Rabbi, I fear that I am only three or four hours ahead of the Kittim soldiers."

Hooba responded, "What did you expect? This is obviously a Kittim saddle on the horse you are riding. Under Kittim law and God's law, you are responsible for your actions! This horse does not belong to you."

Zelo replied, "Your home has been ransacked and I feared it would be unsafe for you to return home."

"And so, you've chosen to make it unsafe at this wedding?" Hooba asked.

"Zelo, I thought your maturity would make you trustworthy to lead my church," Hooba stated.

Akeldama and his men had followed Hooba and Zelo and were listening from a short distance. Zelo noticed them and loudly explained.

"There are Kittim soldiers following me. There has already been a battle and some of your men were killed."

Zelo was standing there feeling sorry for himself.

He thought inwardly: "My house was ruined, my business is gone since I'm selling no fish and Hooba has just embarrassed me in front of all these people. This is Hooba's and the Kittim's fault! Not mine. I just came here to warn them."

Immediately upon hearing this, Akeldama and his three men drew their swords.

Hooba yelled, "How dare you men draw your swords at this wedding?"

"You would just mar the celebration with violence," he added.

Then Hooba said, "Zelo, the Kittims would be within their rights to tie you up like a horse and drag you through the city. Thus, the people of this wedding would be racked with the violence of the Kittims instead of the happiness of the celebration. They would be within their rights to stone you to death."

Hooba jumped up on the horse. "I will return this horse and hopefully, you will be spared."

Bachariko seeing what was transpiring, yelled to Yohanan, "You must stop him!"

Young Philippos, seeing what was happening ran toward the horse, dove and knocked Hooba right off the horse. Then, he jumped on the horse himself.

"Rabbi, in this case, I will return the horse," Philippos told Hooba.

Hooba adamantly responded back, "Philippos, this is the job of a man not a boy!"

Yohanan firmly placed his hand on Hooba's shoulder. "In this case, I would rarely tell you, you were wrong but a boy may be spared and a man may not."

Yohanan turned and threw a bag of gold to Philippos.

Then ordered, "Philippos, pay the Kittims for their troubles, give them their horse and run!"

Philippos took off swiftly for the road heading north. Once he reached the Kittim soldiers, he jumped from the horse, leading it to the most senior man.

He said, "My master has dealt with the man who stole your horse. He ordered me to return your horse and pay you for your troubles."

The Kittim soldier replied, "Turn your back to me!"

He lashed Philippos four times, drawing blood. "Carry this punishment back to your master!" he demanded.

The soldier then asked Philippos, "Where can we find your master?"

Philippos responded, "His home is close to the sea."

Philippos then headed east on foot toward the sea. He stumbled and fell in pain.

He overheard the soldier say, "There is no reason to follow this boy. He will never make it home."

The Kittim soldiers turned their horses and headed north toward Kfar Nahum. They could not see the smile presenting itself upon the lips of Philippos.

Once Philippos no longer heard the hooves of the Kittim's horses hitting the ground, he stood, dusted himself off and headed south.

After the commotion, Hooba returned to the celebration giving a toast to the newly married couple. He motioned for Yohanan and asked that he circulate and round up their group to depart. He found the younger Iakobas.

"We will be leaving by the south road. Please go by the north road, find Philippos and bring him home," Hooba pleaded with Iakobas.

Hilleal heard his request and offered to accompany Iakobas in bringing Philippos home.

Once Yohanan reported back to Hooba that the group was preparing to leave, he also mentioned their trip could only be about one hour south before sunset.

Hooba replied, "It does not matter how far we go. We must not be here should the Kittims return."

They traveled and shortly approached a small community of fifty inhabitants. They set up their tents and afterward Hooba went around to meet some of the people of the community. He invited those that he met to join his group for dinner.

One of the elders of the community suddenly looked at Hooba and remarked, "You are **THE** Hooba!"

"I thought you would be more powerful," the elder remarked.

Hooba then asked, "And, why is that?"

"I thought you would have a great army and would lead us against the Kittims," he replied.

"I have come to teach *The Law* and the greatest law is to love thy neighbor as thyself," Hooba announced.

The elder then responded, "I have heard that you are a great teacher. However, even our small community is not safe from Kittim intervention. The road you are on is well traveled and it is not only our people but also the Kittims that speak of you. My own brother resisted the Kittim tax and was struck down and killed."

Hooba said, "I am greatly sorrowed for your brother but I have come to teach peace and preserve *The Law*."

The elder then asked, "I thought this was our promised land?"

Pointing to his heart, Hooba said, "The promised land is in here and in God's kingdom to come."

The elder then stood up from the table. "Thank you for your hospitality but what good is your message to my dead brother?"

Shortly before sunrise, Iakobas and Hilleal returned with Philippos. Each man had taken turns carrying him through the night. He had been found laying beside the road. The women dressed his wounds with herbs and oils.

Philippos could not wait to explain to Hooba how wise he had been in outsmarting the Kittim soldiers. However, he could hardly speak after losing so much blood and walking until he became dehydrated.

Hooba touched his arm and said, "Save your energy. I am proud of you and my left rib is still bruised from when you knocked me from the horse."

Just after sunrise, they left for the city of The Temple.

While they traveled, Hooba laughed and talked as if nothing was on his mind. Bachariko continually asked him if their destination was the correct choice. She knew there were many Kittim soldiers in the city with The Temple. He reminded her there were also thousands of people living there whose hearts needed to be strengthened.

He continued, "This is our spiritual center, *The Temple*. For many, it represents our faith."

Bachariko was aware that she could not argue with Hooba while he was this determined. When they camped for the evening, she asked Delilah to again stay with Noam and Ruth so she could speak with Hooba alone.

That evening, once alone, they allowed their passion to flow.

Then Bachariko said to Hooba, "I am with child. Please be careful."

The next morning, she awoke to find a wild rose laying on the pillow next to her and Hooba already gone.

Hooba and Hilleal had traveled to the nearby city of his ancestors. They returned with Susanna's mother and her father's father. Susanna had not seen her family in many years. Young Ruth, the daughter of Hilleal and Susanna, had never met her grandmother or great-grandfather. Susanna's grandfather Aramis and Bachariko's grandfather Josephus quickly bonded. This also provided Josephus with a peer of his age during their travels. Hooba also hadn't seen his mother's sister in many years.

Hooba had left hurriedly that morning being fearful that Bachariko would insist that it was not safe for him to go. His efforts were an attempt to help Josephus, Susanna and young Ruth.

Upon the return of Hooba and Hilleal, Bachariko was not upset or concerned with them at all. Delilah had developed a fever while they were gone and Bachariko was busy trying to lower her fever. She had administered turmeric powder and the broth of chicken.

Hooba was visibly shaken by Delilah's illness. He refused to leave her side continually bathing her with cold water. He stayed up through the night with Delilah, advising Bachariko to rest and sleep.

Yohanan reported to their tent door in the morning asking when they would depart.

Hooba said, "Split the caravan. We will not move the child until she is better."

Zelo, Akeldama, the elder Iakobas, the tax collector, the fishermen and fifty others of the caravan left that morning. The remaining twenty-four stayed behind with Hooba, Bachariko and Delilah.

Three days passed. Delilah's fever had still not broken. Hooba would not leave her side even on the Sabbath, continually soothing her with cool water. The next morning, her fever had broken.

Hooba instructed her, "Child … rise and go find your mother."

Chapter 37

The Return

Three years had passed since Hooba visited to the city of The Temple. The Kittims in the north had reported to their Governor Antipas, Hooba could not be located. They also relayed their belief he had traveled south. Governor Antipas sent word to the southern governor, Pechah that Hooba and some of his army, were presumably in the southern region.

Then, the first part of the caravan reached and camped outside the city of The Temple at the Mount. On the Sabbath they traveled to The Temple. In the courtyard of The Temple, Zelo started to teach the people as he had watched Hooba do many times. Zelo announced to the crowd of the coming of the great teacher.

"What the Kittims have torn down, the rabbi will return to its glory," he declared.

Akeldama had gathered some of the men from the city who cheered.

When it came time for The Temple service, it was crowded to the brim with the city people, Akeldama's people and the caravan people. The noise was deafening. Rabbi Zokef grew angry as he could not quiet the crowd to preach.

Some of Akeldama's men mocked Zokef, calling him the puppet of the governor.

The elder Iakobas stood on a bench and yelled, "In my brother Hooba's name, be silent in the presence of God!"

Unfortunately, the entire crowd silenced at the mention of Hooba's name while Zokef grew angrier.

It was so quiet the entire room heard the young boy say, "Hooba fed my mother and me when we were very hungry."

Another man said, "I have heard him speak and it is with the conviction of a man of God."

The Rabbi Zokef feared he was losing control of his service.

Loudly, he declared and asked, "God made the covenant with Abraham, Noah, Moses and King David. Does this man Hooba claim that God has given him a covenant?"

A man from the crowd yelled back, "His mother and father were from the house of David, so this *is* a fulfilment of the covenant with King David."

The man happened to be Akeldama.

Zokef's face flushed red with rage. He yelled, "Beware the false prophet. This ends the lesson for today!"

He spun around and entered the Sanctuary. The veil had been replaced. He was now alone as no others could enter.

He had made a point. Only those clean and pure could enter the Sanctuary.

As the crowd pushed to get out of The Temple, the Kittims held them back, forcing them to pay taxes just to exit.

The elder Iakobas attempted to calm the crowd, "Peace, brothers and sisters. This is not how God would want us to act in his home."

Right at that moment, a man shoved the elder Iakobas, who fell down the stairs of The Temple. He looked up into the face of his offender and later learned his name to be Pseftis.

The elder Iakobas's fall had not been an accident. He tried to get up only to have a Kittim soldier knock him down once again. Akeldama ran over to the elder Iakobas starting to draw his sword.

"Akeldama, lay down your sword and your pride. This is not the way! This is not the lesson of love you should be learning," Iakobas yelled.

He went on, "Have you not been listening? Judgment is God's and God's only."

Zelo helped Iakobas to his feet. He threw two coins into the tax collector's bin as they exited the courtyard.

Once everyone had left The Temple, Rabbi Zokef sent a messenger to the Governor Pechah.

The message read, "The people are at unrest. An uprising will soon begin. This man Hooba must be stopped."

Hooba was still caring for Delilah with the remainder of the caravan. Unbeknown to Hooba, the city he was about to enter was at unrest, all in his name.

Bachariko was relieved with Delilah's improvement as was Hooba. The smaller encampment was peaceful now that so many had already gone ahead. The meal this day was literally with family and the closest of their friends. Laughter filled their camp. Even the small group of Kittim soldiers, about six in view, did not bother with them.

Hooba took their last remaining wine from the marriage celebration and delivered it to the Kittim soldiers. They laughed with appreciation.

Hooba joked with the soldiers. "Relax today. We are not leaving until tomorrow."

One soldier, who answered to the name Odious, said, "Rabbi, why do you share with us?"

"Why would I not share what I have? You have your job and I have mine." Hooba replied.

Odious then asked, "You do not judge me for who I am?"

Hooba answered back, "Judgment is not mine."

"Judgment belongs to my emperor," Odious stated.

Hooba couldn't help but respond, "So, judgment belongs to who you serve? The same is true for me. Odious, be careful. You cannot serve two masters."

"I only serve one master," Odious replied.

Hooba again stated back, "The same is true for me. Peace be with you, Odious."

Before Odious had a chance to gather his thoughts, he had automatically responded back, "Peace be with you also."

Hooba walked away and back toward his camp. He turned one last time and spoke to Odious.

"If we leave early in the morning before you have risen, we are taking the road south to the city of The Temple," Hooba informed him.

The following morning as their small caravan prepared to leave, the Kittim soldiers rode up to their camp and waited. Hooba waved at Odious. Odious waved back.

Hooba walked over to the soldiers and said, "We can only travel about eight hours today otherwise it is difficult for the women and children."

Odious responded, "Well, thank you. The horses will appreciate that."

Hooba said, "We still have ample provisions. You are welcome to join us for the evening meal."

"We will consider it," Odious acknowledged.

Odious and his men then took off south toward the city of The Temple.

The caravan started for the city of The Temple and approximately eight hours later they reached the Kittim soldiers who had cleared a campsite and started a fire to include Hooba's group.

Hooba had prepared the caravan to what could possibly have happened. Therefore, they were not surprised upon reaching their evening destination to find the soldiers awaiting them.

It had taken the greatest amount of convincing of the younger Iakobas that befriending the Kittim soldiers was a good idea. Hooba had explained to him it was hypocritical for them to not invite everyone to their table. The younger Iakobas had argued the Kittim soldiers were not clean to which Hooba's response was that *our cleanliness was our own responsibility and should not be judged.*

"How can I be an example to them if I do not invite them to our table?" Hooba posed the question.

Iakobas still was not completely convinced and neither was Bachariko.

Hooba looked toward Bachariko and inquired, "You are a healer. If this man Odious cut his hand, would you bandage it? Neither could I turn away from an injured soul."

Soon the caravan was ready for the evening while the meal was under preparation. The area to eat was set up. The soldiers appeared to be a bit uncomfortable as were the members of the caravan. Yet, Hooba broke the bread and distributed it as he would have done any other time.

Hooba recited Psalms 23:2 through 23:6 as everyone except the Kittim soldiers joined in.

"Is that some type of oath?" Odious asked as they finished.

Hooba replied, "No."

Then he inquired back, "Did you take an oath to your emperor?"

Odious replied, "Yes."

"We do not believe an oath is necessary in something you believe in. Why would I promise to do something if I did not think it was right? I would not promise; I would just do," Hooba said.

Hooba added, "I am thankful that you prepared our home for this evening just as I am thankful to my God who is preparing my home in Heaven."

Odious stayed silent, trying to wrap his head around those thoughts.

Then, Odious spoke, "My emperor provides for me."

"Or do **you** provide for your emperor? Your emperor gets his power from you." Hooba went on.

Hooba began to tell a story.

"There were two brothers. The first brother went out into the world and was very successful. When he returned home, his father celebrated his return. The second brother went out into the world and accomplished nothing. Yet, when he returned, his father celebrated his return. Would your emperor do the same, Odious?"

Hooba turned to the caravan members.

He said, "This is why all are invited to our table."

Hooba poured wine for everyone at the table. He raised his hand and toasted.

"I celebrate the potential return of all to this table."

Odious raised his own cup. He said, "You have been a gracious host."

Hooba extended his hand toward Odious. Odious reached out and took his hand. The rest of the caravan members gasped in silence. The Hebrew custom permitted touch to be only between family members and close friends.

Hooba turned to the group and scolded, "We are all family and friends under one God!"

Odious thought for just a moment; then smiled.

He spoke, "Peace be with you, Hooba."

Hooba replied, "Peace be with you, Odious."

In the morning, the remaining members of the caravan prepared for the last leg of their journey. Odious's men arrived, helping to load the wagons. The Kittim soldiers, along with Odious, rode ahead of the caravan by a mere two hundred yards as they headed toward the city of The Temple.

Hours had passed during their travel. Hooba noticed that suddenly both sides of the roads were filled with many, many men. Then, he noticed those men were armed and their swords were drawn.

He yelled to Hilleal, the young Iakobas, Philippos and Yohanan to take notice. Hooba began to run toward Odious and his six men to stop any conflict before it arose. The men with swords from the small caravan, now ran behind after Hooba, with their own swords drawn.

Twelve men, eleven of them holding swords, were now surrounded by one hundred men with drawn swords. The only unarmed man was standing between the two groups.

Hooba drew on his culture at that moment and yelled, "There is no part of this sacrifice that would please the Lord!"

One of the men from the group of a hundred ran toward Hooba. Odious ran toward the two men with his sword raised and at that moment, two swords met.

Yohanan gasped as Hooba threw his body into the first man knocking them both to the ground. Hooba jumped up immediately grabbing the sword, driving it into the ground.

"Stop!" Hooba yelled.

Then, he heard the voice of Akeldama also yell to his men, "Stop!"

The large group of Akeldama's men then separated.

Hooba again yelled, "Akeldama, there will be no bloodshed today! Let these men pass in peace."

Akeldama strutted out into the center of the two groups. Hooba walked toward Akeldama with intention.

"Have your men throw down their arms!" Hooba demanded.

Every man present now displayed respect for Hooba including Akeldama. He lowered his sword which, in turn, caused his remaining men to also lower their swords.

Hooba turned to see Susanna and Bachariko treating a wound on the face of Odious caused by the only two swords that had clashed.

He walked over to Odious who lay on the ground and helped him to his feet. Not stopping at this act of kindness, he went and shook the hand of every one of the hundred men who stood with Akeldama. Despite their tradition, Hooba made a conscious decision to acknowledge or embrace each man personally at that point, to display friendship rather than conflict.

Hooba reached for Bachariko's hand. They began to walk down the road toward their destination. Hilleal took Susanna's hand and followed.

Noam took Odious's hand and began to follow along with the other two couples. Philippos joined a Kittim soldier and began to walk. Delilah strode alongside another Kittim soldier. The younger Iakobas held the hand of young Ruth as they also walked along a Kittim soldier.

The rest followed toward the city of The Temple.

Yohanan stood and watched until the last member of the caravan and the last Kittim soldier had begun walking. He walked over to the sword that stood jammed into the ground. He pulled it out and drew a line across the road. He forced it back into the line of dirt.

"Akeldama, beware of the line you cross!" Yohanan warned.

Akeldama stood in shame and silence.

About an hour later, the road busied with traffic, merchants, soldiers and caravans. The road was lined with men, women and children who heard Hooba was coming. The caravan and soldiers would soon reach the city with The Temple.

They could hear people calling out, "Hooba, Rabbi" trying to get his attention. A man offered Hooba a donkey to ride. However, Hooba lifted Bachariko up onto the donkey, leading the animal by foot.

Soon, Yohanan was standing next to Hooba. Hooba instructed him to take the small caravan to the camp on The Mount. Then, he and

Bachariko stood to the side of the road allowing the Kittim soldiers passage into the city.

He turned to see thousands of followers behind him as he and Bachariko entered the city.

Odious and his men had reported back immediately to their commander upon entering the city. When they arrived at the commander's office, their headquarters and barracks, Odious was surprised at the commotion taking place. The commander was yelling, the soldiers were in and out of the building and regiments were marching toward The Temple.

Odious was unaware that the streets of the entire city were filled with people waiting to see Hooba and hear him speak. Merchant carts and tax-payer tables were being pushed over by the crowds and the Kittim soldiers had lost control of the people.

Surprised by all the activity, Odious addressed his commander. "The rabbi, Hooba has entered the city peacefully."

He tried to explain what had occurred on the road outside the city en route with Akeldama and his men and how Hooba had stopped the conflict. The commander just looked at him.

Then he stated, "He is already here. Dispense two more regiments to The Temple. Odious, follow me. We are going straight to the governor."

Odious chased after his commander to the office of the governor. Now, the governor was a calm man. However, the commander was immediately rattling off all the goings on in the city with trepidation.

The commander said, while pointing to Odious, "This man knows of Hooba."

The governor then said, "Well ... speak, man."

Odious began, "We followed him with a small group of twenty. They were unthreatening and unarmed. I spoke to this man Hooba many times. He is a man of peace. He risked his own life for mine. He fed my soldiers and comforted them when they were hungry and tired. He prevented a battle which would have resulted in the deaths of all six of my men. His own men raised their swords to protect my men."

The governor listened and just nodded his head.

Then, he asked, "Is it true that he is over six-foot tall and over two hundred pounds?"

"No, he is soft spoken and does not even stand above my shoulder," Odious replied.

"Does he look like a man who could lead an army against us?" the governor inquired.

Odious answered, "No, he is not a great military leader. What I remember is that his wife treated my wound and was compassionate when I was injured and that he helped me up with his own hand off the ground. He welcomed and toasted us like we were family. My last memory is watching him walk hand-in-hand with his wife almost like a young man and then I saw him lift her up onto a donkey as he looked up at her adoringly."

The governor leaned his chin upon his hand.

He said, "Commander, it appears that the problem is not this man. It seems to be your inability to control the people."

The commander tried to speak but the governor cut him off, "Go do your job!"

Hooba and Bachariko had entered the city. The streets swelled with people. Many were just trying to get a glimpse or touch Hooba's cloak. Every few feet, he stopped and addressed the crowd. The people were cheering. Only about one thousand of the followers had made it through the gates of the city before the soldiers had slammed them closed. Once they finally made it to The Temple, many of the city streets had been shut down. Yet, nearly twenty-thousand people listened to Hooba teach for an hour from the steps of the courtyard. And then, as only Hooba could have accomplished, he dispensed the crowd quietly. The crowd began returning to their homes as Hooba heard a voice from the courtyard.

The Rabbi Zokef yelled to him: "That was quite the spectacle."

Hooba then noticed young Iakobas was standing there as well.

"Why aren't you with the others?" Hooba asked.

"Yohanan sent me to keep an eye on you. Follow me. We will not be taking the path through the center of the city," he said.

The three of them worked their way through the back alleys to avoid people and soldiers. Once they reached the gate to the city, it was closed. To their surprise, Odious was manning the gate. He led them through an interior path inside of the wall and outside the city.

Iakobas, Bachariko and Hooba took a small path through the valley and back over to The Mount and their camp.

Once back at camp, they found the size was no longer eighty people camping with them but closer to eight thousand. The many thousands of people waiting along the road to see Hooba had no other recourse after being closed out by the gates. They had to camp alongside Hooba's people.

The Passover Seder, the ritual feast that marks the beginning of Passover, is about freedom. Freedom from bondage but more important, freedom of spirit. Its meaning comes from The Exodus which is the second book of the Torah. Because the Israelites had so little time to prepare to leave Egypt as slaves, they did not take time to allow their unleavened bread to rise.

Hooba and Bachariko looked at the massive encampment.

Hooba said to Bachariko and young Iakobas, "These people are a free people and have no spiritual bondage. There are so few provisions. Gather all we have and give to the most hungry. Gather all of the flour and flax and do not allow the bread to rise. Bake and distribute it, also, to the most hungry."

Thousands of small fires had been set within the camps which made The Mount glow. The sun set to the emanating songs being sung on The Mount. It was now the Sabbath. You could hear the chorus inside the city walls. Those outside the city walls rejoiced as they heard the echo of song within the walls.

In the morning the gates to the city were open. When men and women should have been traveling to The Temple, people were leaving the city walls. The Temple was empty. Thousands came to the massive encampment carrying food.

Hooba looked out across the entire crowd and watched as people shared their food.

Hooba wept.

Zokef and his scribes, now seeing that The Temple was empty, followed the people. He stood at the base of The Mount and watched Hooba walking toward him. Hooba had been passing bread out to the masses.

Hooba stopped at a leper and said, "I cannot heal you of your disease but your faith can heal your spirit."

Then, he stopped at an injured man. Hooba and Bachariko treated the injury. Zokef called out to him.

"Your presence has inspired the people to break their Sabbath oath. Then you, yourself claim that this man's faith in you can heal his spirit. You actually treat the injured, breaking the Sabbath law yourself," Zokef scolded.

"Do you not preach on the Sabbath and is that not the Lord's work?" Hooba asked.

Hooba turned and climbed to the highest point on The Mount and stood next to an olive tree. He raised both hands above his head and the entire crowd silenced.

"Blessed be the work of God who feeds the hungry and cures the infirmed," Hooba announced for all to hear.

He continued, "Blessed be this olive tree. It has stood for hundreds of years. It represents all of you. Its roots represent the first of God's people that stood here. The roots are strong. The fifteen-thousand people here are as the roots. Strong. They are the base of the faith. Let this represent the tree of life and may we become stronger in God's presence. You are the temple. It is not behind the walls of the city. Let God dwell in you. Let your heart become Eden. Cleanse your heart, mind and soul. Prepare your temple. Then, God will take dwelling within you."

Hooba noticed Akeldama and Zokef were speaking. He continued preaching.

"Do not judge, lest you be judged. Judgment is God's alone. We are to be the peacekeepers and the keepers of *The Law*. That is our roots. Today, celebrate the **Seder**. We proclaim we are free from the early bondage. We feed the hungry of body and spirit. I proclaim the good news. God is in all of you. This is the covenant of Abraham, Noah, Moses and David."

Akeldama yelled to Hooba, "What of the Kittims, the scribes and the priests?"

Hooba replied, "The Kittims have nothing to do with your relationship with God and I call on all of you to be your own personal priest.

For what is the job of the priest but to cleanse themselves to be in the presence of God. We need more teachers not more priests."

Akeldama yelled once more, "But what of the Kittims and their swords?"

Hooba responded, "He who lives by the sword, dies by the sword. Yet, he who lives by the word, dies with the word in his heart."

He continued to preach mostly about love for the next two hours.

Then, he ended by reciting Psalms 23:2 through 23:6 while many joined him including Zokef and with Akeldama mumbling along.

Zokef hurried off, heading back to The Temple with his scribes. It was still the Sabbath, leaving him the only recourse which was to contemplate his actions.

Hooba went straight to Akeldama after he finished.

"I want your men to help me control the crowds. We must release the people slowly as they return to the city," Hooba insisted.

Akeldama asked him, "Why should we control the people?"

Hooba answered, "We cannot leave this up to the Kittims. Our people could be injured and is not your training better than that of the Kittims? We cannot trust this to the Kittims but I am certain that I can trust you."

Chapter 38
The Games

The sun had already risen. Hooba began to stir. He felt his forehead and hair being caressed. He opened his eyes to see Bachariko smiling and lying next to him. He smiled and kissed her softly.

"It seems like it is quite late," he said.

Bachariko replied back, "When do you ever rest?"

"Have you been awake long?" Hooba asked.

"It has been hours," she answered.

Bachariko followed with, "You are beautiful, Hooba. You looked so peaceful."

Hooba started to cry.

He said, "I do not tell you often enough just how beautiful you are."

Bachariko took his hand and placed it on her abdomen.

"I don't know why but I think it's a girl," she said.

Hooba heard the spirit of God speak to him at that moment.

"This is Isaiah. You have done very good work, Hooba. There is a hidden treasure within Bachariko. You should call her Esther."

"Remember the lessons from the book of Esther," the spirit said. *"You can touch the lives of others by acting as a loving example. God uses ordinary people to do extraordinary things. Beauty should not make us boastful. Loving others is the most beautiful thing that we can do."*

Hooba said, "Bachariko? Spirit tells me the name should be Esther."

Bachariko replied, "She was a beautiful queen of our people. I like that name."

"I am sure she will be beautiful like her mother but let's be careful not to boast about our beautiful baby," he quickly reminded her.

Hooba took Bachariko in his arms. They remained entwined for the next two hours. When the two finally exited the tent, they saw Hilleal, Yohanan, the younger Iakobas and Philippos sitting on the ground just waiting. All four men grinned from ear to ear.

Yohanan spoke, "Tomorrow I'll need to travel into the city to gather provisions. The rest of us can't live on love alone."

Both Hooba and Bachariko blushed.

Hooba spoke, "Philippos, gather as many young children as you can."

He took his shawl and tied it into a knotted ball. He gathered olive branches. Once the children arrived, he showed them how to hit the woven ball with the olive branch.

Philippos took all the little boys on his team and Hooba took all of the little girls. Soon, they were all playing and laughing. One little girl fell down and began to cry. Hooba scooped her right up to make sure she was not too hurt. She kissed him right on the nose. He blushed.

Bachariko teased, "No matter how much you practice with the little girls, that blush is still going to happen."

Hooba gathered all the children at his feet. He started to tell them a story.

"Once upon a time, our people had a beautiful queen and her name was Esther …"

Zokef was up early that next morning. He strode through the city of The Temple. He knocked a man off of his feet who stood in his way.

He thought to himself: "My coffers were empty on the Sabbath which means the governor received no tax money. I saw it with my own eyes, **he** worked on the Sabbath. Who does he think he is, God? He blasphemes the very God he says he prays to. He must be stopped."

Zokef pushed straight past the guards and burst into the governor's office. He slammed his fist on the desk.

"Hooba blasphemes our Lord. He must be stopped!" shouted Zokef.

His face was angry and reddened. The governor simply sighed. Then he spoke.

"This man Hooba controls the crowds. He speaks of peace and love. He is kind to Kittim soldiers. I care not what he does to your God for it is not part of our law!"

Zokef sneered, "You collected no tax dollars at The Temple yesterday. He laughs at your Kittim laws."

The governor replied, "He is your problem, not mine. Be gone!"

Two Kittim soldiers took stance on each side of Zokef.

The governor ordered, "Show him out!"

Zokef left angrily. He returned to The Temple. He sat with the scribes and other priests, plotting and planning.

He asked, "What can we do next?"

Then, he turned to one of the scribes, "Tomorrow, find me that man, Akeldama!"

The next day one of Zokef's scribes went in search of Akeldama. Akeldama, along with twelve of his armed men, followed the scribes to the gates of the city of The Temple as asked.

Odious was stationed at the gates that morning. He looked at Akeldama with suspicion.

"What is your purpose within the city?" he asked Akeldama.

The scribe of Zokef spoke up, "The chief priest has requested an audience."

Odious questioned, "With all thirteen of these men?"

"It was Hooba that requested we meet with the priest," Akeldama yelled out.

Odious, still unsure, again inquired, "And, the purpose of this meeting?"

Akeldama responded, "The purpose of this meeting is to bring the *message of peace* to the chief priest."

Odious then allowed them to pass.

Six of Akeldama's men split from them. They went door to door informing the people that Hooba would be gathering an army against the Kittim soldiers.

Their message was that *soon the city will again be ours*.

Akeldama and six of his men met with the priest and six of his scribes.

Zokef began, "Your master presents us with a problem. He incites riots, blasphemes God and ignores *The Law*. Yet, he draws the people to him."

Akeldama said, "I see our problems are different. The Kittims control our city. The people listen to Hooba. If he was not so weak, he could be king. I see only one problem we have in common. Hooba does not want to be king. He wants your job! In one day, by word of mouth, he draws a crowd of fifteen thousand to listen to him. We will not regain the city but you will certainly lose your position."

Zokef stood immediately and slammed his fist upon the desk. "I am the chief priest of The Temple. It is I who serves the Lord!"

"What if I could raise an army, take back the city and still leave you in control of The Temple? If Hooba won't lead the people, maybe they will still fight in his name," Akeldama offered.

As Zokef and Akeldama continued to conspire, the scribes and Akeldama's men set off to collect those within the city who would be supportive of their mission, returning with about one hundred followers. The group was coached for the next hour. Zokef and Akeldama led the group to the governor's office.

During that time, six of Akeldama's men jumped and killed two Kittim soldiers. Once the group arrived at the governor's office, the rumor had already been circulating and had reached him about the murdered soldiers.

Zokef entered the governor's office ahead of the crowd. He looked straight at the governor.

"By breaking our laws, he may not have broken yours but if he wants your job and your city and wants control over these Kittim soldiers, is that breaking your law?" Zokef asked.

The crowd around him began chanting, "King Hooba, King Hooba, King Hooba."

Throughout the entire city, the faint sound was heard, "Hooba, Hooba, Hooba."

Zokef touted, "He has brought about the death of two of your men. Soon, maybe it will be you."

The governor looked toward his commander: "Bring me this man who would be king!"

The commander asked, "How will I know this man?"

Akeldama chimed in, "Tomorrow night, I will have on a red scarf. I will embrace this man who would be king."

The entire group left the governor's office.

Akeldama spoke to Zokef. "Soon, your coffers will be full."

Zokef pulled a small pouch of coins from his cloak and tossed it to Akeldama.

"Just make certain this happens," Zokef demanded.

As Akeldama and his men left the city they came across two more Kittim soldiers, killing them both and leaving them alongside the road.

When Akeldama returned to the camp, he went in search of Zelo and several of the radical followers to tell them what was happening within the city.

"Tomorrow is the day for Hooba to make a choice. He must raise his sword against the Kittims. If he does, I will follow him. My men will follow him. The people will follow him. Any other choice and the repercussions will be of his own doing," Akeldama announced.

Zelo looked shaken. His voice trembled as he said, "I will make one more plea to Hooba."

Chapter 39
Connivance

It was the Wednesday before the Sabbath. In fact, it was the week of Passover. Yohanan had gone into the city and purchased provisions for their feast.

Prior to the meal, Hooba once again heard the spirit of God, Isaiah, speak to him.

"Consider what's going on around you, Hooba. Go off and think about it."

While the women prepared the meal, Hooba found his brother Iakobas and Zelo to take a walk around the grounds.

There was much conversation between the three of them.

Then, Zelo told Hooba, "You see what is going on. You could lead these people. They are listening and following you. It is your choice if you want to save yourself from the disaster that is going to happen."

Zelo was insinuating to Hooba that he wanted him to lead the people in an uprising against the Kittims. Zelo then began to wander off.

Iakobas had been leaning against a tree and had already fallen asleep.

Hooba said to Zelo as he walked away, "My battle is not with the sword. My battle is in the heart. Zelo, in this case, I am afraid that you are the adversary."

A Kittim soldier saw Zelo and asked him while pointing to Hooba, "Do you know that man?"

Zelo answered, "No, I do not."

Zelo wandered off.

Hooba walked over and awakened his brother Iakobas from his slumber.

"I know you are in support of the uprising. I tried to explain to Zelo that this is not a war of swords but rather of faith of the people and I know you understand that, Iakobas. As my brother, if something happens, please speak for me," Hooba asked.

Iakobas responded, "My brother, I know your purpose is just the faith of the people."

Meanwhile, Zelo returned back to the other zealots including Akeldama.

Zelo said, "If all else fails, and Hooba won't lead us, maybe he can become a martyr to our cause."

Akeldama listened intently to Zelo then spoke, "If things get worse than this, *you* will be the man to identify Hooba when I tell you."

Thirty-eight of Hooba's closest friends and family attended their meal that night. Hooba stood and spoke.

He recited Psalms 23:2 through 23:6. He went to each of the thirty-eight present, individually. He took each one's hand into his own.

"Peace be with you," he said, while holding their hands.

Upon reaching Zelo, Hooba whispered in his ear: "Do not disappoint me, Zelo."

Once reaching Akeldama, he whispered, "On your day of atonement, I hope you do not have to explain the blood on your hands."

Hooba broke the bread and passed it to all in front of him. Then he spoke.

"This bread represents our freedom; the promise of God to Moses and to Abraham that we would be the chosen people; that we would bring God's kingdom and God's *law* to the people.

"I will not raise my sword. My God does not need to be defended. I will raise my voice and spread the good news. Holy of Holies, the name of God is in your heart. It is not behind the veil of The Temple in the city. Each of you is God's temple. And, as you provide a suitable, cleansed home for God in this world, God will provide a suitable home for you in Heaven."

Zelo leaned over to Akeldama and whispered, "Hooba has decided not to lead us, so, turn him in."

For one moment, Akeldama felt ashamed. He thought back to the words Hooba had whispered in his ear. Then, he thought back to all that had happened.

Akeldama's father-in-law had been a comfortable businessman. His land and business had been taken by the Kittims and then they murdered him. He remembered his wife crying at the loss of her father. Then, he remembered her complaining that they now had no money as she was accustomed to. Akeldama would have inherited the business. However, now it was gone. This only fueled his negative attitude toward the Kittims and their Emperor.

Before the meal was finished, Akeldama rose from the table.

Hooba spoke, "Akeldama, may God comfort you and bring you peace."

"Rabbi, I am leaving to go pray on the grounds. Come pray with me," Akeldama replied.

He walked off into the darkness. Once he was out of sight, he motioned to a small group of Kittim soldiers. Then, he stood in a small clearing waiting for Hooba to arrive.

Akeldama heard a voice from within speaking to him for the first time in his life: "What have you done?"

He fell to his knees. He began to weep. He started to pray. Then, he felt Hooba's hand on his shoulder.

The Kittim soldiers were soon upon them.

Akeldama yelled to Hooba, "Run!"

But Hooba did not run.

Akeldama spun around and pulled out his sword. One of the Kittim soldiers thrust a sword straight through Akeldama's chest. He fell to the ground as Hooba knelt beside him holding his head.

Hooba could see the panic in Akeldama's eyes.

"I forgive you," Hooba said as he reached to close Akeldama's eyes.

Then he began to recite Psalms 23:2 through 23:6.

The Kittim soldiers pulled Hooba to his feet. Yohanan ran from the darkness to Hooba's side.

"Yohanan, I trust you with all that I love," Hooba said.

Yohanan knew what he meant. He turned and ran back to Bachariko and Hooba's mother.

Hooba heard ***her*** scream as the soldiers dragged him away.

Chapter 40

Tribulation

Hooba was kicked, beaten and thrown into a small cell. He slowly pulled himself to his knees and started to pray. He thanked God for every blessing he had in his life. He thanked God for Bachariko, Esther, Delilah, Noam, Ruth, Susanna and young Ruth, Josephus, both the older and younger Iakobas's, Philippos, Hilleal, Yohanan and Jared.

He was still kneeling and praying when the cell door opened. His eyes were blurry and still filled with dried blood. Then, he smelled Bachariko and felt her warm hands as she washed his face and hair. Behind her stood Yohanan and Odious.

Odious passed him a jug of water and said, "Drink, Rabbi."

They removed his bloodied and dirty cloak and Odious offered him his own outer cloak. Hooba embraced Yohanan and thanked him. Yohanan touched the arm of Odious and the two stepped out of the room.

Hooba looked at Bachariko, "The sight of you is more beautiful than the angels in Heaven."

She kissed him and said, "One moment with you is worth a thousand moments."

He replied, "If only I had a rose but I give you my love."

"I cherish the love, more than the rose," she told Hooba.

Then, in silence, she held *Her Hooba* and he held *His Rose*.

From outside the room, they heard Odious say, "They must leave before any other guards come."

They kissed one last time.

Then, Odious led them all away from Hooba's cell.

Two additional Kittim soldiers appeared at the door of Hooba's cell.

Odious said, "Rabbi, do not struggle. It will only make this worse."

Hooba looked up at Odious and replied, "Thank you."

The other two soldiers led Hooba down a narrow hallway and into the governor's courtroom.

The governor looked at Hooba and thought to himself: "This pathetic little man would lead a nation?"

Hooba looked around in the brightness of the room. He saw his brother Iakobas and Yohanan. He saw Zokef and six scribes. He noticed the Kittim commander present and two other Kittim soldiers. No one else was present for his trial. As was the custom, women were not allowed in the courtroom.

Then the governor demanded aloud, "Read the charges!"

The commander read, "1. Conspiracy

2. Murder

3. Treason against the emperor."

The governor asked, "Who speaks against this man?"

Zokef spoke first. "This man claims to speak for God and the people. He claims he would be king. I am a man of God. He does not speak for God. It is a sham to control the people. Nothing but subterfuge … lies, garbage, conspiracy."

The governor asked again: "Who else speaks against this man?"

The commander came forth. He said, "I have witnessed the results of this man's actions. It has resulted in the death of the emperor's men."

"Who speaks *for* this man?" the governor asked.

Iakobas stood. "This man is my brother and my friend. The two statements you heard before are twisted. They speak nothing of the character and the love of this man."

The governor then spoke again. "I would expect his brother to speak for him."

Yohanan immediately rose up. "This man is not my brother, nor my relative yet I know him well. He is the most peaceful man I have ever met. He discourages war and violence. I have heard him say to give Caesar what is his. There is no conspiracy here or treason."

"Before I ask this man to defend himself, is there any other testimony?" the governor asked.

Odious walked into the center of the room from the hallway. "I have witnessed this man prevent death and support peace."

The commander stood up again in anger, "We would call Akeldama, the follower of this man if he were not dead. This man has caused the death of many Kittim soldiers. Akeldama did what this man said. When we went to detain this man who is on trial, Akeldama drew his sword to defend him. My men defended themselves or certainly they would be dead at the hand of Hooba."

The governor looked at Hooba and ordered, "Defend yourself, man who would be king!"

Hooba spoke, "It is *you* who call me king; my only king is God in Heaven. He is the king in my heart. We reap what we sow. I so underestimated hate. I was once asked, what could be the sins of a man who was born blind. My answer was the sins of his past. Why would I be a king? Look at the kings of our people; King Saul, King David and King Solomon. Each man failed. This is a lesson of the past. Certainly, there is no value in the spoils of war. Yet, it would easier to forgive King Saul if he had not judged himself and ended his own life. All judgment belongs to God. But today, it is you who brings judgment. What would I learn if I followed in the steps of Saul, David and Solomon? War has never served any purpose. The kingdom of God will come without a sword; only by the word."

The governor asked, "Then, who is responsible for the atrocities?"

Hooba replied, "It is the hate in man's heart."

"So, you take no responsibility for your actions?" the governor asked.

"No, I take full responsibility for my actions yet I only respect the judgment of God," Hooba submitted.

The governor asked, "Are you not a citizen of Caesar?"

Hooba replied, "I submit to the rule of Caesar in all earthly things except where the rule of God supersedes Caesar."

The governor inquired, "Do you have anything else to add?"

"I plead for mercy because of my wife and unborn child. The same mercy I would plead for you," Hooba stated.

"Is there any accuser who would plead for mercy?" The governor asked the courtroom.

None of the accusers spoke up.

"Is there any man present who would take this man's sentence?" he asked.

Yohanan tried to step forward. Iakobas held him back.

"Can you not see the love they have for this man?' yelled Odious.

His commander acted swiftly, lifting the butt of his sword and smashing it into Odious's helmeted head, knocking him to the ground.

"Do not speak, unless the governor speaks to you!" he demanded of Odious.

The governor asked, "Can any accuser speak to the valor of a lesser sentence?"

Again, the room stood silent.

The governor pleaded to the audience. "I could not simply flog him to near death and satisfy the accusers?"

Again, not one response.

The governor lowered his head.

"Under the authority of Caesar and his law, I condemn this man to death; to hang from a pole, to commence before noon tomorrow," his voice quivered.

The governor could not look up for there was a tear about to roll down his cheek.

The commander spoke up. "May I make a request? I recommend that Odious attend the execution."

Without raising his head, the governor answered, "So be it, commanded."

While the courtroom was clearing Zokef approached the governor. He knew that the normal way was to leave the hanging bodies to rot but the people would rebel against Hooba's body being left on the Sabbath. Zokef was laden with guilt. He did not want a reminder or to go against his own beliefs, he told himself.

"Sir, in all due respect, you want to avoid an uprising so you are getting rid of the cause of the uprising. However, carrying out this sentence past sunset tomorrow would be entering into the Sabbath. I am afraid it would stir the people." said Zokef.

The governor turned to the commander and ordered, "Send a man with Odious that will ensure his death by sundown."

Yohanan stood dejected. He thought of Hooba, his friend and rabbi. Then, he thought about his friend lying in a mass grave with paupers. He couldn't imagine the feelings of Noam and Bachariko having their beloved thrown into the Valley of Gehenna without the means to purchase a proper burial tomb.

Yohanan was aware that he had the means to purchase a burial tomb but he was also aware that he could only do so by standing in the presence of Zokef and asking to do so. Zokef had control and the authority to allow a tomb.

He shook with anger as he awaited an audience with Zokef.

His thoughts were, "I would rather sever his head than ask him respectfully!"

Yet, he took a deep breath when Zokef finally entered the room.

"With the utmost respect, I have a bag of gold and I beg a resting place for my friend," Yohanan stated.

Zokef responded, "He deserves no more than any other illegitimate king."

Yohanan threw a bag of gold at Zokef's feet and ordered, "Fill your coffers so you can do God's work!"

"Your request is granted," Zokef replied.

Under his breath as he exited the room, Yohanan said, "What a sham that I have to pay an illegitimate priest for a place of burial for a legitimate rabbi."

Yohanan then went to his warehouse. He selected twelve feet of his finest linen as a burial shroud, carefully folding it. Then, he went to find Noam to present it to her as he announced the verdict of Hooba's trial.

Chapter 41

Evanescent

*H*e stood in his cell alone. Then, he began to shiver and shake. Yes, he felt a chill but it was much more.

"What have I done?" Hooba yelled out.
"Was this not my purpose?"
"What of my wife and children?"
"What of my family and friends?"
"What of the people?"
"How could I have underestimated hate so much?"
"Was it my arrogance; did I think I could be king?"
"Did I think I could change the world?"
"I just wanted to bring the kingdom of God to the people."
"My God, my God, have I failed thee?"
He fell to his knees and began to cry.
Then he whispered, "Forgive me."
Hooba felt a pure white light encompass him. He felt warmth and comforted.
"Eli, Eli (*most high God*). Thank you for my blessings."
A guard at his door said to another guard, "Is he calling for the prophet Elijah?"
The other guard answered, "I think he is asking his God for mercy."
Then Hooba heard the spirit of God reciting Psalms 23:2 through 23:6. It calmed him as he fell into slumber.

The next morning, Odious ran into Hooba's cell.

He said, "Rabbi, drink this water. The day will become long and you will be parched. Save all you have, so that you can speak to those you love."

Soon, four more guards appeared at the door. They tied his hands and placed a rope around his neck. Hooba did not struggle. They led him down the streets of the city like a dog with the rope around his neck and barefooted.

People were watching and leaning out of windows. Women were crying. Hooba saw Zelo standing in the shadows of an alley. Twenty Kittim guards walked up and down the streets pushing people away.

A small boy ran out from the crowd.

"Rabbi, Rabbi, you fed me and my mother when I was hungry," he cried.

One of the Kittim soldiers backhanded the boy.

Hooba fought back and picked the little boy up off the ground. The soldiers pulled him right off his feet and dragged him on the ground. Odious stopped them, helping him to his feet.

Bachariko, Noam, Ruth, Susanna, young Ruth and Delilah appeared and walked directly behind Hooba. They sang as they followed him. Then came Beatrice, Joanna and Rebecca. Other women of the community joined in and followed.

Philippos ran out from the crowd. He removed his own sandals and quickly tied them onto Hooba's feet. Yohanan and both the younger and older Iakobas fell into procession with the women. Josephus and Aramis followed suit.

Hilleal appeared from within the crowd. He walked right next to Hooba. When the guards suspiciously looked at him, he spoke.

"I represent the men who raised him; they cannot be present but would be proud to walk where I am."

Over Hilleal's shoulder was a leather pouch embossed with the letter J, for Jared.

As they approached the hill of stone, Hooba turned. Bachariko ran to him. She reached for his hands that were bound together. Their hands touched for just a moment before the guards pulled them apart.

He was led into the pit. Odious gave him a small piece of leather wrapped in cloth. He began to speak to Hooba but Hooba silenced him.

"Thank you," Hooba said, then placed the leather between his teeth.

He was laid down on a pole, his hands tied above his head. Two guards held his feet. Odious looked directly into his eyes and Hooba stared back. A third guard drew up a mallet and drove a six-inch nail through both of Hooba's feet and into the pole. Tears ran down the cheeks of both Hooba's and Odious's eyes.

The guards thrust the pole up into the air. Hooba gasped as the weight of his body pulled on his shoulders.

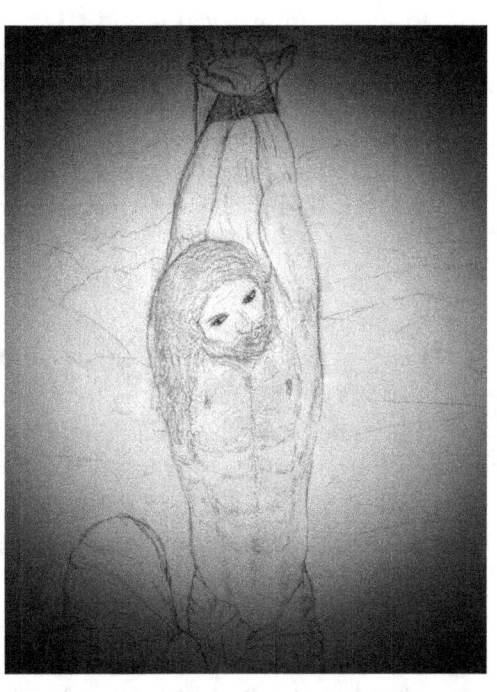

The guard who had been ordered to ensure Hooba's death before sunset, drew his sword and thrust it up under Hooba's rib cage. Blood gushed out from the gash. Hooba shuddered in pain.

He struggled to gain his breath, trying to hold part of his weight up with his nailed feet.

Hooba looked at all of his family and friends, one by one. After each one caught his gaze, they fell to their knees in tears.

Finally, while looking into the eyes of Bachariko, she did not kneel. She held his gaze in hers.

Josephus came forward and took Bachariko's hand. As the hours passed, Susanna took Bachariko's hand, then Hilleal took Susanna's hand until each and every one of them were holding one another's hands.

Hooba tried to speak. But his lips were so dry. Josephus removed a bottle of wine from the leather embossed pouch. He soaked a sponge with the wine. Odious offered his sword to lift the sponge to Hooba's mouth.

Josephus, lifting it to Hooba's mouth, said, "Drink all you can, Rabbi."

Within moments it appeared that Hooba's agony lessened. He had the strength to speak.

He looked at Bachariko and simply murmured, "I love you."

A tear rolled down Bachariko's cheek. She saw the pain in his face. She prayed.

"My God, my God, end his suffering."

She watched as his left shoulder dislocated. He was gasping for breath. Blood dripped from his feet. She watched as he used every strength to pull himself up by his right arm against the rope.

Then she thought to herself: "I will teach Esther all about her father."

Josephus emphatically said, "Drink more wine, Hooba!"

Hooba gasped once more, then screamed in pain. He summoned his last strength.

Hooba began reciting Psalms 23:2 through 23:6. His vision became blurred. He was mumbling the words. All the others were chanting along with him. He heavenly gasped and his body went limp. His agony had ended.

At that moment, Bachariko screamed. Then, she felt the baby move inside her.

Josephus announced, "This man has died!"

Odious confirmed, "This man is a physician."

Then, he pried the stake from Hooba's feet. He cut the rope above his hands and caught his lifeless body as it fell toward the ground.

Hilleal and Yohanan carried the body to the cart for transport to the tomb. Bachariko stood motionless and in shock. Then, Susanna's and Hooba's grandfather took Bachariko's hand and led her toward the cart.

Odious turned to the guards and said, "I will secure the tomb until tomorrow. Back off and let this family grieve."

Josephus jumped into the cart with the lifeless body of Hooba with the energy of a much younger man. While the crowd watched, he anointed Hooba's head with oil.

The younger Iakobas was in control of the donkey and cart as it drove off. Bachariko had not yet reached the cart with Aramis.

Josephus ordered, "Drive the cart now! Do not wait!"

And the farther they got from the city, Josephus pulled out a crudely shaped funnel passing it down Hooba's throat. He began forcing water down the tube and funnel; alternating filling his stomach, then throwing his weight on Hooba to expel the liquid from his stomach. Josephus continued this routine for the next many minutes until they reached the site of the tomb. Part of the family had followed along behind the cart including Hilleal, Susanna and Joanna. Aramis and Bachariko were slowly walking much further behind.

Yohanan had led the remainder of their group back into the city. He, along with Philippos, announced the death of Hooba to his followers. Then all returned to the camp outside the city walls. Shortly before sunset, Zelo stood up to pray for Hooba's fallen soul.

It was the elder Iakobas who, at that same time, stood up and said, "Do not challenge me the right to pray at this my brother's death."

Zelo remained standing but did not speak.

Josephus yelled to Iakobas, "Faster!!!"

Iakobas turned around to look back into the cart. He saw Hooba's hands starting to contract. He had no experience with death. He saw Josephus placing pressure on Hooba's abdomen as fluid spewed from his mouth.

He thought, "Josephus, why do you desecrate the dead?"

Young Iakobas nearly ran off the road when Hooba's back arched up and air was drawn into his chest.

He thought again to himself, "What witchcraft is this?"

Josephus yelled once more, "Watch the road. He just may live!"

Iakobas's eyes were wide open in both panic and fear. He hurried the donkey onward.

Approaching the tomb, Hilleal was running to catch up to the cart.

Josephus yelled to him, "He is alive!"

Hilleal scooped him up without help and carried him into the tomb.

Hilleal yelled to Iakobas, "Guard the entrance to the tomb! Let no one enter!"

Josephus called out, "I need the women."

Joanna and Susanna arrived first. Josephus had Joanna pack Hooba's abdominal wound created by the soldier's sword. He ordered Susanna to wrap his feet and legs as tightly as possible up to his torso to force fluids and blood to his vital organs.

Susanna leaned forward and watched Hooba's chest rise and fall. Then she watched, hoping it would rise again. She waited. His chest again rose and fell.

The packing in his abdomen was soon soaked with blood. Josephus yelled to Iakobas, "Get Bachariko too!"
Aramis escorted Bachariko into the tomb.
She stood there, horrified.

Her grandfather ordered her, "Remove your scarf, pack it into the abdominal wound then push and hold it with all your might!"

"Joanna … help Susanna finish wrapping the legs!" Josephus ordered.

When Joanna was finished she stood at the entrance of the tomb with Iakobas, watching for anyone.

Odious approached the tomb. Iakobas reached for his sword but Joanna stopped his arm to prevent him from lifting his sword. Joanna stepped forward.

"Please allow the family to grieve," she stated.

Josephus watched Hooba. His breaths were occurring more frequently and deeper. Josephus removed his own head covering and tied the bolster around Hooba's waist. He could find no more active bleeding.

The tomb was completely silent at that moment.

The smallest moan was then heard.

Josephus thought, "The opium is wearing off. He will have so much pain."

Hooba's body started to shiver. It was Susanna's and Hooba's grandfather who placed his cloak over Hooba's body. His body began to convulse.

Josephus thought, "My God, my God, do not make her watch him die twice."

He pulled out a small pipe. He lit the pipe and took deep breaths of the opium into his own lungs. Then he slowly blew it across Hooba's face. The convulsions stopped.

Every few seconds, Josephus blew another small amount of smoke toward Hooba's face. Then, Josephus noticed Hooba's dislocated shoulder. He placed his foot in Hooba's armpit and pulled for all his might. The shoulder popped and Hooba's eyes opened widely!

Hooba looked right into Bachariko's eyes.

He thought, "Do not stop looking for I am still here. I do not want to miss one moment of this life with you."

Then, she touched his face and said, "I love you too."

Hooba thought to himself, "Good, she heard me. It is getting dark. This must be what it is like to die."

Hooba thought he was talking to himself when he heard his words, "God is good. He has given me one more glimpse of your beauty."

But he had spoken these words aloud.

Bachariko leaned over and kissed his cheek.

He again spoke aloud without his knowledge, "I can even smell her hair."

He attempted to reach for his *Rose* but moaned with pain.

"I hurt. I am not dead," he realized to himself.

"Bachariko?" he called.

Then he heard her answer him, "Yes, my Hooba?"

It all went dark once more for Hooba.

Josephus leaned forward and said, "It is up to God now. He will be in and out of awareness."

All of the women were staring at their bloodied hands, Josephus noticed.

Hooba asked, "Bachariko, are you still here?"

Bachariko replied, "Yes, Hooba."

She thought a smile came across his lips.

Hilleal looked up for the first time. Everyone was just staring at Hooba including Odious who was now standing in the entrance of the tomb.

Hilleal yelled, "Iakobas, detain the guard!"

Odious's jaw dropped open when Hooba spoke, "Do not harm him. He is my friend."

Odious then said to all of them, "His God must be very powerful. He has raised him from the dead."

"I am so thirsty," Hooba said.

Odious passed in his jug of water. Bachariko held his head as he drank from the jug.

"Can he be moved? There will be new guard here tomorrow. No man deserves to die twice. Certainly not this man," Odious stated.

The sun had set. It was now the Sabbath.

Josephus answered Odious, "I would prefer not to move him but if we must, we must."

Hilleal, Iakobas, Odious and Josephus carried Hooba to the cart. He moaned softly. Bachariko climbed into the cart and laid next to him. Josephus and Aramis also climbed into the cart.

Young Iakobas began steering the cart toward the east. Hilleal looked at Odious.

"Will you come with us? We are heading north. Then there will be at least two tracks to follow," Hilleal pleaded.

Odious removed his helmet to reveal a large, bruised area on his head.

He said, "I must stay."

Hilleal asked, "What will you tell them?"

"That I only remember being hit in the head. No one would believe it if I told them the truth anyway," he responded.

Susanna, with haste, picked up the scraps of dressings and looked back to the place where Hooba had laid. It was stained with blood. She looked at the shroud that been laid on top of Hooba's body and carefully lifted it up, folded it and placed it where Hooba's body had been.

Hilleal headed north with Susanna and Joanna while the cart headed east. Odious followed the cart for the next two miles, dragging brush back and forth across the road, covering the tracks. He then returned to the tomb, took out his sword and pried the large stone until it crossed the opening of the entrance.

The next morning which was the Sabbath, two Kittim guards arrived at the tomb. They found a dazed Odious without his helmet, sitting in front of the stone that crossed the opening to the crypt.

One guard inquired, "Odious, why do you not stand guard?"

"I do not know. The last thing I remember was the stone being rolled across the entrance," Odious replied.

That same guard asked, "Is your mind with you?"

Odious answered, "I believe my mind is solid. I just need rest."

Odious placed his helmet on his head, mounted his horse and headed back to his barracks.

Noam awakened on that Sabbath day beside herself with grief. The older Ruth sat with her. She began to wail.

"I should be attending the body of my son," she cried.

The older Ruth said, "It is the Sabbath and your son would want you to rest."

There was much commotion in the camp that morning. Noam believed she heard preaching. One end of the camp stood the older Iakobas preaching peace and forgiveness.

Noam thought she heard Iakobas say, "I am preaching in my brother's name."

The other end of the camp stood Zelo. Noam could also hear his words.

"I am but a simple fisherman who followed my master. I have learned that I am to be a *fisher* of men," he shouted.

Yohanan stepped into Noam's tent at that moment.

He spoke to Hooba's mother, "I beg your forgiveness in this time of your grief but the two fools are prophesizing a new world order."

Noam responded, "Yohanan, I must visit my son."

He replied, "Mother of Hooba, it is the Sabbath and with all due respect, your son is no longer there. Tomorrow, I will take you to your son's tomb."

Noam said, "Then take me to my daughter Bachariko."

"Noam, I do not know where she is. I pray she is safe," Yohanan answered.

Delilah entered the tent just then holding the hand of young Ruth. They fell at Noam's feet and began sobbing.

Yohanan thought to himself: "These women are my responsibility. I promised Hooba."

He said to the women, "Tomorrow we will visit the tomb and today you should just pray."

Yohanan sat outside of their tent until sunset when he gathered and brought them food. In Hooba's name he would protect and care for them through their grief.

He noticed a single man slowly walking through the camp. His head was covered and bowed low to disguise himself. The man paused but one moment in front of Noam's tent.

He said to Yohanan, "Ask no questions. Bring the women to the city within the walls. Tell no one. First, head north."

Yohanan did not speak but had recognized the voice of Hilleal. He was relieved knowing that Hilleal probably knew the whereabouts of Bachariko and the others.

It was morning. Yohanan led the small group of women to the tomb. Upon arrival, they found Zelo and his men at the tomb. He was arguing with the guards. As Noam approached, Zelo called out.

"This is his mother. Let us roll back the stone so she can pay her respects!" he ordered.

Because the guards were obviously outnumbered, they did as was asked and rolled the stone from the opening.

Noam entered the tomb alone, finding it empty. Then, she noticed the shroud carefully folded.

She thought, "Certainly, a woman has folded this shroud."

Noam exited the tomb and said, "The tomb is empty."

Yohanan helped her back into the cart with the other women.

Zelo yelled at the guards, "What have you done with the body of my master?"

The two guards spoke, "The stone was in place at the time we arrived at our post."

They pointed and accused, "Maybe it was you men who stole the body!"

The men with Zelo had previously been followers of Akeldama. Swords were drawn and the Kittim guards were threatened.

Yohanan said, "I will be heading north, possibly to the city by the sea. I am looking for the mothers of these children."

Yohanan hurried the cart away from the tomb. They departed to the screams of the two Kittim soldiers being killed by Zelo's men.

Zelo's men threw the soldiers into the tomb, rolled the stone back over the opening and headed back to the encampment outside the city of The Temple. Zelo's head was spinning as they traveled.

They first passed a man while en route.

The man asked, "Zelo, do you not recognize me? I am traveling to the tomb of Hooba."

This man had also been following Hooba and was camped outside the city of The Temple.

Zelo answered, "No, I do not recognize you! Turn back; the tomb is empty."

When Zelo returned to the camp, he shared part of the story with those who were waiting.

He explained, "I arrived at the tomb and the mother of Hooba said that he was no longer there; that he had left the tomb. Then, a man approached me and asked why I did not recognize him."

He continued, "I now know this man was our master and through the power of God, he has overcome death!"

One of the men said, "Zelo, I know you were close to the rabbi yet I find it hard to believe. Until I place my hand in his side where he was cut open, I cannot trust what you say."

Zelo yelled, "Shame on all you doubters! Blessed will be those who have not seen and still believe. Theirs' will be the kingdom of Heaven on Earth."

The elder Iakobas asked, "Why has my brother not appeared to me?"

Zelo answered, "Because it is upon my testimony that this church will be built."

Yohanan hurried the donkey with the cart as fast as he could. He began to whip the back of the donkey in his panic.

Young Ruth reached forward to Yohanan and said, "Hooba would not like that. Where are my mother and father?"

"I spoke with your father and I am taking you home," he replied.

Yohanan did not whip the donkey again.

"What is happening? Please tell me!" Noam demanded.

Yohanan answered, "I promised to protect those Hooba loved. We are going to the city within the walls and I know nothing else."

"Then, why are we traveling north?" She asked.

"Because I want no one to know where we are truly heading," he admitted.

Delilah asked, "Where is *my* mother?"

Yohanan replied, "I do not know. I do not know anything."

Then Noam asked, "Where is the body of my son?"

Again, Yohanan had to respond, "I do not know."

Chapter 42

Shrouded

Bachariko clung to Hooba's body. He passed through moments of awake with pain and asleep in absence. Each time a wheel hit a rut, he moaned; yet, she held on all the tighter.

Josephus would yell out to the younger Iakobas, "Can you not drive this any more careful?"

Iakobas admitted, "I cannot see the road."

Within moments, the moon rose up over the horizon lighting the valley in front of them. They could see a small stream.

Josephus ordered, "Stop! We must get him fresh water."

Once they stopped, Josephus made Hooba drink the water. Then, he lit a pipe and blew the smoke over Hooba's face once more. Hooba drifted off into sleep.

"Iakobas, keep traveling while we have some light," Josephus said.

Aramis got into the front of the cart with his grandson, the younger Iakobas.

Iakobas looked at his grandfather and asked, "What has just happened?"

"It is a miracle, son," he answered.

Aramis did not give the details to his grandson at that moment. He chose to keep secret about the words Josephus had revealed to him. He knew something had transpired but was not understanding of what had happened.

Josephus had told him, "I have an idea. I can relieve Hooba's pain while he hangs on the pole. It will ease his suffering."

What Aramis did not know was that when Hooba slumped and all believed him to have died, Josephus was aware there was still a shallow breath. It was his moment to act. He could declare Hooba dead then cut him down and hope to revive him.

Meanwhile, as Aramis talked with Iakobas, Josephus seated in the back of the cart still feared for the death of Hooba. He was still concerned that Azrael the Angel of Death would appear.

In the moonlight, Josephus could see that Hooba's feet were dark. He began unwrapping the tight cloths Joanna and Susanna had woven around his legs. The color returned to his feet. However, Hooba could not be awakened. Josephus waited a few moments then began rewrapping the legs.

Josephus repeated this routine every hour. He would wrap the legs, awaken Hooba and force water into him, then unwrap the legs once again causing Hooba to drift back into unconsciousness. While he was unconscious, Josephus washed the wound in his abdomen with wine.

The sun rose and fell and still they traveled. It had been nearly forty hours since they left the tomb.

Aramis reached back, touching Josephus. "You are not a young man. We must stop and rest. Even young Iakobas is past the point of exhaustion. The donkey cannot go on."

Bachariko and Hooba remained laying in the cart once they stopped. Iakobas fed and watered the donkey. Josephus and Aramis both passed into slumber under the stars. Iakobas slept for nearly three hours then he woke and fed and watered the donkey again.

Then, he awakened Josephus and Aramis.

He asked the two older men: "Do you think you can walk? I am going to lead the donkey as he cannot carry all of us."

Josephus thought to himself, "I am so sore, I do not know if I can move." "Yes, I can walk," he said aloud.

Aramis agreed.

Every two hours they stopped. They fed and watered the donkey, unwrapped and rewrapped Hooba's legs. Soon Josephus noticed that Iakobas and Aramis were both pulling the cart with the donkey.

During one stop, the donkey went over and peered into the cart nuzzling Hooba.

Hooba responded in all his delirium, "Naomi, is it you?"

"Mother, are you there?" Hooba asked.

Bachariko answered, "No Hooba, your mother is not here."

"Isaiah, you sound just like Bachariko," Hooba said.

"It is me, Hooba," Bachariko soothed.

"My *Rose* ..." he whispered.

Then, as if talking to himself, he continued, "My *Rose* is so beautiful. I can see her red hair flowing.

"Bachariko, I lived for the look in your eyes. Did I tell you that I love you?" he spoke with eyes closed.

"Rest, Hooba. I love you too," she replied.

Very soon the donkey was tied to the front of the cart and they were once again on their way.

Hooba spoke up, "Bachariko, I can smell the salt of the sea. Tell Jared I love him and that I wasn't scared."

She shushed him, "You wait and tell him yourself."

Hooba laid there with Bachariko's arms wrapped around him and within his arms was a leather pouch embossed with a letter J.

The sun was once more starting to set. Jared broke bread with the men of his community. They all recited Psalms 23:2 through 23:6.

Yohanan was breaking bread and passing it to the women while they camped. He was also reciting Psalms. 23:2 through 23:6.

Meanwhile, Hilleal passed bread to Joanna and Susanna and recited Psalms 23:2 through 23:6 while they rested at camp.

Young Iakobas still drove on in the dark, reciting Psalms 23:2 through 23:6. He could see the community and the walls.

Chapter 43
The Lost Sheep

When the meal was finished, Jared walked the walls as he always had. He looked north, east, south and then west from the gate.

He saw two men and a donkey pulling a cart. Another man walked behind the cart.

Jared carried a torch in his hand. Iakobas could see a man standing with a torch.

Iakobas yelled, "Open the gates! Our Rabbi Hooba requests entry to the city."

Jared wondered if he had heard correctly. He replayed it in his mind.

"Identify yourself!" Jared yelled out.

Iakobas recognized Jared's voice. He yelled again.

"It is Iakobas and I have Hooba."

Jared's head was spinning as he jumped down off the wall. He rang a bell. Men came running. The gates were pulled open.

Jared ran to the cart. He saw in the back of the cart a red-haired woman holding Hooba in her arms. Hooba was bruised and covered in blood. Jared gathered his strength.

"Hooba?" he called.

Hooba's eyes opened, "Rabbi, brother, friend. I believe this pouch is yours. It has probably weathered better than I. I have missed you."

Jared scooped the frail and beaten man into his arms carrying him inside the gates and into the Great Hall. Some of the men began throwing their cloaks on the floor as bedding.

Bread, date-fruit and water were brought to them.

Hooba asked Jared, "Help me to my knees. It has been a long time since I prayed at the altar of the Lord."

Soon, two hundred men were kneeled next to Hooba. Jared looked as the red-headed woman kneeled next to Hooba. It was not ordinary for a woman to be inside the walls let alone kneeling in the Great Hall with the men.

Hooba smiled at his friend saying, "Jared, this is my wife, Bachariko and my daughter Esther."

Bachariko reached out and touched Jared's face. He blushed.

She looked into Jared's eyes and said, "Thank you."

Jared looked back and replied, "Thank you."

Bachariko was thanking Jared for helping to raise the good man Hooba had become.

Jared was thanking Bachariko for loving and caring for his friend, Hooba.

Hooba was thanking God for everything.

Josephus asked for water and bandages. It was again time to rewrap Hooba's legs, force water and cleanse his wound.

Josephus also asked Jared for clay. Then, he instructed Bachariko and Jared to each take the hands of Hooba. He once more wrapped Hooba's feet and legs tightly. Then molded each of Hooba's feet back into place. He packed the clay into the wrapping of his feet to hold the position and bones in place.

Hooba grimaced in pain.

Then he asked, "May I have some dates?"

This was a sign Hooba was healing.

Bachariko smiled widely in hope.

Next, Josephus flushed Hooba's abdominal wound with water. One of the men of the community handed Josephus a needle and twine. Josephus passed the needle through Hooba's skin four times pulling it closed then tying a knot.

Josephus asked Jared if he could borrow the leather pouch for another moment. He pulled from the pouch dried garlic and turmeric, giving it to Hooba to swallow.

Hooba admitted to Jared, "I must rest."

Jared stood up and ordered, "Clear the hall! Find rooms for these men."

Josephus lit his opium pipe and blew the smoke over Hooba's face again. Hooba drifted off to sleep.

Jared turned to Bachariko and said, "I will be just outside the front door. Make yourself and your husband comfortable."

Jared sat on the front steps of the Great Hall. The younger Iakobas joined Jared on the steps and also sat down. He shared with Jared the story of thousands of followers who came to listen to Hooba and how they had traveled all over the country sharing a message of love. He explained how the Kittim soldiers had come and dragged Hooba off. He explained how Hooba had been hanged on a pole to die by the Kittims.

Iakobas started to tell the story of the escape from the tomb when he fell into slumber, head held on Jared's lap. He had slept only three hours in over three days.

Jared cradled his head in his lap and pondered.

As the sun started to rise Jared noticed that the gates were still wide open. He could see a single young man running toward the gates. The young man ran through the gates without wearing sandals. His feet were raw and bloodied.

He reached the middle of the courtyard and fell to his knees. Jared ran over to the young man.

Philippos declared, "He is risen from the dead!"

Jared scooped up the collapsed young man and carried him into the Great Hall. Iakobas rose and followed him in.

Jared placed him onto a pile of the cloaks and turned to Iakobas. "Do you know this boy?" he asked.

"Yes, he is Philippos, chosen by Hooba," Iakobas answered.

They heard Hooba speak in that moment, "I do not know if I have the official station but I recommend this boy as a member of the community within the walls."

Jared snickered, "I think rising from the dead gives you enough station!"

Jared stood in the center of the courtyard looking directly up into the sky.

"I thought he was to be the great teacher. They tried to make him king. And, now they think he has power over death."

Then he heard the voice of Susanna yelling his name. She ran across the courtyard and threw her arms around his neck. She was talking as fast as she could, trying to explain to Jared what had happened. Joanna and Hilleal walked through the gates behind her.

"We don't know where Hooba is or how he is doing," she continued.

Jared shushed her, "He is fine. He is behind these doors."

Susanna, Hilleal and Joanna hurriedly entered the Great Hall.

Within just a few minutes, Jared could see another cart coming toward the gate. He stood and waited knowing it must be related to Hooba.

Jared watched as Yohanan drove the cart into the courtyard. He saw his own mother in the cart with Noam, and two young girls. He recognized young Ruth as one of them.

His mother immediately began talking, "Hilleal your brother and his wife are missing. Hooba was killed and someone has stolen his body from the tomb!"

Jared immediately turned to young Ruth and said, "Your mother and father are fine."

Then he turned to Noam and said, "Mother, your son has not been stolen and he has not died."

Yohanan caught Noam as she fainted, nearly falling to the ground. Yohanan looked questioningly at Jared.

Jared said, "Follow me."

He opened the doors to the Great Hall. As they entered, there was Hooba seated on a bench talking and listening to everyone. Noam ran to him as did Delilah. Young Ruth ran to her mother and father. Yohanan waited patiently to speak to Hooba while listening to parts of the story everywhere in the room.

Finally, the time arrived for Yohanan to approach Hooba. He stepped forward.

Hooba said with a laugh, "Yohanan, forgive me if I do not stand to embrace you."

Yohanan said, "Peace be with you, brother."

Hooba replied, "Thank you, brother. All that I love is present."

Hooba looked at Jared and said, "Jared, do you think I could get some fresh air?"

Jared leaned over and lifted Hooba right off the bench and down the steps to the open air.

And as he carried him, he chuckled, "Hooba, you've caused quite a stir."

The business of the day had already begun. People were coming and going through the courtyard. Two of the brothers from inside the walls had carried over a bench for Hooba to sit. Small children had already gathered and listened as he told stories.

Hooba told the story of a young little lamb who had wandered far from his home. The lamb had faced wolves and danger but had survived to return home and how the shepherd had rejoiced at the homecoming of the lost lamb.

Then he leaned forward and said, "God is a lot like that shepherd."

Little Ruth ran over and sat on Hooba's lap.

He moaned a bit in discomfort but when she touched his face and said, "We are glad you are home, Hooba," he simply blushed.

Chapter 44
Ameliorate

Over the next few days, bits and pieces of the story were added together. Some of the most valuable parts of the story came from Philippos.

Every time the part of the story arose that *he* had risen from the dead, Hooba shook his head in disbelief.

Then he thought, "If Philippos can find me, Bachariko, Esther, Delilah and my mother are not safe."

The following day, the men of the community within the walls were busy at work, guided by Jared. A wooden chair was crafted with two long poles to help lift Hooba and transport him from place to place. It would be another eight weeks before Hooba would be able to walk again.

That same day, Jared walked through the gates of the community and over to a large tree. With one swing of his sword, he struck the tree removing the largest limb. Jared carved the limb with an intentional curve and handle for Hooba to use along with his other staff.

Then Jared found a spot within the courtyard where he sat for the next two hours, intricately carving a small rose into the end of the new staff. He went to find Hooba who was talking with Delilah. As he approached he heard part of their conversation.

"Delilah, even though you are young, you will soon reach maturity. I need your help. I must send your mother away until I know it is safe for her to stay here. She will not want to go. Your mother is with child and she will need your help. I will be sending my mother and the elder Ruth away also," Hooba explained.

Jared spoke, "Rabbi, while your *Rose* is away, you will learn to walk again. I have created this *rose* for you to lean on."

Hooba said to Delilah, "Can you bring your mother to me?"

Delilah ran off to find her mother. Hooba turned to Jared and spoke.

"Jared, I have arranged for Yohanan to take my mother and the elder Ruth to care for them. He is also preparing for passage on a boat for Bachariko and Delilah from the port close to Damascus. They will head north to a land that is safe. Jared, I need you on that boat with them."

Hooba then smiled, "I know you do not find travel by boat comforting. However, I do know you will be discreet."

"I will do my best to stomach the trip," Jared replied.

Hooba explained that Yohanan would be leaving to take his mother and the elder Ruth to a safe place. He would then return and travel to the port close to Damascus with Bachariko and Delilah and wait for Jared to arrive to accompany them.

Hooba continued, "At the port, you will find a flamboyant young man dressed in a coat of many colors. This is my brother of whom I have never met. I only know him through what my mother has told me. You will book passage with my brother. Yohanan has connections at the port. He will introduce you to a dear friend called Massa who works near the port. Bachariko and Delilah already know Massa. Massa will be the connection at the port back to us. No one else knows this plan."

Hooba handed Jared a small bag of gold and silver coins in a small alabaster jar. Jared placed the jar in his leather pouch.

Jared looked at Hooba and said, "I will make sure they arrive at their destination."

"My friend, I expect to see you walking when I return!" Jared ordered.

Jared went to seek Hilleal and Susanna.

Jared found Hilleal at his home outside the walls. He gave instructions to his brother.

"I will not tell you the details. Tomorrow, take Hooba to the caves until I return. You must help him recover. Take Josephus, Aramis, young

Iakobas and Philippos. Men from within the walls will come daily. Hooba will teach and the men shall write his words. Take all of our scrolls and make copies before hiding them. Hilleal, you must preserve *The Law*."

Hilleal nodded and said, "It will be so."

Delilah returned to Hooba with Bachariko. Raised voices could be heard. Yet, at the end, the loudest voice was Hooba's.

That night, they all broke bread together. Yet there was no conversation occurring at the table.

Shortly after sunset, a single, hooded figure left on foot with a leather pouch on his shoulder. Not long afterward, Yohanan left in a cart with four women.

Chapter 45
Flee

Jared walked nearly sixteen hours a day until he reached the coast of the sea. He followed the coast to Kfar Nahum.

Jared kept his head covered and spoke to no one. He did, however, stop to listen to a man preaching on the beach. This man stood on the rock that was once Hooba's.

There were four hundred men standing and listening. What Jared heard was part of Zelo's speech.

"He has power over death. Certainly, he will have power over the Kittims. He will return us to a great nation under our God. I saw him risen. He told me to come here to the north where he would meet me. There were those with me who doubted but they also saw him. He commanded that I come to his rock to build his church and army. This way, we will be prepared as God returns his kingdom on Earth to us."

In the morning, Jared ritually bathed in the sea then headed farther north to the port near Damascus.

Once arriving at the port, Jared inquired about a man called Massa. Massa introduced Jared to the man with the red coat of colors.

During the meeting with the two men, Jared showed both men the alabaster jar.

"If you see this jar in the hands of another, word must be sent to me at the community within the walls," Jared empathetically explained.

He then purchased passage and hid in the hull of the boat.

Yohanan and the four women had headed south by cart. They stopped at an oasis called David Stream where Yohanan's daughter and husband now lived. He considered this a safe place away from the city of The Temple.

Yohanan gathered provisions from the ample garden of his daughter and son-in-law and once again began the journey with Bachariko and Delilah to the port.

They traveled north along the sea and sought shelter in the former home of Bachariko's grandfather in the area which was still unoccupied.

The road from there and north to Kfar Nahum was well traveled. They passed many travelers along the road but Yohanan purposely did not stop for fear of being recognized. Unfortunately, however, they were, indeed, recognized. A man recognized the woman with the cinnamon-red hair.

He told Zelo later that day he had seen a man, a young woman and the woman with the cinnamon-red hair heading north.

Zelo, thinking the man was Hooba, decided to tell the man that the woman with the red hair was never close to Hooba.

"She was nothing but a mere prostitute that Hooba showed pity on along with her illegitimate daughter," Zelo lied.

"If it was, indeed, her and she was fleeing north, it is so not to be associated with Hooba and she flees to protect herself," he went on.

Zelo went off to find the Kittim guards.

He told the guards: "The wife of the man you called Hooba was seen heading north from Kfar Nahum."

"Weren't you associated with Hooba?" one guard asked.

For the third time, Zelo responded, "I do not know the man."

A few miles before reaching the port, they came upon three homes and a garden. While passing these homes a larger, covered cart pulled by four horses came out from between the homes.

A man Yohanan long recognized yelled, "Peace be with you!"

"Peace be with you, Massa," Yohanan replied back.

"Tie up your cart and donkey. The last bit of your travel will be faster. The boat departs within hours," Massa instructed.

Yohanan strutted down the dock with the women's meager belongings. Bachariko and Delilah followed behind then boarded the ship with him. The man with the red coat who was the captain of the boat greeted him.

"Everything else is in order on the boat," Jude stated.

Yohanan replied, "This cargo is precious."

Jude responded, "I am aware."

Massa called to them desperately from the deck: "Yohanan, the port is filled with Kittim soldiers."

Jude dropped a small boat over the bow of the ship.

He said, "Brother, row to the ship sitting out in the water. It is soon departing to the port near the city of The Temple."

Yohanan jumped into the boat and rowed toward the outer ship. The sails of Jude's ship filled with air as it exited the dock. Their ship passed Yohanan's small boat.

He smiled back as they all waved from the deck. He looked back at the shore as two Kittim soldiers dragged Massa away.

For a moment, Yohanan considered turning the rowboat around.

But he thought, "What can I do?"

What Yohanan could not see was a young man on horseback charging straight toward the Kittim soldiers. The soldiers let go of Massa running in all directions as Philippos pulled him onto the horse and fled.

Hooba had asked Philippos to follow Yohanan and the women without their knowledge; this was to secure their destination and safety.

As Philippos and Massa, along with their horse, outran the Kittim soldiers on foot, Philippos screamed, "Massa, which direction should I go?"

"Head east. I know the road to Damascus well," Massa answered.

Yohanan returned by boat then made his way on foot to the community within the walls. He reported to Hooba that the women were safe and headed north to the area of Gallia. He also told Hooba of Massa being detained.

Hooba feared for his friend and for Philippos as he had not yet returned.

His thoughts were, "They think I am dead, yet hate is still costing men's lives."

Hooba crawled across the floor of the cave to a secluded corner and wept.

He thought, "They are safe but I may never see *her* again."

Young Ruth saw Hooba crying. She sat with him, holding his hand.

Weeks passed. Two men on horseback arrived. Hooba could only hear yelling coming from who he believed was Philippos.

"I am delivering a friend," Philippos yelled.

By this time, Hooba could still not walk but he could pull himself into a standing position. He stood in the entrance of the cave smiling at young Philippos.

Chapter 46
The Vessel

Delilah usually remained at Bachariko's side as her mother was frequently nauseated during the sea travel. Delilah herself was not particularly fond of the rocking of the boat or the rough sea waters.

In the evenings, Delilah would venture outside the quarters to hang her head over the side of the boat. Each time she saw the same tall, cloaked-man standing with his head also hanging over the side of the boat.

Sometimes, she noticed him talking with the captain who wore the red coat. She never noticed him during the daytime. One night she observed him talking with her mother but as she approached, he disappeared. That night, when she returned to her quarters, she saw the alabaster jar sitting next to her mother's bed.

Many weeks had passed when Delilah could first see green, lush land in the distance. She thought they were arriving none too soon as her mother would soon be approaching her confinement.

She thought to herself, "No baby should be born on this boat!"

Nightly, Delilah worried as she noticed her mother crying herself to sleep.

When finally arriving on land, Delilah watched as the cloaked-man followed them two hundred yards behind. They made their way up the cliff only to have Bachariko stumble. The cloaked-man ran up the hill, lifting Bachariko and carrying her the remainder of the way to the top. He continued to carry Delilah's mother to a small community.

The women of the town began to realize they needed help and started to gather and assist Bachariko. This was the first time that Delilah remembered Jared as his hood fell backward. She recognized him although he had not shaved his head or face in weeks.

Delilah touched his face in recognition. He blushed.

Then Jared was startled. He heard Bachariko's piercing scream. He jumped to his feet only to be stopped by the women at the door of the small hut where they had taken her.

Delilah rushed by as Jared heard a baby cry. He looked all around and found a wild rosebush. He plucked a single flower. Delilah came out and took his hand guiding him into the hut.

Jared laid the rose next to Bachariko's head. She smiled as she held baby Esther. Delilah took the child from her mother's arms and turned, handing her to the giant, crying man. He sat on the floor, awkwardly holding the baby.

Jared softly touched Esther's cheek with one finger. She suckled on the end causing him to blush again. He returned the baby to her mother's arms.

He said, "Send the alabaster jar if there is a need or a concern and I will find you.

"Tomorrow, the ship will leave once more. I will return and deliver the news to Hooba. When it is safe, I will return for you," Jared explained.

Bachariko looked up and said, "Tell my *Hooba*, his *Rose* misses him."

The next morning, Jared ritually bathed at the edge of the sea, shaved his head and face, then boarded the ship for return.

Jared traveled by boat back to the port close to Damascus. He took a second boat to the coast by the city of The Temple. It had been over four months since he had last seen Hooba.

He bypassed the city of The Temple and traveled on foot directly to the community within the walls. Another five days had passed.

Jared arrived at the community within the walls but immediately walked up the embankment to the caves. He listened at the entrance as he heard Hooba reciting The Torah. Hooba was standing, leaning on his two staffs.

Jared announced loudly, "The baby has a healthy cry and reminds me of her outspoken mother, yet she has her father's eyes. Your *Rose* misses her *Hooba*."

Hooba turned slowly. His left foot appeared still very weak. He threw down his staffs and crawled over to Jared's feet. He looked up with tears streaming from his eyes.

"Rabbi, thank you," he cried.

Soon, the younger Iakobas, Hilleal and Philippos began filling Jared in on everything they knew including that there had been only one small group of Kittim soldiers who passed by the community. One fisherman and a small band of men from Kfar Nahum had visited.

"We shared nothing and acted to be shocked when told of Hooba's demise. We were advised to be aware of the rising Kittim presence and the oppressiveness of them," the three blurted out.

Philippos shared his daring story of the rescue of Massa from the Kittim guards and how they barely made it out of port before the area was filled with Kittim soldiers.

Hooba was now standing with one hand on the shoulder of Philippos.

Jared asked, "Is there any among us that would stand and recommend this man, Philippos, to the community within the walls?"

Hooba spoke immediately, "I do."

"Philippos, can you recite Psalms 23:2 through 23:6?"

Philippos began reciting as all the men joined in. Jared turned to Hooba.

"Will you take responsibility for the rest of his training?"

Hooba replied, "I will."

Jared removed his own sword and lifting it said, "I have carried this for years. Today, I give it to you, Philippos."

Then he turned to the younger Iakobas: "It is your responsibility that he learns to use it."

Hooba embraced Philippos and turned to Jared. The two men embraced.

Jared whispered into his ear: "I fear safety is not upon us yet. The fisherman from Kfar Nahum still put you at risk. I do not believe they came to warn us but rather this truly was a fishing expedition."

Flowers were blooming in Gallia. The land was green and lush. There was cool mist unlike their homeland. Summer was approaching but the heat was nothing like back home.

Esther was thriving and growing. The locals were charmed by the new, young baby. Bachariko's hair color drew no attention. Many cultures inhabiting the area were fair of skin and hair.

The women of Gallia did not cover the head thus Bachariko soon allowed her hair to flow down her back, uncovered.

During the day Bachariko played with the baby, walked in the sunshine, learned about root vegetables and how to raise chickens. And, on these days, she could be seen smiling and laughing. However at night, Delilah knew the truth. Bachariko would kneel to pray and nearly always it was with tears.

Bachariko was quite confused. There were so many gods to the people in the area when she only knew one God. She also believed the food of the area to be bland and could not develop a taste for cows because she knew it was not ritually cleaned and couldn't physically handle it. However, she would cook chicken because she could ritually kill and handle the chicken.

She quickly introduced the women of the community to herbs and cooking with different root vegetables that provided more flavor. Ginger, horseradish, onion and garlic hadn't been normally used at home but in Gallia they were plentiful and seldom used.

What interested the women more was her ability to heal with those same herbs.

Bachariko soon tired of trying to explain that God provided the herbs for healing. The women of Gallia believed that Mother God of the Earth provided the herbs. She soon became known as the local sorcerer or in their language *sorciere*.

Many women traveled to learn healing from Bachariko and the women of her community. These women began to worship a single Mother God versus many other gods. Each week on Friday evening, which was the beginning of the Sabbath, Bachariko would pray and the women would gather to join her as the sun would set.

Days, weeks and months had passed. The leaves were changing on the trees.

Delilah would go to bed each night watching her mother rock the baby. Esther could now stand on her mother's lap, gripping her mother's fingers.

There was a chill in the air one evening causing Bachariko to light a fire in the hearth. The light danced around the room and shone off the alabaster jar. Delilah could see her mother staring at the jar. From her bed she inquired to her mother.

"Mother, are you thinking about Hooba?"

Bachariko replied, "Every day, dear. He would come for us if it was safe."

Delilah asked, "Do you think he can walk now, Mother?"

Bachariko looked over her shoulder to Delilah. "I would not care if he could not walk. Besides, he would send Jared."

Then looking at Esther, she said, "He is missing so much."

Delilah replied, "You are missing him too."

Bachariko then said, "Delilah, I can only hope you can feel this kind of love."

Delilah then responded, "Mother, the boys here are barbarians and do not believe in God. Sometimes they don't bathe for weeks."

"I know, Delilah. I must return you to our homeland because you are reaching the time when you will need a suitable match," her mother stated.

"Mother, how do you think things are at home?" Delilah inquired.

"Not knowing is the worst, Delilah. But it's time to go to sleep. It's not for you to worry about," she answered.

Delilah continued to watch her mother's tears fall from her eyes holding Esther tightly, before she fell off to sleep.

The following morning, one of the young men walking by Delilah's hut yelled to her.

"Delilah, I have manure on my boots. However, I know something that you do not," he taunted.

Delilah looked out but simply rolled her eyes. He had just confirmed what she told her mother just the night before.

"What could you possibly know that I would want to know?" she nonchalantly asked.

He replied, "I plan to walk to the shore to wash my boots in the sea and watch the great vessel come in. Would you join me in my walk to the sea?"

"Why not just walk down to the sea and wash your boots? Then come here and tell me they're clean. Maybe then, I'll walk to the beach with you," she answered.

The young man did as Delilah suggested. He walked to the sea to wash off his boots. As he walked away, Bachariko chimed in.

"Delilah, are you toying with the boy's emotions? Hooba was once that awkward also, yet maybe cleaner," she chuckled.

"Mother, may I walk down to the sea and watch the vessel come in?" Delilah asked.

Bachariko answered, "Delilah, would you consider this boy an appropriate match?"

"No, Mother, I would not." Delilah replied.

"Then, I find walking down to the beach with him inappropriate," her mother decided.

"Delilah, would you like to join Esther and me as we visit the women?" Bachariko asked.

She replied, "I choose not to go, Mother."

Bachariko and Esther left for the day and not long afterward, Delilah left for the sea, carrying the alabaster jar.

Delilah walked down the cliff toward the sea. She passed the young man with the now clean boots. She informed him she was finding her way to the sea by herself.

She thought, "I must find the man with the red coat and deliver this alabaster jar to him. It will find its way back to Hooba and he will send for us."

The vessel was docking upon her arrival. She boarded the boat searching for the man with the red coat. She inquired about the well-dressed man but was told the captain would be back soon, pointing her in the direction of his quarters. She slipped into his quarters and waited.

Soon, a storm approached outside. The waves threw the boat against the rocks on the coast. Delilah heard the men running around the boat. She ran from the captain's quarters. However, the door to the hull was closed. She could not get onto the deck. She could feel the boat swaying from side to side and realized she was out in the middle of the sea and the boat was battling the storm.

Bachariko scurried home as it was already late afternoon. She thought how Delilah would undeniably scold her and would already have begun cooking dinner. She also thought how her day had been a good one. The women had distracted her from her loneliness.

Esther had been smiling all day long which warmed Bachariko's heart. The early morning storm had gone out to sea and the sun shone brightly throughout the day. But, when she entered their hut, it was empty. Her mood quickly changed from worry to anger to worry.

Her thoughts went from, "Where would she go? Why is she not here? Did she leave with that boy? Did something happen? I wish I would have known which boy he was."

Bachariko ran to the nearest two huts. She asked if anyone had seen Delilah. Yet, no one had.

The neighboring men went out to search. One older boy ran down to the beach while Bachariko returned home to wait. The older boy saw men camping with the wares they were selling.

He asked them, "What became of the vessel that docked this morning?"

The men replied, "When the storm arrived the captain set out to sea to prevent it from crushing against the rocks. We stayed camping in case he returns tomorrow."

The boy ran back to Bachariko's hut to report there were no signs of Delilah at the beach and that the vessel was gone but mentioned it could return.

Soon, one of the men appeared at the hut with a young man wearing clean boots.

Like any mother her first question was, "What have you done with my daughter?"

The young man replied, "She refused to walk with me but went to the beach by herself."

Bachariko quickly thought, then, "He says she went to the beach but the men say there are no signs of her being there."

Her eyes shot around her hut and noticed the alabaster jar was missing. She ran next door and handed Esther to the woman.

"Please watch my baby. I am going to the beach," she said.

Bachariko lit an oil lamp as the sun was setting and darkness was falling. She hurried down the path to the beach.

"Did you see my daughter?" she asked over and over again.

She blurted out to all who were listening, "Do you know who the captain of the vessel was? Did he wear a red coat?"

One man stood and said, "I know the captain you speak of and it was not he."

Bachariko stumbled back up the path to the neighbor's hut for Esther. Esther was crying and hungry. It was getting late.

She quickly lit a fire, fed her baby, laid her down to sleep and began to pray. Just before sunrise, she again fed Esther and walked to the edge of the bluff. She stood watching, hoping the boat would return but it never did.

Two days had passed. The vessel had been thrown many miles off course. The men had not slept but the boat was whole. Only two men had been washed overboard and lost. The water was calm, the doors to the hull were now open and at the bottom of the ladder lay a single, young, disoriented woman.

The first man to reach her kicked at her feet, fearing she was dead. The young woman moaned.

Then she looked up at the man and said, "Are you the little man that held my hand last night?"

"No, you were alone. We were all on deck," he explained.

"Captain! We have an unexpected passenger," he yelled.

"There were no passengers booked on this vessel," the captain yelled back.

Delilah looked up to see the captain through the opening to the hull, standing in the bright sunlight.

"Where is your red coat?" she asked him.

The captain yelled down, "Bring her to my cabin."

Soon Delilah was seated at a small wooden table once again in the captain's quarters. In front of her was a cup of a warm, bitter tea. She drank it only because she was thirsty.

The captain tried to speak in both broken Aramaic and broken Greek to communicate with her.

"What am I to do with you? What good is a woman on a ship of hungry men?" he asked her.

"We have a cook. What other service can you provide?" he inquired.

Under his breath he said to himself, "What am I going to do? These men have been at sea. She is a woman of the right age."

Delilah looked up at him and asked, "Sir, can you take me home?"

"No, young lady! We are so far south now, the only two ports we can reach are a port in Egypt and a port close to the city of The Temple," he explained.

Delilah threw up the bitter tea. The captain was frustrated and concerned.

"You are certainly not suited for the sea," he said.

Then he poured her a glass of water.

Then he continued, "Young woman, I have not slept for two days and that is my cot. Lay on it! Do not leave this room! Do not speak to the men! I must rest. Do you understand?"

Delilah answered, "Yes, master."

The captain left the room, closed the door and started to walk away. Then he stopped.

He pulled a chain from around his neck. On the end of the chain was a key. He walked back to the door and locked it for the first time in years.

Each morning and each night, the captain brought food to Delilah. He stood outside her door late each night, listening to her pray. One particular evening he heard her mention Hooba.

He became very excited. He unlocked and opened the door to his quarters.

"I have heard Hooba speak. I am of Greek and Syrian descent. But, after listening to Hooba, I now pray to his God," he told Delilah.

He then went on, "Young woman, you are lucky to not have known me before my conversion. I killed many men. I pirated these seas. My life was harsh. You would not have survived this trip had you known me before."

Delilah was so shocked, she exclaimed, "I know Hooba too!"

The captain sat down.

He said, "I will tell you the story from one of the witnesses."

The captain began, "One of Hooba's followers who witnessed his death barely escaped the city of The Temple. He boarded my boat at the port. He told me that God so favored Hooba that God would not let Hooba die; that he resurrected three days after his death. He said Hooba had appeared to him and commissioned him to build his church, a church based on God having power over death and to believe in God means we will never die."

Delilah blurted out, "Hooba sat with me and healed me. He was a great man."

The captain said, "That same man, Zelo, told me he had been involved in many miracles."

"Can you take me to men that know Hooba?" Delilah asked him.

"I can only take you to men who *knew* Hooba. Zelo told me Hooba has gone to be one with his God," he answered.

With those words, Delilah burst into tears.

The captain tried to console her, "He is with his God now though he still appears to mere men. At the port near Damascus, I have heard of a man who claims to have seen him also on the road to Damascus. God still works through this man, Hooba."

Delilah thought to herself, "Maybe Hooba was coming from Damascus to get us. What if I never find him?"

"Do you know Yohanan? He has run the trade route," she asked the captain.

The captain replied, "I do not know him personally but I do know that he was a wealthy trader. I once sunk one of his boats. I now pray that Hooba's God has forgiven me."

He got up and walked out of his quarters. Delilah heard him yelling.

"Change course to the west. We will land at the port closest to the city of The Temple."

The captain thought to himself, "I have ruined so many lives. Maybe I can help this young one."

He then returned to his quarters.

He said to Delilah, "Peace be with you. The food I have been bringing is clean."

He used his key and locked the door once more.

Chapter 47

Trade Routes

Yohanan ran all his trade routes from the city of The Temple but he personally delivered all goods within the walls of the community. However, he frequently returned to the city of The Temple to maintain his business and glean the current atmosphere concerning the Kittims.

He was expecting a large shipment of woven cloth from Egypt and asked Jared to provide him with one man to accompany him in returning the shipment to the community within the walls. Jared chose Philippos to ride along with Yohanan. Jared understood the resourcefulness of Philippos should a situation arise. Philippos, in Jared's eyes, needed the challenge and the change.

Yohanan and Philippos reached the port, west of the city of The Temple before the shipment had arrived. Against Yohanan's advice, Philippos went off to explore.

Philippos watched as ships came into port. Then he saw a man carrying a small alabaster jar. Philippos had only seen an alabaster jar like that one time and it belonged to Hooba. Unbeknown to Philippos, it was the captain of the ship Delilah remained on.

He began to follow the man with the alabaster jar. The man was repeatedly asking who knew Yohanan or Zelo. The captain continued to search for someone Delilah might know and Philippos continued to follow him.

Philippos finally approached the captain.

"Peace be with you."

The captain turned and replied, "Peace be with you."

Philippos then responded, "I am traveling with a wealthy man who would be interested in your beautiful jar. His name is Yohanan."

"Is this the man that runs the trade routes?" he inquired.

Philippos replied, "Yes, it is he."

"Can you take me to him?" the captain asked.

Philippos said, "Follow me."

As they headed toward the place where Philippos had left Yohanan, four men approached and questioned the captain.

"You asked for Zelo?" they said.

Philippos immediately recognized one of the men as a fisherman. He acknowledged all of them right away.

"Peace be with you," he said.

All four men awkwardly responded with a greeting.

Philippos was hoping and his wish came true when the captain did notice the strained response of the four men.

For just a moment, the captain turned his back on the four men. He handed Philippos the jar.

He said, "Run onto the boat and prepare things."

He turned back to the men, "I met Zelo one time. I was looking for him. He always knew men willing to work on my boat."

The four men luckily had not recognized Philippos. His head was now shaved and he had matured.

Philippos continued to search for Yohanan. Once he was found, Philippos pulled out the alabaster jar and questioned.

"Yohanan, what does this mean?"

Yohanan's eyes widened.

"Who gave you the jar?" he inquired in concern.

"The captain from the boat over there, asked about you and Zelo," Philippos informed.

"Was he wearing a red coat?" Yohanan asked.

"No, he was not. But he did hand me the jar and tell me to go to the boat and prepare," Philippos said.

"Then, we must go to the boat now!" Yohanan commanded.

Approaching the boat, Yohanan stopped abruptly. He could see the captain just ahead of them about to board.

He reached for his sword.

Philippos saw this and quickly yelled out, "Peace be with you, brother."

The captain turned around and repeated back to Philippos, "Peace be with you."

He looked into Yohanan's eyes, slowly drew his sword and placed it on the ground.

Yohanan had recognized the former pirate and destroyer of his ship.

"This is a bad man, Philippos," Yohanan was thinking to himself.

He was unsure of what was about to happen. The captain reached down to Yohanan, took his hand and helped him onto the vessel. Yohanan took his own sword and placed it on the deck next to him.

The captain looked into his eyes and asked, "Do you know a young woman called Delilah? She is highly religious and has somehow found her way onto my boat."

Yohanan asked, "And, her mother?"

The captain replied, "The girl is alone and safe."

"Sir, can you take us to her?" Philippos asked.

The captain gestured down the stairs to the hull. They followed him down and waited as he unlocked the door to his quarters.

Philippos ran into the room. Delilah threw her arms around him.

"Help me," was all she muttered.

She ran to the captain. "Thank you. It is a blessing that I met a man of God," she said.

Yohanan stood, trying to believe the words she spoke when his experience had been very different with the captain.

Yohanan asked, "Delilah, where is your mother?"

Delilah began to cry and Philippos jumped to comfort her.

Once Delilah explained what had happened to her and how she ended up on the boat, Yohanan pulled out a bag of gold coins. He placed them on the captain's table in his quarters.

"How much would it cost to book this boat back to Delilah's origination?" he asked the captain.

"I have many men to pay and very little to trade," the captain replied.

"If you can wait, I have a shipment soon coming with the finest linens to trade with you," Yohanan offered.

The captain went to a small door in the wall of his quarters. He pulled out a bag of gold.

"If I take what you have offered and what I offered with the linen, I may be able to pay my men," he said.

Yohanan replied, "I will work without payment."

"Philippos, see if some men from the boat will help you unload the linen," Yohanan ordered.

After Philippos and the men returned from unloading the linen shipment, Yohanan spoke to Philippos.

"She is in your hands now," he said.

He, of course, was referring to Delilah. Philippos took Delilah's hand.

He placed a note in her clutch. She opened her hand and read the note.

"He is alive," it read.

Delilah closed her hand around the note. Then she walked to the alabaster jar sitting on the table where Philippos had placed it while unloading the linen, dropping the note inside of it.

She looked up at Yohanan, "Please deliver this jar to my mother."

Yohanan turned to the captain and said, "We will and I will bring her home."

―――

Philippos and Delilah returned by a different route to the community within the walls. Yohanan set off to sea with the captain and their crew.

―――

During their travel to the community within the walls, Philippos and Delilah were stopped only once by the Kittim guards. The guards asked Philippos with whom he was traveling and why.

His immediate response was, "I am traveling home with my wife."

Delilah thought to herself, "This is a clean young man. I wonder what my mother would think?"

Chapter 48

They Return

Philippos and Delilah traveled by day and camped by night. Each one of those nights, Delilah slept in the cart with Philippos on the ground below her.

It had been three days since either had eaten when they finally arrived back to the community within the walls.

Jared was standing on the wall as they approached the gate. He ran out to greet them.

"Philippos, go in and rest," he said.

Philippos responded, "I am responsible for this woman until I return her to her father."

Jared turned the cart around and guided the donkey, the cart, Delilah and Philippos toward the caves. Philippos helped Delilah from the cart once arriving. He took her hand and guided her to the entrance.

"Delilah needs food and water," he yelled out hoping someone was listening.

Hooba awkwardly stumbled across the rocks and embraced Delilah. He began asking question after question only to be stopped by Philippos.

"Rabbi, please let her rest and eat," he begged.

"Yohanan travels to Bachariko to bring her back to you," Philippos explained.

Philippos made sure Delilah ate and drank. Then he, himself, drank and ate. Hooba just watched and thought how Philippos, the young man, had matured.

Hilleal had already left the caves but soon returned with Susanna.

"I will prepare Delilah. You will be invited to our home for dinner tonight," Susanna said to Philippos.

Susanna winked at Jared and Hooba, "I suppose you two can attend also!"

Yohanan and the captain worked together to pull the forward sails of the vessel into place. They tied down the rigs. The sails billowed as they pushed away from the dock.

That evening the captain walked Yohanan to his quarters. There was a large basin of water on the table where the captain allowed Yohanan to wash with first.

He broke bread and served Yohanan a piece ahead of himself. The two men bowed their heads and prayed.

The captain looked to Yohanan and asked, "Can you handle this boat?"

"I believe I can," Yohanan replied.

"I will sleep during the day and you may sleep at night. My quarters are your quarters," the captain said.

In the morning, the captain awakened Yohanan and on the deck announced to his men, "This man has my authority on the boat while I sleep."

Each night, the two men broke bread together. When a storm approached neither of the men slept. Only four short weeks had passed while the two men became the best of friends.

That evening the captain announced, "Tomorrow, we will hit land."

He looked at Yohanan and spoke, "It has been four weeks. Why is this woman of such importance to you?"

Yohanan replied, "This woman is Delilah's mother and the wife of Hooba. She is also the mother of Hooba's daughter, Esther, who will be returning with us."

The captain shook his head and said, "I see. May we deliver them home, safely."

Each day Bachariko walked to the bluff realizing it had been over two months since Delilah had left. She would go back to her hut each time and cry when there was still no boat.

Esther was now walking. She was more than ten months old and would now sleep through the night.

Every night when Bachariko laid her baby down to rest, she would tell her, "Hooba says goodnight."

One night, Esther answered back, "Ooba?"

The following morning, Bachariko walked to the bluff with Esther in tow, only to be surprised to see a boat on the horizon.

She picked Esther up and hurried down the path to the shore. She scanned the boat for a tall imposing man with a shaved head, hoping for Jared. Then scanned again for a man with a red coat. She saw neither.

She began to walk back up the bluff with Esther. She heard a voice call to her.

"Bachariko, Hooba sends his love," Yohanan yelled.

She halted in shock. She turned back to see Yohanan running toward her.

"Your daughter has sent you a message in this alabaster jar," he said.

She emptied the jar into her hand and found a crumpled-up note that read, "He is alive."

Bachariko looked into Esther's eyes and said, "Your father is alive."

Esther's response was not so surprising. She babbled, "Ooba?"

The captain yelled from the deck of the boat to Yohanan, "I will return in one week. I shall leave for a port that will pay for the linens."

Yohanan cradled Esther and rocked her into the evening. He then laid her down to sleep.

"Bachariko, there are things you do not forget as a father," he said.

They continued to talk into the night.

Bachariko and Yohanan spent much of the next week preparing for the journey home. Seven days later, the ship returned.

The morning of their departure, the women of the small community lined up, each presenting Bachariko with a piece of clothing for Esther. And as she later stood on the deck of the boat with her baby in arms, she looked up to see the women waving from the bluff.

She said to Esther, "I have missed your father but this has been a good experience."

Esther only responded, "Ooba?"

Yohanan and the captain slept with the men on the ship and gave the quarters to Bachariko and Esther each night; the captain always locked the door.

The sea was smooth and they could soon see land. Three weeks had passed.

As they approached land, the captain went to Yohanan. He handed him the key to his quarters.

"Yohanan, I can truly never make amends. But this ship is now yours," the captain offered.

Yohanan replied, "I will accept this ship on only one condition, if you will continue to pilot it."

And with those words said, Yohanan placed the key back into the hand of the captain.

Bachariko stood on the deck watching the shoreline. Men were loading other boats as she observed. Then she noticed one single, tall man with a shaved head. He had been camping at the shore for the past seven days awaiting their arrival.

Jared slowly walked to where the boat was docking. He helped Bachariko down from the vessel.

"Welcome home," he said to her.

Bachariko looked up at Jared and replied, "Peace be with you. This is our child, Esther."

Jared pulled a single red rose from his cloak and said, "And this is a rose for *His Rose*."

"Would you like to hold her?" she asked.

And as Jared held Esther, she reached up and touched his face … and he blushed.

Jared motioned down the shoreline to a young man and woman on horseback. Delilah and Philippos rode up to greet them.

Philippos carefully helped Delilah from the horse. She ran to her mother's embrace.

Delilah turned and walked back to Philippos, reaching up for his hand. Their hands lingered together for a moment, long enough for Bachariko to take notice.

Philippos took off with great speed and determination toward the community within the walls carrying the news of Bachariko's arrival.

Jared helped Bachariko, Esther and Delilah into a small cart pulled by a donkey. Yohanan, meanwhile, headed toward the Ein Gedi to retrieve Noam and the elder Ruth also with news of the arrival of Bachariko and Esther.

Two days later, Philippos arrived at the community within the walls. He couldn't wait to announce the arrival once he reached Hooba in the caves. A single tear rolled down Hooba's face. He placed a staff in his right hand and then his left and began to climb down from the caves.

Hilleal and the younger Iakobas followed quietly behind Hooba. Once he reached the road to the city of The Temple, he turned and continued to walk. He slowly placed one staff in front of the other to follow. After an hour, he had barely covered half a mile.

Hilleal spoke up, "Rabbi, even though you are walking quite well, at this pace, you would only see them twenty or thirty minutes earlier. We believe you should save your strength."

"Can you get me a cart, Hilleal?" Hooba asked.

Hilleal ran back inside the walls and returned with a cart. Iakobas helped Hilleal load Hooba into the cart.

It was then that Hooba heard Isaiah speak, "Consider how long they have been traveling to ensure all of your safety."

Hilleal turned the cart around unaware that Isaiah had been speaking to Hooba. Hooba sat quietly without protest. He spent the remainder of the night within the walls.

In the morning, he ritually bathed, then he prayed and walked to the gates and stood. He saw the dust from the cart approaching from down the road. He tried to run.

Bachariko handed Esther to Delilah as they approached the gates of the community. Jared helped her down from the cart. Bachariko ran four hundred yards to meet *Her Hooba*.

"Hooba!" Bachariko screamed.

They finally met and clung to one another, tears streaming from their eyes.

"The sight of you is even more beautiful than I remember," Hooba said.

His voice quivered as he barely murmured, "My *Rose*."

Jared lifted Hooba off his feet and carried him toward the cart that held Esther and Delilah. Bachariko reached up to Delilah and took Esther from her arms.

Jared softly placed Hooba back on the ground in time for Bachariko to lay Esther into his arms.

Esther's and Hooba's eyes met for the first time. He smiled and she smiled back.

Three hours passed before dust was again noticed arising on the road. There was a call from up on the walls.

"Yohanan returns with two women," Jared announced.

"Hooba, one is your mother and has not seen you since she believed you died," Jared continued.

Esther responded when she heard the name Hooba, "ooba, ooba, ooba, ooba."

Hooba began to walk toward the oncoming cart but quickly turned in response to Esther's babbling. She had begun to follow after *her Ooba*.

The cart approached as Noam started to cry and for a moment was angry.

"I thought you were dead. I was separated from my family."

Hooba sympathetically replied, "Woman, it was safer."

Bachariko ran to Noam and embraced her, "It was months until I knew he was alive. It was months until I knew my daughter, Delilah, was alive. Yet as we stand here today you have a granddaughter."

Jared assisted his mother, the elder Ruth out of the cart. From the gate Hilleal could be heard.

"Susanna is already preparing the meal for the celebration tonight. Family is one," he stated.

Philippos was heard calling out, "Am I invited?"

Delilah looked to her mother for an answer.

Bachariko looked to Hooba.

"The custom is for the young man to ask me," Hooba responded.

Then he inquired, "Philippos, just what are your intentions?"

"Rabbi, my intentions toward Delilah are honorable," Philippos declared.

Hooba asked Delilah, "What are your intentions?"

"The same," Delilah answered.

Hooba replied, "I need to spend time discussing this with my wife and mother."

Bachariko picked Esther up in her arms. Noam, Hooba and Bachariko had a very quiet discussion between themselves. Hooba embraced his mother then Bachariko placed Esther in her arms.

Noam again had tears streaming from her eyes.

Hooba turned to Philippos, "You're invited."

A banquet table had been set by Susanna. Young Ruth baked the bread with help from the elder Ruth. Noam sat with Esther. Aramis and Josephus were seated next to the elder Ruth.

One end of the table sat Delilah, Bachariko, Hooba and Philippos. Jared was seated next to Philippos, then the younger Iakobas, Yohanan, Hilleal and Susanna. The younger Ruth sat with her grandmother, the elder Ruth.

Hooba stood at his place. He asked Philippos to recite Psalms 23:2 through 23:6.

Then Hooba said, "This table represents many generations under God. Including those who are not with us."

Susanna spoke up, announcing, "There are more generations to come."

Susanna and Hilleal were with child once again.

"Philippos, this is what family means to us," Hooba directed.

Hooba broke the bread and slowly limped around the table serving everyone except for Philippos and Delilah. Once approaching Philippos he handed him two servings of bread and sat down.

Philippos stood from his place and walked to Delilah. He placed both pieces of bread on her plate. By the time he stepped back to his own seat, Hooba had placed his own bread onto Philippos's plate. Bachariko had placed her bread on Hooba's plate and Delilah had placed one piece of her bread onto her mother's plate.

Susanna yelled, "Please, everyone, eat; I am starving!"

There was much conversation at the table.

Jared suddenly announced to the younger Ruth, "If I look around this table, I believe you are the next to be betrothed."

The elder Ruth chimed in, "Her skills in the kitchen are already preparing her."

The younger Ruth blushed.

Jared jumped in, "Thankfully a comment I made caused one of the women in that family to blush!"

The laughter roared around the table.

"I may have to look for a suitable match for you," Jared teased.

Hooba couldn't help but respond, "Usually it is the custom that an elderly unmarried woman do such a job, Jared. However, I imagine, you will do."

Young Ruth took her turn next. She got up and walked right over to Jared. She rubbed his head.

"Could my betrothed at least have hair?" she tormented.

Jared blushed, of course. Then responded.

"I know a few young men who are studying *The Law*, live outside the walls and still have hair. Are there any other requirements?" he asked young Ruth.

Young Ruth replied, "I only wish that they would have the character of you, my father and of Hooba."

All three men blushed.

Chapter 49

The Times Were Changing

The small community inside and outside of the walls became more isolated. The only people who ventured outside the community were Yohanan and Philippos when retrieving supplies or trading. Yohanan traded only with the captain who had given him his boat and Jude. He had turned all of his trade routes over to the two men. There were no longer Zadokites or Zadokite priests to refer candidates to the community within the walls.

The outside world now consisted of Kittims, nationalists and Ebionites; who were a poor, Jewish/Hooba-following sect who viewed poverty as being holy. These Ebionites followed the elder Iakobas's teachings.

A new gentile/Jewish group had also emerged who followed Zelo and his band of men. Additionally, a new teacher appeared who had previously persecuted both Jews and followers of Hooba. His new followers called him Pseftis. He preached a different message than *The Law*.

All of these groups persecuted each other while vying for power and control. However, the Kittims were somehow continuing to hold their power and control.

Membership in one group meant hatred from another group. Meetings were held in secret by most of these sects. Letters were sent corresponding with one another but not signed in fear of discovery. Men were imprisoned, hanged or beheaded by the Kittims once discovered.

The people fled to many countries away from their homeland. Even the followers of *The Law* became influenced by the Romans and Greeks.

The community within the walls continued to preserve *The Law* and the message of love.

Philippos soon married Delilah. Young Ruth married Samuel, a young man from outside the walls of the community as recommended by Jared.

Delilah, young Ruth and Bachariko were soon with child. Aramis passed before the births of the new children and then Josephus passed as well. The elder Ruth was quickly approaching her demise and was being cared for by her namesake, the younger Ruth.

Beatrice lived in the *Marriage House* outside the walls although still unmarried. Women who stayed in the Marriage House were those unmarried or betrothed to men who lived within the walls.

Rebecca married Timothy, Beatrice's brother and also lived outside the walls of the community.

The younger Iakobas lived within the walls and sat at Jared's table, yet married a woman outside the walls of the community and therefore frequently visited the Marriage House.

Daily, Hooba continued to teach all the children.

Jared and the younger Iakobas trained the novitiates of which there were few.

Susanna, Delilah, the younger Ruth and Bachariko also taught the children.

Yohanan along with his and Bachariko's wealth, paid exorbitant taxes to keep the Kittims away from their community inside and outside the walls.

Delilah and the younger Ruth gave birth to daughters. Ruth and Samuel named their daughter Miriam. Delilah and Philippos gave their daughter the name of Beatrice.

The younger Iakobas and his wife named their son Thomas.

Bachariko reached the time of her confinement and Esther was then capable of saying the word *Hooba*. However, she then called him father.

Hooba cradled young Esther in his lap as she cradled her little brother in hers. His face was slightly fair complected. His hair was a lighter brown than his father's.

Bachariko said, "I believe he will be unable to hide it when he blushes."

Hooba then added, "Then, I think his name should be Jared."

Noam spent the next three months after the birth of her grandson at Bachariko's side. On that third month, Yohanan approached Hooba.

"Rabbi, your mother and I are getting old. I miss my daughter and family. I once promised I would protect your mother. I will soon be taking leave of the community and moving to the Ein Gedi. Your mother wishes to accompany me," Yohanan admitted.

Hooba responded, "You are one of the three men I would proudly call *Father*."

Many years had gone by, in fact about seventeen. The world outside the community was worsening with each passing day.

A day came when Timothy, the husband of Rebecca, approached Hooba.

"Rabbi, I would like to take the teachings outside the wall. I understand you can speak Kush. I would like to travel to the region of Kush with my family. Could you teach me Kush, Greek and help me with my Aramaic?"

Hooba replied, "I understand, Timothy. I will help you. It will help me to remember the language of Kush."

"My daughter will soon be of the age to marry. I understand. She also tires of this place and wishes to return to Gallia the land of her birth with a new husband. She has heard her mother speak of the lush, green lands and abundancy of herbs," Hooba stated.

Timothy spoke up, "Rabbi, my son Nicodemus is quite taken with your daughter Esther."

Hooba replied, "And my daughter Esther is quite taken with your son. They both have an adventurous spirit. Nicodemus has also been a good student of *The Law*."

He continued, "Jared will soon travel to the port by the city of The Temple and once again place my daughter in the safe hands of my younger brother Jude. If you find the land of Kush open to the teaching, please make me aware. My purpose was to teach everyone not preserve *The Law*."

Later that night, Hooba placed a single rose on the pillow of Esther. Bachariko spent time with Esther, preparing her. That evening, Nicodemus and Esther were betrothed.

The Passover week was approaching. Susanna prepared the meals for the family throughout the week. Bachariko was tearful during the entire week as Esther prepared to leave the community.

The family gathered for the Passover meal and the elder Jared stood. He recited Psalms 23:2 through 23:6 as all joined in.

Hooba then stood and spoke, "Just as we exited the Promised Land when we left Eden at the Passover, we became no longer slaves. Then, we entered a new Promised Land at Gil Gal. Symbolically, this land became our new Eden. The center of this land became The Temple just as the center of Eden symbolized the Tree of Life. Soon, God no longer lived in that Eden but then in The Temple; again, separated from the people. The *Ark of the Covenant, the Ten Commandments and The Law* lived within The Temple, sheltered from the people. Then a veil was placed around the Sanctuary again separating the people from God. And now my fear is the only remaining home of *The Law* and God is separating or keeping us here in this community. I honor all who preserve this law. I must read a letter from our brother Timothy."

He began, "The people of Kush have no temples. They crave the messages of God. No veils are hung. The people find great need in Rebecca's healing. Peace be with you, Timothy."

Then Hooba continued, "I find great pleasure that my daughter, Esther, will carry healing and the word of God to Gallia. God does not exist only in this Eden. We must take God to the people. Bachariko and I have discussed this at length. We will soon be leaving to spend the remainder of our days in Kush."

Samuel looked at the younger Ruth, his wife.

Then he stood, "We do not believe they should travel alone."

Young Ruth looked at her parents, "With your permission, we would travel with Hooba, Bachariko and young Jared."

Thomas the son of Iakobas then stood, "I would go along to be with Miriam."

Susanna began to cry and Hooba placed his hand upon her shoulder.

"Love has overflowed from this family. We will love them like they are our own," he stated.

The elder Jared spoke, "May these children of this family grow as Hooba grew and may they bless the world."

Philippos stood and removed the sword from his side.

Handing it to the young Thomas he said, "I received this sword from Jared to serve next to Hooba. Now, Thomas, you serve next to Hooba."

Bachariko and Susanna embraced to comfort one another. They had become like sisters. Then Hooba went from person to person, embracing each one.

The next week was in preparation of Miriam's and Thomas's wedding, packing for travel and saying their goodbyes.

In the city of The Temple, Zelo, the elder Iakobas and Pseftis met to discuss the future of their church; that is, the one that was begun by Hooba and changed by their individual embellished stories. Unbeknown to them, soon all three would be imprisoned or killed by the ruling Kittims.

Chapter 50

Revelation

The day before all were to depart, Jared searched for Hooba. He found him in the Sanctuary praying at the altar.

He entered the Sanctuary and kneeled beside Hooba; the two men in prayer.

Jared first spoke, "Son, if boasting was not a sin, I would declare before God how proud I am of you."

"Father, I was just thanking God for you," Hooba said.

Hooba continued, "Rabbi, the spirit of God speaks through me. I must do God's work. I believe God works through you too. The spirit of God has spoken to Abraham, Moses, Enoch and you. There is also a spirit who has spoken through Hagar the mother of Ishmael, Jochebed the mother of Moses, Susanna your cousin and Bachariko my wife. These men and women have moved me and led me to God's work as has the voice of God within them. Neither God nor this spirit has ever abandoned me.

"In the caves, there is a copy of *The Law* and in my heart is a copy of *The Law*. Your love and the love of so many have taught me the true meaning of life. God is within us. We are his temple. We bring God to this world through our love. The kingdom of God is now and forever."

"Yes Hooba, I also hear the spirit who speaks to me. Each time the spirit has told me I must let you go," Jared confessed.

At that moment both men heard from the spirit within them, "Peace be with you."

They stood and walked out of the Sanctuary.

Hooba and Bachariko stood in the courtyard the following morning. Hooba noticed Philippos loading a cart meant to deliver Esther and her husband to his brother Jude's boat. He looked directly at Philippos and smiled. This nice, young man now stood over six-foot tall. His head was shaved and he reminded Hooba of the elder Jared in his younger days.

He thought to himself, "Just as I felt safe with Jared, I feel Esther will be safe with Philippos. Jude would be delivering Esther and Nicodemus to Gallia, the land of her birth."

Hooba gazed across the courtyard and saw Bachariko talking with Esther. A tear rolled down his cheek.

He thought, "My *Rose* with *our Rose*; how these two have blossomed."

Esther looked up and saw her father sobbing. She ran across the courtyard, throwing herself into his embrace.

She spoke, "Father, I love you."

Hooba replied with tears streaming, "I love you, too, Esther. Be as strong as your namesake and your mother."

"Father, I am ..." she began.

Hooba raised one hand and said, "You're with child. Teach her to be a healer like your mother."

Timothy approached the two. He held two small leather pouches of dirt. He handed one to Esther.

"This is from the shore of the River Jordan; a small piece of the Promised Land where the people of Moses first crossed. When you arrive in Gallia, empty this upon the land so that you will always be a part of your heritage," Timothy advised.

He handed the other pouch to Hooba, "We first met in Gil Gal. I watched you cross the River Jordan into the Promised Land. Through you, I know the Promised Land is much greater. With this, I know you and your daughter will always place your feet on the same land."

Hooba, Esther and Timothy walked to where Rebecca, Bachariko and Nicodemus were talking in the courtyard. Each of the two mothers held small woven blankets.

Bachariko first spoke, "Noam gave me this blanket. I first wrapped you in it, Esther, in the land of Gallia. Noam first wrapped Hooba, your father, in it."

She handed the blanket to Esther.

Rebecca then spoke as she handed her blanket to Esther. "This is the blanket I first wrapped Nicodemus in."

Philippos, standing across the courtyard, yelled to them, "It is a long way to the boat and Jude will be waiting."

Nicodemus and Esther climbed into the cart. Philippos sat in the front to lead the donkey. He could not turn around for fear they would see the tears streaming down his face. He began to shoo the donkey when he heard Hooba call to him, then halted.

"Philippos, I would call you son even if you had not married my daughter," Hooba yelled.

Philippos jumped down from the cart. He knew when he returned from this journey, Hooba and Bachariko would already be gone … forever. This six-foot giant who once upon a time had stood next to Hooba as a small boy, embraced the much smaller Hooba, his father-in-law. Simultaneously, as the two men embraced, they began reciting Psalms 23:2 through 23:6 in its entirety for the last time.

Hooba looked into Philippos's eyes and said, "Sometimes, it is the least of my brothers that makes me the most proud to call them rabbi."

Bachariko was now standing next to them. She kissed Philippos on his cheek.

"Philippos, just as Hooba entrusted Jared with all that he loves, I entrust you," Bachariko told him.

Bachariko leaned over and quietly said to Philippos, "Last night, I had a dream that Esther would have a little girl and you would name her Sarah."

"I will honor your daughter and your dream," Philippos replied.

Philippos jumped into the cart and drove off for the port.

Bachariko, Susanna, Delilah and the other women all stood talking. Hooba yelled out, "Has anyone seen young Jared?"

Bachariko yelled back, "He's much like his father. We never know where he'll run off to."

Hooba searched the camp until he found the elder Jared, the younger Jared and his cousin David carrying out a lively conversation on *The Law*.

"They both seem quite advanced, Jared," Hooba teased.

Jared replied, "Yes, they both remind me of another young man I knew."

Hooba said, "Boys, go find your mothers."

Young Jared took off to find Bachariko as David ran to find Susanna.

Hooba looked directly at Jared. "Those two may be the last of their kind; train them well."

The two men walked together into the center of the courtyard. The entire community from inside and outside the walls stood waiting. Over eight-hundred people came to say goodbye to Hooba, Bachariko, young Ruth, Samuel, Thomas and Miriam. Sons, daughters, mothers, fathers, families and friends all embraced.

Hooba walked over to stand with the elder Jared. The now, younger-adult Jared walked out into the middle of the crowd.

The younger Jared addressed the crowd: "Peace be with you my brothers and sisters. God made a covenant with Adam; then Abraham, Noah, Moses and David. This covenant has made up *The Law*. Here within the walls of the community we preserve that covenant. My father has made a new covenant to share *The Law*. Today, he continues that purpose. The veil has been torn from the Sanctuary. The word of God is shared with all the people. The kingdom of God is within us just as my father is within me. Peace be with you, Rabbi. I look forward to seeing you again in the House of the Lord."

Hooba passed through the crowd with Bachariko reaching his hand out to touch everyone. He embraced the younger Iakobas, Hilleal, Susanna and then Delilah. Bachariko embraced the men immediately afterward. She stopped at Susanna.

"You have been like a sister and my best friend. I will miss you. Take care of these men I leave you with. They are all much like Hooba and need guidance." Bachariko cried and laughed.

Susanna tearfully replied, "Take care of Hooba and be like a mother to my child, Ruth."

Bachariko stepped over to Delilah.

"Daughter, you have grown into a beautiful woman. May you and your husband be blessed with a beautiful life and the happiness that I have found."

"Mother, with you as an example, how could I expect anything else?" Delilah responded.

Hooba approached his son.

"My son, continue to preserve *The Law*, continue with your training. If someday you wish to teach like your father, take this silver coin just as my father passed a silver coin to me. Thus, you can gain passage anywhere. Love God with your whole heart, mind and soul. Love your neighbor as yourself and the most important lesson I learned with your mother ... it's what's inside the vessel that counts."

Hooba tapped his hand on young Jared's heart just as Bachariko kissed Jared on the cheek.

Hooba searched around the courtyard for the elder Jared. Once found, he immediately walked over to speak. The two men embraced and remained silent to what appeared to be the longest time. Then Jared handed his leather pouch, embossed with a J, back over to Hooba.

"Hooba, just take this part of me with you," Jared said.

Hooba replied, "Jared, I take a much greater part of you with me than just this."

Then Hooba took the staff given to him by Massa and handed it over to Jared.

"Rabbi, I no longer need a second staff. This staff has carried me for years and now I give it to you. Let it represent *The Tree of Life*. The tree that gave us birth, your mother, my mother and God. Then, let it represent the tree that nearly cost my life. Let this tree carry you as you have carried me," Hooba sincerely offered.

Once all had said their goodbyes, Hooba and Bachariko climbed into the front of the cart. Thomas, Miriam, Ruth and Samuel got into the back.

For one moment, there was complete silence. Hooba took the reins as the elder Jared began reciting Psalms 23:2 through 23:6. The cart exited the gates and headed south along the Dead Sea.

A thousand yards from the city within the walls, Hooba stopped the cart. He stood and turned back. He raised his hand and waved at the lone man standing on the wall. Jared raised his hand and waved back.

He whispered to himself, "Peace be with you, Hooba."

Chapter 51

The Ritual Bath

The small cart rattled as it moved down the road. Bachariko was silent. Hooba reached over and took her hand.

"I miss them too," he said.

In the back of the cart, the young people were laughing and excited because, for them, this was an adventure and not an ending. For Hooba and Bachariko, this was a purpose and yet an exile.

They traveled south toward the region of the Ein Gedi. The Dead Sea stood on their left and a small range of mountains stood on their right, separating them from their homeland. Nearly three hours had passed since they left home until they reached the Ein Gedi.

Camp was set up at a small stream just before a waterfall. From this vantage point, they could see lush gardens and a small, thriving community in the valley below.

Bachariko and Hooba stood there in awe viewing the cascading, wild roses growing close to the waterfall.

She said to her husband, "How very heavy in my heart I feel when I think of any of our people leaving such a beautiful existence."

Samuel and Thomas just then returned with fresh fruits and vegetables from the valley.

Hooba asked Samuel and Thomas, "What do the village people call this area where we stand?"

It was Thomas who responded, "They call this David Stream."

Hooba replied, "How fitting. At the most southern tip of the land of King David lies a beauty, reminiscent of Eden. If only they knew when cast out of Eden, that they were ... *The Temple* and God resided within them and the Promised Land resided within them. The war was never about this land but rather the hearts within."

Hooba reached for Bachariko's hand and waded into David Stream. Here, the two together ritually bathed for the last time in their homeland. As they exited the water, Hooba knelt and carefully removed the water and sand from Bachariko's feet.

"Just as our journey began as we together crossed the water at Gil Gal, I am washing the last bit of this land from your feet. This land has served its purpose. It has preserved *The Law* and now we must continue the purpose which is to share *The Law*," Hooba mourned.

He continued, "Tomorrow, we will leave this land, follow the River Jordan and cross at the mouth of the Red Sea far south of the trade routes to Egypt. We will enter the area of Kush as it has been isolated for thousands of years. Here we will share the love of God."

The land of Kush was still very much the land of Pharaohs and old Egypt as opposed to modern day Alexandria which was filled with Greeks and Jews. It was still not yet well traveled and less inhabited than larger areas. Hooba and Bachariko would be safe and not recognized in this place. The home they left behind was over a thousand miles away.

The next sixteen days were filled with travel. It was after eight days of travel before they did not hear about *a risen son of God*. They traveled south along the eastern shore of the Red Sea not aware of what would later develop on the opposite side of the water into the western shore of Mecca which would become the holiest city of the Muslims, hundreds of years later.

Each small community they reached, Hooba would teach the people. Each day at least one man would convert from Paganism.

As the years passed, many followers went out to teach *The Law*.

Thomas and Miriam gave birth to six children. Ruth and Samuel brought four children into the world.

Each day, Thomas would hear Hooba teach of *the temple within us*, where God resides.

And years later, none of them were aware when the city within the walls and outside the walls had fallen. The Kittims had destroyed and killed all of the eight-hundred residents who remained.

On that particular day, however, Hooba said to Thomas, "I have heard that people speak of Timothy, your father who traveled to Asmara. Take your family and travel there. Then continue the work. I fear I can no longer travel."

Each day, Samuel helped Hooba walk fifteen feet from their small hut to a single tree where Hooba sat and taught the people. On those days, Ruth brought him water and fruit and, on those evenings, she and Samuel helped Hooba back to the hut.

Every night, Bachariko held the ailing, elder Hooba in her arms.

And every night, he looked into her eyes and said, "You are more beautiful than the day I met you."

Bachariko would smile; the color of cinnamon-red no longer in her hair.

"My *Rose*," Hooba would whisper.

She would reply back, "Yes, my *Hooba*?"

He would say, "I love you."

Bachariko would always respond, "I love you, too, Hooba."

One day, Hooba asked, "Bachariko, can you hear the angels singing?"

He looked up into her eyes. "I look forward to the days when I will meet you again in the house of the Lord."

Clouds cleared in front of the full moon that night. It appeared Hooba was being bathed in bright light.

Hooba heard Isaiah speaking to him, "You have pleased your God."

He felt Bachariko's hand in his own. He saw in his altered state the gates to the community within the walls and Jared standing in the gates holding the staff he had given him.

He heard a voice that felt warm and ritually bathed in love. "Welcome home. I have missed you."

Hooba could still feel the last kiss from Bachariko lingering on his lips.

Chapter 52

The Unblossoming of the Rose

Bachariko kissed Hooba on the lips, then laid beside him. She still cradled his head.

She answered, "Yes, Hooba. I can hear the angels singing."

The next morning, it was Ruth who found them wrapped in an eternal embrace.

Ruth knelt beside them and anointed both with oil that she had removed from Jared's leather pouch. Ruth then called to Samuel.

Samuel prepared a small grave. He sprinkled the sand from Gil Gal into the grave with both bodies.

Samuel, Ruth and their four children stood at the grave.

"These two temples of God have joined with God above," Samuel spoke.

Unbeknown to Samuel, Ruth and their family, the city of Jerusalem had burned and The Temple had fallen to the ground by the Kittims at the same time.

Samuel and Ruth's youngest daughter asked, "Father, may I speak?"

Samuel answered, "Yes, Aster, you may."

Aster began reciting Psalms 23:2 through 23:6.

"He maketh me to lie down in green pastures.
He leadeth me beside the still waters.
He restoreth my soul.
He leadeth me in the path of righteousness for his name's sake.
Yea, though I walk through the valley of the shadow of death,
I will fear no evil for thou art with me.
Thy rod and they staff, they shall comfort me.
Thou preparest a table before me in the presence of thine enemies;
thou anointest my head with oil; my cup runneth over.
Surely goodness and mercy shall follow me all the days of my life:
and I will dwell in the house of the Lord forever."

Appendix I
List of Characters

Name	Hebrew, Greek or Aramaic Meaning
Aahan	Gift of God
Akeldama	Field of blood
Antipas	Against his father
Aramis	Promised by God
Bachariko	Spice
Beatrice	Bringer of joy, blessings
Bhuti	Well-being; existence
Chari	Grace
Cyrus	As miserable as air
David	Beloved
Delilah	Delicate
Hilleal	Praise
Hooba	Dear to my heart, both a feeling and an action
Iakobas	To follow or be behind
Isaiah	Yahweh is salvation
Isoep	Add to me
Jared	He descends
Josephus	God will multiply
Jude	Praised
Khedenn	Sorrowful or repentant
Massa	A lifting up or gift
Miriam	Drop of the sea, bitter, beloved

Naomi	Straight and beautiful, pleasant one
Nicodemus	Victory to the people
Noam	Pleasant one
Odious	Disgraced
Pechah	Governor
Philippos	Lover of horses
Pseftis	Liar
Rebecca	To tie, to bind
Rose	Love, confidentiality, balance
Ruth	Friend
Samuel	God has heard
Susanna	Lily or rose
Thomas	Twin or look alike
Timothy	Honoring God
Tyrus	Strength, rock, sharp
Yohanan	Yahweh has been gracious
Zachariah	God remembers
Zelo	Zealot
Zeruiah	Pain or tribulation of the Lord
Zokef	Bent

About the Authors

We consider ourselves to be spiritual authors as the writers of this book. We do not believe the world is just black and white like one of our cats but rather gray ... like the other!

Together and separately, we hold significant interest in both history and religion.

This is our first historical novel that delves into the events that changed mankind.

Just like ourselves, sometimes the names were changed to protect the innocent.

Our purpose as always, is to spark curiosity and conversation motivating all to learn more about their core beliefs and historical past.

We hope your journey is both entertaining and enlightening!

Love, Dave & Carla

We hope you enjoyed this book.
Would you help us, please?

*L*ike all authors, we rely on online reviews to encourage future sales in order to further our message. Your opinion is invaluable. Would you take a few moments now to share your assessment of our book at the review site of your choice? Your opinion will help the book marketplace become more transparent and help spread our message to all.

Thank you very much!

www.ingramcontent.com/pod-product-compliance
Lightning Source LLC
Chambersburg PA
CBHW071953070526
44583CB00015B/1176